MORAL STATUS AND HUMAN LIFE

Are children of equal, lesser, or perhaps even greater moral importance than adults? This work of applied moral philosophy develops a comprehensive account of how adults as moral agents ascribe moral status to beings – ourselves and others – and on the basis of that account identifies multiple criteria for moral status. It argues that proper application of those criteria should lead us to treat children as being of greater moral importance than adults. This conclusion presents a basis for critiquing existing social practices, many of which implicitly presuppose that children occupy an inferior status, and for suggesting how government policy, law, and social life might differ if they reflected an assumption that children actually have superior status.

James G. Dwyer is a professor of law at the College of William and Mary. He previously taught at the University of Wyoming and Chicago–Kent. He received a PhD in philosophy from Stanford University in 1995 and a JD from Yale University in 1987. Dwyer has written three other monographs on the rights of children and parents in connection with child rearing, as well as numerous law journal articles on child welfare issues. He serves on the board of child advocacy organizations and has advocated for children in court proceedings.

T0370819

Moral Status and Human Life

THE CASE FOR CHILDREN'S SUPERIORITY

James G. Dwyer

College of William and Mary, School of Law

CAMBRIDGE
UNIVERSITY PRESS

CAMBRIDGE UNIVERSITY PRESS
Cambridge, New York, Melbourne, Madrid, Cape Town,
Singapore, São Paulo, Delhi, Mexico City

Cambridge University Press
32 Avenue of the Americas, New York NY 10013-2473, USA

Published in the United States of America by Cambridge University Press, New York

www.cambridge.org
Information on this title: www.cambridge.org/9781107637610

First published 2011
First paperback edition 2013

A catalogue record for this publication is available from the British Library

Library of Congress Cataloging in Publication data
Dwyer, James G., 1961–
Moral status and human life : the case for children's superiority /
James G. Dwyer.
p. cm.
Includes bibliographical references and index.
ISBN 978-0-521-76691-3
1. Children. 2. Social status – Moral and ethical aspects. I. Title.
HQ767.9.D99 2010
305.23–dc22   2010031691

ISBN 978-0-521-76691-3 Hardback
ISBN 978-1-107-63761-0 Paperback

I dedicate this book to my darling daughters,
Anna and Maggie, who inspired it.

Contents

Introduction

Historically, children have occupied an inferior *social* status, in the sense that adults – who dictate the norms of social interaction – have generally regarded children as less worthy of consideration than themselves. A paradigmatic example of this phenomenon is the ancient Roman law under which parents had legal power to sell or kill their offspring (Maine 1930, 153). In addition to having an inferior social status, children have historically been viewed, by many philosophers in the Western intellectual tradition, as occupying an inferior *moral* status. Especially in the post-Enlightenment Western world, when the rational capacities of the individual were central to political theories supporting liberation from monarchy, philosophers maintained or presupposed that only rational, autonomous beings are "persons" belonging to the moral community, a proposition that could explain and justify children's inferior social status.[1] The prevailing view of childhood was as mere preparation for adulthood, a state of being unfinished relative to the human *telos* of cognitive and physical maturity.[2]

However, beginning in the seventeenth century, and accelerating greatly in recent decades, children's position in Western society and in political and moral philosophy has been substantially elevated.[3] Today, international

---

[1] See Annette Ruth Appell, "The Pre-political Child of Child-Centered Jurisprudence," 46 *Houston Law Review* 703, 737–50 (2009) (discussing the impact of Enlightenment political theories on attitudes toward children); Martha C. Nussbaum, *Frontiers of Justice: Disability, Nationality, Species Membership* (Cambridge, MA: Harvard University Press, 2006) 130–1 (discussing Kant and the Greek and Roman Stoics); Arnulf Zweig, "Immanuel Kant's Children," in Turner and Matthews (1998).

[2] Brocklehurst (2006) 3; David Archard, "Children," in LaFollette (2003), 92–3.

[3] See Ariès (1962) 38–39; Peter O. King, "Thomas Hobbes's Children," and David Archard, "John Locke's Children," in Turner and Matthews (1998) (both discussing early liberal political theorists' efforts to justify parental power over children by reference to some sort of contract, based on an acknowledgment of children's moral standing).

and domestic children's rights documents, national ombudsmen for children in many countries, professionalized child welfare agencies, public debates over the acceptability of corporal punishment, and a culture of more child-centered parenting testify to the enhanced respect for children in society. Scholarly work on the moral and legal rights of children has proliferated since the 1970s, with many philosophers and legal academics devoting all or most of their attention to children's issues.[4] It is less common today for philosophers to contend that children occupy a moral status inferior to that of adults. On the contrary, some contend that "[t]he principle that all humans are equal is now part of the prevailing political and ethical orthodoxy" (Singer 1979, 14), and that one fundamental commitment of a liberal democracy is "the proposition that each and every human being has equal inherent dignity" (Perry 2010, 61).

Philosophers have also paid increasing attention in recent decades to the concept and theoretical underpinnings of moral status in general. That work suggests general principles concerning, and criteria for determining, moral status. Those principles could now be applied to the case of children, in order to think through in a more rigorous way what moral status we *should* attribute to children relative to that of adults. But that task has not yet been undertaken, at least not in a sustained way. Whereas in the past three decades "a veritable industry" of work on animals' moral status has developed,[5] and an extensive environmental literature has analyzed the idea of our owing duties to nonanimal entities, moral status theorists have paid little attention to children. Moral theorists concerned with childhood have generally simply stipulated that children have a particular moral status relative to adults, and have focused on the implications of that presumed status.[6] Long overdue is a concerted examination of this most fundamental question in moral theorizing about proper treatment of children – that is, are children of equal, lesser, or perhaps even greater moral importance compared to adults? Undertaking such an examination can help us assess whether popular attitudes and scholarly assumptions have evolved in a direction consistent with sound general principles and

---

[4] For references to some of the more important theoretical and legal writings on children's place in society, and a critique of the field, see Appell, supra note 1.

[5] R. G. Frey, "Animals," in LaFollette (2003) 161.

[6] Two fine collections that exemplify this phenomenon are David Archard and Colin M. Macleod, eds., *The Moral and Political Status of Children* (Oxford: Oxford University Press, 2002), and Michael Freeman, *The Moral Status of Children: Essays on the Rights of the Child* (The Hague, The Netherlands : Martinus Nijhoff Publishers, 1997). Despite their titles, neither book offers an analysis of what moral status children have relative to adults and why.

criteria of moral status and, if so, whether they have moved far enough in that direction. The basic task of this book is to identify those general principles and criteria, assess how they should apply to children relative to adults, and consider some implications of that assessment for legal and social treatment of children.

In the course of accomplishing this aim, I uncover some deficiencies in general theorizing about moral status and suggest ways to correct them. This book therefore aims to improve theorizing about moral status more generally. In particular, most ethical theorists have supposed that only one criterion of moral status exists, while differing as to what that criterion is, and that moral status is an all or nothing thing – that is, a being has either "full" moral status or none at all. I show that neither a single-criterion nor an either/or view about moral status is defensible, and neither is consistent with the way our moral psychology operates. Holding onto those mistaken views is the primary reason ethical theorists have had such difficulty fitting their theories with settled convictions about specific cases – in particular, convictions that certain beings, such as adults in a coma, anencephalic infants, human fetuses, and nonhuman mammals, have some moral status but not the same status as normal humans after birth. Widespread specific moral beliefs or intuitions reflect an acceptance of moral hierarchy, but most theorists writing about moral status go to great lengths to deny such hierarchy, for reasons I will address.

I ultimately find that a more plausible and complete account of moral status – one that incorporates multiple criteria, recognizes that each morally relevant trait can be present to different degrees, and accepts that moral status exists in degrees – generates a quite novel and surprising conclusion about the relative moral status of children. To the extent philosophers in recent decades have addressed directly the status of children, most have simply stipulated that all human beings (at least after birth) are of equal moral status, so that children are the moral equals of adults, against the traditional notion that there is a moral hierarchy among human beings tied to age or stage of cognitive development.[7] At the same time, some still assert that children are inferior in moral status because of their lesser mental capacities relative to adults. Adherents to the view that "personhood," defined as having cognitive capacities that include at least self-awareness, is a necessary condition for having moral status are likely to say either that young children do not matter morally

---

[7] See, e.g., Noggle and Brennan, "The Moral Status of Children: Children's Rights, Parents' Rights, and Family Justice," 23 *Social Theory and Practice* 1, 2–3 (1997).

at all or that moral status is initially slight and then increases during normal human development.[8] My critique of the existing literature on moral
status, however, supports an altogether different and novel position –
namely, that if it is possible to arrive at any rationally defensible conclusions about the relative moral status of different beings (and it might not
be), we should conclude that children occupy a moral status *superior* to
that of adults. Various traits associated with youthfulness elevate beings'
moral status, and in general children are more youthful than adults.

Chapter 1 explains what moral status is and how it operates in
moral reasoning; demonstrates how assumptions about beings' moral
status underlie all areas of law, public policy, and personal morality; and
describes the status currently imputed to children, explicitly or implicitly,
in these domains. The last of these – how society views children – is a
very complex matter; no single, uniform attitude toward children prevails
among people or is reflected throughout the legal and political system in
Western society. But I identify several phenomena that appear to reflect
an implicit assumption that children are less worthy of moral and political consideration than adults.

Chapter 2 begins the project of developing the best account of moral
status, by getting at the root sources of attributions of moral status in
human moral psychology. This approach differs from standard theorizing
about moral status. Most theorists begin with assertions as to the relative
moral status of particular beings – for example, competent human adults,
persons in a coma, fetuses, or nonhuman mammals – and then argue that
certain features of those beings justify according them that status.[9] Some
attempt to ground conclusions about moral status in conceptual analysis
of things such as duty and interests. The approach taken here is more
comprehensive and foundational (in a nonrealist sense), first asking in
the abstract what all the plausible criteria for ascribing moral standing
to any beings are. It is also naturalistic, resting conclusions regarding
the plausibility of possible criteria ultimately on observations about how
our "moral brains" operate.[10] It pays particular attention to Humean
and Kantian accounts of human moral psychology – grounding moral

---

[8] For the view that the youngest children have no moral standing, see Michael Tooley,
"Personhood," in Kuhse and Singer (1998) 124–5; Narveson (2002) 267. For the view
that moral status increases during development, see Tooley (1998) 122–3; Walters
(1997) 61.

[9] See Dombrowski (1997) 28 (describing examples of this approach).

[10] Many other moral theorists appear to do this as well, though generally without acknowledging it. See Franklin (2005) 69–70 (discussing Carruthers and Narveson).

attitudes in, respectively, sympathetic identification with others and the inherently objective nature of demands for respect that we make on our own behalf. These accounts capture, as a descriptive matter, much of the social practice of assigning moral status. Chapter 2 suggests, though, that the Humean and Kantian accounts, even in combination, do not provide a complete picture of our practice of attributing moral status. Awe is an additional trigger for intuitions that other entities matter morally for their own sake, and disgust can trigger intuitions that other beings matter less or are less worthy of protection. My approach does share with many others writing on the topic a "coherentist" rather than "foundationalist" (in a moral realist sense) orientation, aiming not to establish any truth of any beings' moral status, but rather to assess whether current prevailing views as to children's standing in society are consistent with, or cohere to, general principles and criteria of moral status that arise from our moral psychology and that we apply in other contexts.[11]

Chapter 3 develops a list of criteria for moral status arising from these three sources or triggers of moral intuition – that is, from sympathetic identification, rational extension of our self-estimation, and awe. I demonstrate the implausibility of both single-criterion and all-or-nothing views of moral status, which predominate in the literature. Any plausible account of moral status, I contend, will allow for more than one basis for having it and will allow for degrees of moral status, in recognition of the fact that different beings have some status-conferring properties but not others and/or can possess any particular status-conferring property to different degrees. Moral status theorists have, to date, failed to grapple adequately with this latter reality in particular – that is, that characteristics such as rationality, sentience, and aliveness come in different degrees. Many simply assert that any being possessing a characteristic to any degree or passing some threshold level of the characteristic has "full" moral status, while offering no argument in favor of ignoring clear differences of degree.

Chapter 4 addresses potential objections to assigning moral status on the basis of multiple criteria and with reference to degree of manifestation – namely, that doing so might justify discriminatory treatment among humans in unacceptable or dangerous ways, and that such a complex

---

[11] Wood (2007) 44 characterizes this as the "dominant model" of moral theorizing today. Other theorists explicitly taking this approach to the topic of moral status include DeGrazia (1996) and Carruthers (1992). DeGrazia characterizes the test of coherence as "consistency among a wide array of judgments under constraints of adequate reason giving" (15) and offers an extended defense of the approach (11–35).

rubric for moral status makes the enterprise of assigning it too difficult, even indeterminate. It explains how a more comprehensive and complex rubric of moral standing actually provides a stronger basis than do standard accounts of moral status for assumptions about respect owed to certain groups of humans, such as mentally disabled adults and anencephalic infants. Such a rubric also offers a better justification than standard accounts for discriminations that we still collectively embrace – that is, of our intuitions that some beings, such as nonhuman animals, have *some* moral status but less than that of humans, so that it is morally permissible to have greater solicitude for the interests of humans than for equivalent interests of nonhumans. Chapter 4 also suggests that while the complexity of the rubric of moral status I offer might make fine distinctions between similar groups infeasible, some rough rankings are possible and, indeed, indispensable.

Having developed and defended a general theoretical approach to moral status, I undertake in Chapter 5 to apply the identified criteria to children and adults, in just a preliminary way, to see if any defensible conclusion might be reached as to which group of humans, as a general matter, occupies a higher moral standing. A thorough application would require incorporation of an immense empirical and theoretical literature, which is not possible in one chapter, so this assessment is meant to be suggestive and provocative rather than definitive. To make even a preliminary comparative assessment manageable, it is necessary to simplify by focusing on a narrow age range within each category of child and adult. It is not the case, of course, that there are just two phases of normal human life – childhood and adulthood – and that within each phase humans are static in terms of the traits they possess that could be relevant to moral status. There are dramatic changes from neonatal status to infancy to childhood to adolescence to early then middle then late adulthood. It might be that we should assign a different moral status to infants than to school-aged children, and to middle-aged adults than to the elderly. Throughout the book, I make some references to humans at all stages of life, but Chapter 5 principally compares preadolescent school-aged children (roughly six to twelve) with middle-aged adults (forties and fifties). Middle school children present a good test case, because many adults view them with a fair amount of dread. Should we revere rather than denigrate them?

Chapter 5 offers reasons for concluding that children come out ahead on nearly every criterion of moral status other than certain aspects of cognitive functioning, that adults' superiority in those aspects does not outweigh all the considerations that favor children, and that, in any event, children's potential to develop those aspects of higher-order cognitive functioning nullifies adults' advantage even on that measure. If these preliminary conclusions were to hold up following a more thorough examination of empirical evidence, then we should regard children in general as occupying a moral status superior to that of middle-aged adults. Strictly speaking, the conjecture is not that chronological age per se gives rise to superior standing, but rather that youthfulness does – that is, a collection of attributes that typically characterize younger members of our species. Thus, contrary to the traditional view that young humans rise in status by emulating older humans, my analysis suggests that adults could seek to preserve their moral status by emulating children, by holding on to their youthfulness or childlikeness (which is not the same as what "childishness" commonly connotes). To the extent adults fail to do this, we might appropriately regard their interests as less weighty in our moral deliberations relative to like interests of children. Coupled with an assumption that children often have greater interests at stake in connection with many moral, public policy, and legal decisions, such as decisions relating to primary education, this conclusion regarding moral status would support much more child-centered reasoning about many aspects of social life affecting children.

Last, Chapter 6 considers some specific practical implications that might follow, for legal, social, and moral practice, from attributing a moral status to children superior to that of adults. How might we act differently as individuals, spend resources as a community, and assign legal rights if we assumed that children's interests trump equivalent interests of adults? Considering how we might privilege children illuminates some ways in which current practices appear to presuppose the moral inferiority of children despite whatever rhetoric about children's equal personhood might be current.

The project as a whole might be described succinctly as follows: The core of the book advances a general theory of moral status, by developing a naturalistic account of the normal human practice of assigning moral status and identifying the general principles and criteria inherent in that practice. Surrounding the core are, first, an explanation of what moral status is and how current social practices reflect an implicit denigration of children, and then, after the general theory is developed, a sketch of how the principles and criteria generated by the general theory might be applied to the specific case of humans at different stages of life, yielding the counterintuitive conjecture that children might in fact occupy a higher moral status than adults. Finally, I envision an alternative set of attitudes and policies toward children that would be consistent with this conjecture as to the superiority of youth. Along the way, the book identifies ways in which the general theoretical points shed new light on perennial ethical debates about beings other than children, including debates on abortion, animal rights, and environmental protection. I have chosen to maintain a primary focus on children, however, rather than broaden the topical scope to address these other debates in a substantial fashion, because the moral status of nonhuman entities has received great attention but that of children has received almost none. Children are certainly deserving of special philosophical attention.

One last point about methodology: A starting assumption underlying the analysis is that general criteria of moral status can provide a basis for critiquing more specific attitudes toward particular beings, because specific attitudes might reflect unattractive nonmoral influences on beliefs – in particular, self-interest and ignorance. That assumption underlies much extant theorizing about the moral status and proper treatment of specific categories of beings. For example, proponents of greater respect for nonhuman animals contend that we adult humans have failed to afford sufficient protection to animals because our self-regarding desire to use animals in various ways blinds us to the reality that those animals share with us a characteristic – sentience – that we generally believe to have moral significance and that underlies, at least in part, our sense of why others owe us moral duties. Self-interest and ignorance seems also to have underwritten the tendency, historically, for adult humans to have treated children as nonpersons or of lesser significance in normative discussions.

Conversely, unshakable convictions about specific moral beliefs – for example, that among conscious adult humans no distinctions of moral status should be drawn – might cause us to question use of one or another general criterion of moral status, or might push us to look for a more sophisticated general account. Ultimately, it could be that some such "fixed points" in our moral attitudes cannot be reconciled with any plausible general theory of moral status, yet abandoning those specific convictions would make us very uncomfortable and would serve no purpose other than logical consistency. As a possible way out of such a dilemma, I will suggest that in some instances nonmoral, pragmatic considerations might license us to ignore certain status distinctions that the best theory of moral status generates. But before considering possible untoward implications, I proceed unconstrained to construct a general account of moral status based on our moral psychology.

I

What Is Moral Status
and Why Does It Matter?

Moral status is a characteristic that we human moral agents attribute to entities, by virtue of which they matter morally for their own sake, so that we must pay attention to their interests or integrity when we consider actions that might affect them, regardless of whether other beings are concerned about them. When an entity has moral status, I may not act toward it in any way I please, disregarding its well-being, preferences, or continued existence. I owe some moral obligations to that entity itself. As a moral agent, I must care to some degree about what it wants or needs, or simply what it is; this imposes some limitations on how I may act toward it. This is importantly different from having obligations *in relation to* some entity (e.g., my neighbor's house) that are actually owed to some other entity (i.e., my neighbor). It is the being to whom duties are owed that has moral status.[1] Moral status is also importantly different from moral goodness; persons' intentional conformity to moral principles might be one of the characteristics that enhances their moral status, relative to persons who routinely act immorally and to beings who are incapable of moral action, but being worthy of consideration in others' moral reasoning is quite distinct conceptually from acting morally oneself.

Because moral status gives rise to moral obligations, what moral status different beings occupy is crucial to all of social existence and to every area of law. With respect to some contemporary legal issues, the moral status question is apparent to all and openly discussed. For example, discussion of legal issues relating to preservation of human life

---

[1] I treat as synonymous with "moral status" several other terms that more clearly connect with the notion of moral agents owing duties – namely, "moral considerability," "moral standing," "moral importance," and "worthiness of moral consideration."

often focuses on the question whether the being whose life is at stake is a "person" – an ontological category believed to entail the highest moral status. The abortion debate has turned, to a substantial degree, on the moral status of fetuses, and specifically on whether a fetus has yet become a person. Developing legal rules for treatment of humans who have fallen into a coma or persistent vegetative state has required consideration of what moral status those humans possess, often couched in terms of assessing whether they remain persons. Outside the human realm, advocacy for protection of endangered species and of natural resources has raised the question whether individual animals, species per se, and non-animal entities, even if not persons, nevertheless have moral standing, such that they matter for their own sake and not simply because of any benefit humans might derive from them.

Truly, though, moral status is critical to every area of law, and much legal debate simply presupposes that the beings under discussion occupy a particular moral status. For example, scholarly analysis of the rights of convicted criminals typically presupposes that convicts remain persons no matter how heinous their behavior, and thus are entitled to a certain level of respect and fair treatment. Yet a society conceivably *could* adopt a practice of demoting some convicted criminals to a status less than personhood, or less than "full" personhood, if such a notion of partial personhood makes any sense.[2] In fact, actual conditions in some prisons today might suggest an unstated popular view that some criminals do have a diminished moral status and are therefore undeserving of the same concern and protection they received prior to committing their crimes. Some people express an "anything goes" attitude toward how prisons treat, for example, murderers and child molesters, equating such prisoners to animals, thereby implying they possess a diminished moral status.

Other groups in our society that once occupied a subordinate social position – for example, African Americans and women – were regarded as having a lower moral status than a socially superordinate group (i.e., white male adults), and those in power invoked this supposed inferior moral status as justification for the subordinate treatment. Though their equal moral status is no longer a matter of serious dispute, moral status remains crucial to their treatment, and many believe once subordinate groups must still fight for recognition of their equal moral status.

---

[2] Some Kantians have suggested a partial, but not complete, demotion in moral status as a result of criminality. See Colin Bird, "Status, Identity, and Respect," 32 *Political Theory* 207, 227–8 (2004); Franklin (2005) 78.

These particular examples suggest both that it is not entirely foreign to common attitudes to differentiate among humans in assigning moral status, and that prevailing views on the appropriateness of particular differentiations can change over time, considerations I return to in later chapters. I consider, for example, how, within the coherentist approach to assigning moral status that I advance, it would be possible to avoid arbitrary discrimination and subordination, and whether there is such a thing as moral progress.

As noted earlier, moral status matters, concretely, because it determines whether and to what extent moral agents, including political and legal decision makers, should give consideration and weight to a being's wishes, interests, or integrity.[3] We might assume, as is generally taken for granted in the literature on moral status, that when a being has *any* moral status, then moral agents must give it *some* consideration for its own sake. Many moral theorists, however, argue for – or, more commonly, simply assume – the more specific position that if a being has any moral status, then it must have "full" moral status, equal to that of all other morally considerable beings. As discussed in Chapters 2 and 3, such an all-or-nothing view of moral status is theoretically unsupportable, whatever appeal it might have as a political matter. The concept of moral status clearly allows for variation in magnitude from one being to another, with corresponding degrees in the amount of consideration owed to a being, and many common social practices appear to reflect an implicit assumption that some beings matter morally less than others while nevertheless mattering to some degree – for example, cattle relative to dogs and fetuses relative to children after birth. Gratuitous torture of cows would be universally condemned, but there is still widespread acceptance of

---

[3] In this book, I speak principally of interests rather than wishes and integrity. According to one philosophical view, satisfying others' wishes can be subsumed within the idea of satisfying their interests, by recognizing that people have an interest in their preferences being satisfied and/or by supposing that their wishes are generally consistent with their interests. But it is not important to my analysis to establish whether there are reasons other than promoting interests for respecting others' wishes. I include the concept of integrity, which I understand to mean remaining intact, free from destructive action, principally to allow for the possibility, explored later, that some entities might have moral status even though we do not commonly speak of them as having interests – for example, the Grand Teton Mountains, the Amazon rain forest, or the Hope diamond. Accepting that possibility is not essential to my analysis of children's moral status, however, because children clearly do have interests, and that should suffice for any theorist to concede that human children are the sorts of beings that can have moral status (though some might nevertheless insist that they do not).

practices in the beef industry that would be widely condemned if inflicted on golden retrievers.

Assuming that moral status can vary in degree, the higher a being's moral status, the greater the consideration moral agents should give it. If two beings have moral status, but one's is higher than the other's, then moral agents should assign greater moral weight to an interest of the former that is identical to an interest of the latter – for example, an interest in avoiding a certain amount of pain – and thus give priority to satisfying that interest in the former being. If some beings have equal moral status, on the other hand, moral agents should give those beings equal consideration in their decision making, giving the same weight to identical interests of both. Thus, if dogs and humans were of equal moral status, legislators would be morally required to give the interests of dogs consideration and weight equal to that given to like interests of humans – for example, in making decisions about use of public space for recreation.

Importantly, though, moral consideration is not the same as social or legal treatment. It is a common mistake in the scholarly literature to conflate the two. That two beings have equal moral status does not mean that moral agents must treat them exactly the same. Equal consideration of their respective interests might actually compel disparate treatment, if they have very different interests or different characteristics that dictate different means of satisfying similar interests. Thus, for example, most advocates for children's rights acknowledge that attributing moral status to young children equal to that of adults would not entail giving the two groups all the same legal rights. Because the needs of very young children are predominantly for nurturance and guidance rather than for freedom, equal consideration of interests would likely lead to conferring more rights to assistance on children and more rights to freedom on adults.[4] Similarly, if dogs were of the same moral status as human children, that would not mean dogs have the same moral right to schooling that children are generally deemed to have. It might, instead, mean

[4] Tamar Schapiro thus errs when she concludes from the fact that Western society treats children paternalistically to a greater degree than it does adults, and does not afford children the same set of rights it affords adults, that it "is implicit in our moral and legal practice [that] children, as a class, do not share the same status as adults" and that we "think of children as second-class moral and political citizens." Tamar Schapiro, "Childhood and Personhood," 45 *Arizona Law Review* 575, 578 (2003). Schapiro's argument for the justifiability of our being more paternalistic toward children than we are toward other adults therefore does not accomplish her stated aim of justifying attribution of inferior moral status to children; paternalistic treatment and attribution of moral status are conceptually distinct.

that dogs are entitled to whatever would allow them to have flourishing dog lives to a degree comparable to the extent we aim to give children flourishing human lives. Thus, disciplining children and imposing restrictions on them are not necessarily incompatible with their having a moral status equal to that of adults. Indeed, even a being recognized as having *greater* moral status than others could be treated more paternalistically than those others. Think, for example, of how the guardians for an infant emperor in China or a child goddess in Nepal might be expected to train their revered wards to fulfill their roles.[5]

In addition, one type of being might simply have lesser interests to protect than another, so that even if the two are of equal moral status, the former might receive less legal protection on the whole than the latter. This supposition allows even proponents of all-or-nothing views of moral status to reconcile their positions with widespread intuitions supporting different levels of legal protection for the lives of different types of beings. For example, one who concludes that all sentient beings have equal moral status might nevertheless endorse more severe punishment for wanton killing of a human than for wanton killing of a robin, by assuming that a robin simply has lesser interests at stake in remaining alive than does a human. Some utilitarians emphasize this point in defending the view that every being's pains and pleasures are of equal moral significance, against the concern that this view might require a radical transformation of human social and personal life (e.g., Singer 1975). My criticism of all-or-nothing views will not, therefore, rest on their incompatibility with fixed beliefs about proper levels of legal protection among different types of beings (though some widely endorsed current practices do appear incompatible with all-or-nothing views), but rather principally on their failing to provide any good argument for treating moral status as having a binary "you either have it or you don't" character.

Having unequal moral status, in contrast, would mean that beings' interests, wishes, or integrity should receive unequal degrees of consideration. One being's interests would simply count for more, command more attention and concern, than like interests of another. Unequal consideration does not, however, necessarily result in different treatment for all purposes. For example, the law could include a prohibition against killing one class of beings that is just as strongly expressed and enforced

---

5   See Neela Banerjee, "In a City of Power Brokers, a Young Visitor Who is Truly Worshipped," *New York Times* A19 (June 14, 2007) (discussing visit to Washington of a ten-year-old Nepalese Goddess, who is worshipped in her society but who must rise early for prayers – to her – and who must attend school).

as a prohibition against killing a morally superior class of beings. This might be so because all beings exceeding some threshold of moral status are deemed to have an absolute right against being killed. Among different classes of beings who pass this threshold, other kinds of rights might be unevenly distributed, but all have that right not to be killed. Alternatively, two beings of different moral status might receive equal treatment for pragmatic reasons – for example, that having different rules for the different beings is inefficient, or that affording to an inferior class of beings the same legal rights that a superior class enjoys as a matter of moral entitlement indirectly protects the interests of those in the superior class. Prohibiting killing of a broader class of beings might habituate people to respecting life or guard against mistakes in identifying a being as a member of the superior group. Thus, for example, the U.S. Supreme Court, in upholding a federal law outlawing "partial birth abortion," recognized as a valid justification for the ban Congress's explanation that "the abortion methods it proscribed had a 'disturbing similarity to the killing of a newborn infant,' and thus it was concerned with 'draw[ing] a bright line that clearly distinguishes abortion and infanticide.'"[6]

Because equal moral consideration can produce unequal treatment and unequal moral consideration can allow for equal legal protection, it is often difficult to determine when decision makers are systematically treating one group as occupying a lower moral status than another, or are instead treating them as moral equals. It is fairly clear, however, that governments and societies throughout the world have in many ways treated children as occupying a moral status lower than that occupied by adults. Children have been treated differently from adults in ways that cannot be explained in terms of their having lesser interests at stake or of efforts to serve their distinct interests equally well or their like interests in different ways. To be sure, children's interests are no longer uniformly subordinated to those of adults. As noted in the introduction, the social status of children has risen considerably in recent decades throughout most of the world. And it is plausible that some parents unduly sacrifice their self-regarding interests for the sake of their children. Yet in both public and private realms, one can still find manifestations of a view that children do not matter as much and may be treated in ways unacceptable for adults even when they have similar interests at stake. This might be more true

---

[6] *Gonzales v. Planned Parenthood Federation of America,* 550 U.S. 124, 127 S.Ct. 1610, 1633–34 (2007). See also Franklin (2005) 26 (discussing a pragmatic response to the "argument from marginal cases").

in the United States than in other Western nations; the U.S. government, after all, has the dubious distinction of being the only government in the world not to ratify the UN Convention on the Rights of the Child. But examples can likely be found in any nation.

In particular, the law governing, and much scholarship addressing, child rearing in the United States and the United Kingdom has in many ways implicitly treated children instrumentally, as mere means to the satisfaction of their parents' desires or the supposed needs of their parents' community, even in contexts where the interests children had at stake were much greater than those of the adults involved. A prime example is the U.S. Supreme Court's 1972 decision in *Wisconsin v. Yoder*, which is still a controlling precedent in the United States.[7] The Court in that case effectively treated Amish children as conduits of the Amish way of life and as appendages or possessions that parents could use to gratify religiously infused desires, in holding that states must grant Amish parents an exemption from compulsory school attendance laws. Driving the Court's decision was a concern that if states forced Amish parents to send their children to school beyond the eighth grade, the children might learn enough about the non-Amish world to be able to decide that they don't want to be Amish. The attrition this would cause would pose a substantial threat to the survival of the Amish community. So, to gratify Amish adults' desires for the survival of the Amish way of life, the Court created for them a constitutional right to block application of state child welfare legislation, legislation designed to serve what the state views as children's fundamental interests in developing toward autonomy and in enjoying an equal opportunity for a wide variety of careers. Paul Meredith describes education law in England and Wales as similarly focused on gratifying parents rather than serving the interests of children.[8]

This is not to say that child-centered arguments for parental freedom in child rearing cannot or have not been advanced, but rather that the legal system has focused principally on parental desires in education and some other contexts, with little independent consideration of children's interests in, for example, equal opportunity to pursue careers suited to their natural talents and abilities. If children's welfare were at the forefront of judges' thinking about parent-state conflicts over education, one might expect to see analysis in terms of children's rights rather than parents' rights, but one rarely does. Political theorists debating the propriety of

[7]   406 U.S. 205 (1972).
[8]   Paul Meredith, "Children's Rights and Education," in Fionda (2001) 203–22.

the *Yoder* decision and more generally addressing control over children's education likewise manifest a predominantly adult-centric outlook. For the most part, they divide into three camps: defenders of parental entitlement; advocates for "cultural rights," who view education as a means for adult members of cultural minority communities to preserve their culture; and proponents of "democratic education," who contend that all adult members of society are entitled to have some say in how children are educated, in order to create the kind of future society they want.[9] All three camps implicitly treat children's minds and development as means to satisfying the ideologically driven desires of adults. Consideration of whether children have any rights or independent interests at stake is generally entirely absent or just a cursory afterthought. Yet viewed objectively, as an empirical matter, children's interests in cognitive development are far greater than the interests of adults in dictating how the next generation develops and what children come to believe.

Later U.S. Supreme Court decisions concerning grandparent visitation, school vouchers, and gay scout leaders also rested on an adult-centric analysis, one reflecting little or no regard for the interests and moral rights of the children whom the decisions would impact. The Court's plurality decision in a grandparent visitation case, *Troxel v. Granville*,[10] was based *in part* on an assumption that parents presumptively know what is best for their children, which is plausible in that context. However, an additional underlying assumption was that parents are entitled to control their children's associations with others, regardless of whether this is best for the children, so long as the parents do not harm the children. Yet children's social lives are quite important to their development, whereas parents' desire for control over their children's lives, in and of itself, is not central to parents' well-being. Denying children a relationship with grandparents could deprive them of a benefit (without causing them what courts would deem "harm") far more important than the supposed benefit to parents of giving them this increment of control over children's lives.

In *Mitchell v. Helms*,[11] the Court upheld a school voucher program in Cleveland that allowed for transfer of students from public schools to religious schools, without once considering what quality of education the religious schools provide or acknowledging that religious and other

---

[9] See James G. Dwyer, "Changing the Conversation About Children's Education," in Macedo, ed. (2002), and Dwyer (1998) ch. 4.

[10] 530 U.S. 57 (2000).

[11] 530 U.S. 793 (2000). For an extensive analysis of the school voucher question from a children's rights perspective, see Dwyer (2002).

private schools are virtually unregulated, and thus subject to no account-ability. The educational interests of the children appeared irrelevant. And the Court's decision in the conflict over a gay man's application to serve as a boy scout leader, *Boy Scouts of America v. Dale*,[12] treated the legal analysis as purely one of balancing the gay man's right to pursue an avocation against the Boy Scout organization leaders' wishes to use the organization to communicate a message to the world and to decide with whom scouts would associate. The Court gave no consideration to the wishes or interests of the boys with whom the applicant would have inter-acted, or the interests of boys throughout the organization who might be affected by the adult leadership's decision. Certainly, a complete disre-gard of the educational and developmental interests at stake for children in connection with their schooling and afterschool activities suggests a moral devaluation of the children relative to the adults involved.

These U.S. Supreme Court decisions are just the tip of a global iceberg. Innumerable examples in legislation and other decisions by many nations' legal decision makers' confer on parents an entitlement to sacrifice what the legal decision makers *themselves* regard as in the interests of chil-dren, for no reason other than to gratify the parents' wishes, especially those resting on religious belief. Thus, parents are allowed to deny their children medical care, in some jurisdictions up to a point approaching death, if it conflicts with the parents' religious beliefs.[13] Governments throughout most of the Western world empower parents to place chil-dren in virtually unregulated religious schools and home schools, even though government education officials know quite well that some do not even *aim* to provide a good secular education.[14]

These special exemptions and authorizations for parents rest largely on a belief that parents have a moral right to control their children's lives however they wish, as long as they do not damage the child so badly as to raise concerns that the child might later become dependent on soci-ety for subsistence. This is inherently demeaning to children, just as the supposed moral rights of husbands with respect to control of wives in bygone years inherently demeaned women.[15] Because of the nature of

---

[12]   530 U.S. 640 (2000).

[13]   See James G. Dwyer, "The Children We Abandon: Religious Exemptions to Child Welfare and Education Laws as Denials of Equal Protection to Children of Religious Objectors," 74 *North Carolina Law Review* 1321, 1356 (1996).

[14]   See ibid. at 1329–53.

[15]   For an extended critique of the notion of parental child-rearing rights, see Dwyer (1998) ch. 3.

rights, these notions necessarily entail thinking about children instrumentally, as means to further the ends of others. Yet even the UN Convention on the Rights of the Child affirms the principle of parental *entitlement* to effectuate religious aims through child rearing, because in all or most signatory nations an adult-centric view of child rearing still prevails.[16]

In contrast, with adults – even incompetent adults – the law generally adheres to a principle of not treating persons instrumentally, in the sense of authorizing some to direct core aspects of the lives of others so as to gratify or serve the interests of the former. In contexts of guardianship for and treatment of incompetent adults, the law reflects an assumption that such adults have a moral status equal to that of competent adults, and that this equal status is incompatible with treating them instrumentally (Dwyer 1998, 73–75; 2006, ch. 3) Thus, the law conceptualizes care taking for incompetent adults as a fiduciary role held as a matter of privilege, with such fiduciaries having no claim in their own right to object to, or demand an exemption from, laws imposing uniform standards of care. Rather, guardians for incompetent adults can object to interference by the state or other private parties in their decision making only by contending that the interference conflicts with the interests and rights *of the ward*, and judicial analysis of such a contention would focus exclusively on the interests and rights of the ward. John Locke might be interpreted as having urged a similar, fiduciary conception of parenthood,[17] but that conception has never become predominant. Significantly, one finds in no human rights documents or statutes relating to treatment of mentally disabled adults, nor in any treaties or legislation concerning domestic violence toward or trafficking in women, exceptions for people motivated by religious belief to treat mentally disabled adults or women in ways the state deems harmful.

Some of the most striking examples of state decision making that deprecates the interests of children, though, relate not to state regulation of child rearing after families have been formed, but rather to state creation of families in the first instance, a topic that political theorists and children's rights conventions have largely ignored. For example, legal rules throughout the world governing assignment of legal parents to children at birth pay no direct attention to the welfare of children, and cannot

[16]   United Nations Convention on the Rights of the Child, Articles 3 and 5 (1989).
[17]   See John Locke, *Second Treatise of Government* § 67, at 37 (C.B. Macpherson, ed., Hackett, 1980) (1690) (parents' authority over the child "to speak properly ... is rather the privilege of children, and duty of parents, than any prerogative of paternal power").

plausibly be explained or justified in terms of children's interests. These rules automatically bestow legal parenthood on a child's biological parents regardless of how unprepared the biological parents are to raise a child. Thus, drug addicts, prison inmates, and people who have already terribly abused other children have parenthood bestowed on them as automatically as anyone else whenever they conceive a child. Only after attempting, with predictable futility, to "rehabilitate" those biological parents who predictably turn out to be abusive or neglectful, do we attempt to find suitable parents for their biological offspring, after the offspring are damaged, through a lengthy process that is designed assiduously to protect the relational interests and due process rights of the parents, giving them every opportunity to show some improvement and thereby reclaim "their" children.[18]

Attributing to children equal moral status and giving full effect to that status would surely entail affording them some sort of legal right in connection with family formation that is comparable or analogous to that which adults enjoy, to choose the best available willing persons for family affiliation (Dwyer 2006). One need not go so far as to require licensing of anyone who wishes to become a parent, though there is much to be said in favor of doing so.[19] More realistically, we might say that children have a moral right that state parentage laws at least screen out the most manifestly unfit biological parents or that in certain circumstances a court make a best-interests decision as to whether their biological parents should become their legal parents.[20] That children presently enjoy nothing like such a right suggests that the law of family formation is implicitly premised on a view that newborn children are less deserving of protection of their relationship interests than are adults, even though a newborn child's interests at stake in the state's selection of parents are enormous,

[18] See James G. Dwyer, "A Taxonomy of Children's Existing Rights in State Decision Making About Their Relationships," *William & Mary Bill of Rights Journal* (2002); James G. Dwyer, "The Child Protection Pretense: States' Continued Consignment of Babies to Unfit Parents," 93 *Minnesota Law Review* 101 (2008).

[19] For arguments in favor of some form of universal screening of parents, see Hugh LaFollette, "Licensing Parents," 9 *Philosophy and Public Affairs*, 182–97 (Winter 1980); Westman (2001); Dwyer (2006), ch. 8.

[20] In fact, I have argued that existing judicial doctrine in the United States supports attributing to newborn babies a constitutional right, as a matter of substantive due process under the Fourteenth Amendment, against the state's placing them into legal relationships with and in the custody of birth parents whom the state knows to be unfit. See James G. Dwyer, "A Constitutional Birthright: The State, Parentage, and Newborn Persons," 56 *UCLA Law Review* 755 (2009).

which in turn implies that newborn children are assumed to occupy an inferior moral status.

The examples of implicit denigration in the law could be multiplied. Courts are dismissive of young people's privacy and dignitary interests, in public and private settings, authorizing searches and forms of discipline in schools that would not be tolerated with adults.[21] They likewise too readily assume that children have lesser interests than adults in receiving due process before being involuntarily committed to a juvenile detention center or psychiatric facility.[22] The penal system in the United Kingdom is more tolerant of the use of force and violence to control detained juveniles than to control adult criminals.[23] In divorce cases, children's interests are considered only after their parents' rights of association and residential choice have been satisfied, and children, rather than the parents who cause the family dissolution, must shuffle around among residences in order to maintain relationships with their parents and extended family members. Though infanticide is no longer legally permissible in Western society, the law permits more violent behavior toward children than it does toward adults, as evidenced by the legality in the vast majority of countries of parents' hitting children for purposes of discipline. Western nations no longer permit such treatment, regardless of the purpose or motivation, with respect to spouses or even adult criminals, even though corporal punishment might be just as effective in deterring adults from engaging in bad behavior.[24] Defenders of corporal punishment typically assume that the only relevant question is "Is it effective in controlling

---

[21]   The U.S. Supreme Court has authorized increasingly broad and intrusive suspicionless searches of pupils in public schools. See *Board of Education of Independent School District No. 92 of Pottawatomie County v. Earls*, 536 U.S. 822, 847–9 (Ginsburg, J., dissenting) (criticizing decision of majority of Court to uphold school district policy requiring all students who participate in competitive extracurricular activities to submit to suspicionless urinalysis drug testing). In *Ingraham v. Wright*, 430 U.S 651, 685 (1977), the Court noted that hitting adult criminals in jail for any purpose would violate their dignity, but went on to find that disciplinary hitting of children in schools was constitutionally permissible, with no consideration of children's dignity.

[22]   See, e.g., *Parham v. J.R.*, 442 U.S. 584, 637–9 (Brennan, J., dissenting) (criticizing decision of Court majority to uphold state practice of committing minors to psychiatric institutions without preadmission hearing).

[23]   See Tim Ross, "Report Condemns Discrimination Against Children," Press Association Newsfile (June 9, 2008).

[24]   See Susan H. Bitensky, "The Constitutionality of School Corporal Punishment of Children as a Betrayal of Brown v. Board of Education," 36 *Loyola University of Chicago Law Journal* 201 (2004); Susan H. Bitensky, "Spare the Rod, Embrace Our Humanity: Toward a New Legal Regime Prohibiting Corporal Punishment of Children," 31 *University of Michigan Journal of Law Reform* 353 (1988).

behavior?" rather than "Is it absolutely necessary?" or "Do children have a dignitary interest that precludes it even if it otherwise sometimes does more good than harm?"[25] Discounting of children's interests relative to adults also appears implicit in the quite high threshold for state action to stop child abuse, which cannot plausibly be explained in child welfare terms.[26] John Harris writes: "it is precisely because children have been treated as children and not as equals that they have been fair game for adults, exploited, abused, and even tortured and arbitrarily done to death."[27]

Many everyday social practices also suggest ascription of lower moral status to children. One cannot say there is a uniform or consistent attitude toward children. As with old age (Nelson 2002, 137), a variety of conceptions of childhood have popular currency, some positive and some negative. They range from a romanticized idealization of children to the view that children are inherently wicked and dangerous and need severe correction and restraint. (Fionda 2001; Krinsky 2008). However, some specific practices suggest a widespread tendency to discount the interests of children relative to adults. Even many parents, in dealing with their own children, make many decisions for their families, from what to have for dinner to where the family will live, based principally on their own preferences and aims, with the preferences or well-being of their children at best receiving secondary consideration. Traditionally, family households have been organized around adult preferences, and though it is increasingly common to see children's needs and preferences dictating a family's schedule and use of space in the home, it appears still to be the case that children are routinely compelled to conform to an adult rhythm of life and to adult preferences for where and when they engage in their preferred activities. To give one small example, in many American households parents require all family members sit down to eat at the same times for three meals a day. If children ask for food at other times, parents tell them it is not time to eat. If children stand and walk around the table while eating, parents tell them that this is inappropriate and insist that the children sit in their chairs. Few such parents consider that a three-sit-down-meals-a-day regimen might not be the ideal regimen for active little people with small stomachs; parents impose on children a routine that works for the parents and that they assume to

---

[25] See James G. Dwyer, ___ *Law & Contemporary Problems* ___ (2010).
[26] See Dwyer (2002), supra note 9, at 952–66.
[27] John Harris, "Liberating Children," in Leahy and Cohn-Sherbok, eds., (1996) 138.

be the "right way" to live. Of course, there are also many families that rarely eat together at all (though the notion that dining is *the* time for parent-child socializing seems to be an adult-driven one). And there are parents who impose little or no structure on their children's lives or who capitulate to every demand of their children, which can be quite deleterious to children's development. But such phenomena might more often reflect a lack of parenting motivation than respect for children. Another example is family relocation. It is usually parents' career aspirations or geographical preferences that drive family moves, rather than parents' determination that a move would make the children better off, though parents might assure themselves that it would.[28]

In dealing with other people's children, most adults appear to discount the interests of children relative to adults even more. For example, while the poverty rate for the elderly in the United States in the past four decades has declined from roughly twenty-five to ten percent, Americans have allowed the poverty rate for children to climb during that same period. The rate of poverty among children now is higher than that in any other age group. One third of children in the United Kingdom live in moderate or severe poverty. Schools in many poor urban areas are left to wallow in dysfunction.

In addition, adults appear generally less reluctant or embarrassed to interfere with the legitimate activities of children than they are with the activities of other adults, and adults appear generally to assume that in a conflict of preferences between adults and children (e.g., regarding how much noise should be tolerated in public places) adult wishes are objectively superior or more important. Children are pretty much the only group of humans it is socially acceptable to exclude from social settings. Many restaurants, housing developments, vacation properties, stores, and other public facilities have in recent years adopted policies of prohibiting children altogether, something they could not do to adults who have disabilities making them similarly distracting.[29] The UK Children's

---

[28] I am not suggesting here that any parents make all decisions for their families in such a self-centered way; many make even some larger decisions based primarily on the well-being of their children. But certainly a substantial percentage of the decisions that millions of parents make every year to move to a new locale cannot plausibly be justified in terms of the welfare of their children and entail a significant cost for the children, a cost that might outweigh the gain for the parents by objective measures.

[29] For examples of restaurants that exclude children, see Kirstin Cole, "CBS 2 Exclusive: Restaurant Doesn't Serve Kids," CBS2, (Feb. 27, 2007), http://wcbstv.com/topstories/cbs.2.anti.2.242509.html; Chris McCann, "No Delivery, No Children," *The Stranger*, (Oct. 10, 2006), http://www.thestranger.com/seattle/Content?oid=87856;

Commissioners recently reported widespread use of the "Mosquito" device, "a privately marketed product that issues a high frequency noise generally only heard by those under the age of 25," which "is used to repel teenagers from public places."[30] In addition, adults seem generally to regard their time as more valuable than children's, their opinions more valid or worthy of expression, and their use of public space more important.

I do not offer these observations as objective proof of anything. My account of children's status in law rests on my interpretation of certain rules, and that interpretation is contestable. My account of children's status in society rests on many empirical suppositions and on interpretation of the facts assumed, and is therefore contestable and susceptible to refutation. And I emphasize again that there is no uniform attitude toward or treatment of children, among philosophers, government officials, or the general public. It is not important to the analysis of moral status that follows, however, whether the accounts just given are true, persuasive, or representative of prevailing views or practices. Even if children are now largely viewed and treated as equals

Adults Exclusive Dining – Disney Cruise Line, http://disneycruise.disney.go.com/ships-activities/onboard-activities/dining/adult-exclusive/ (last visited Jan. 28, 2010); Mode's Bum Steer, http://www.modesbumsteer.com/ (last visited Jan. 28, 2010); Victoria & Albert's, http://disneyworld.disney.go.com/resorts/grand-floridian-resort-and-spa/dining/victoria-and-alberts/ (last visited Jan. 28, 2010); The Vortex Bar and Grill, http://www.thevortexbarandgrill.com/ (last visited Jan. 28, 2010).

For examples of communities that exclude children, see Christopher Caldwell, "Childproof," *N.Y. Times Magazine* 18 (Aug. 13, 2006); Kelly Greene and Jennifer Levitz, "Retiree Havens Turn Younger To Combat the Housing Bust," *Wall Street Journal* (Dec. 1, 2008), A1; Phillip McGowan, "New Housing Caters To 55-And-Older Set," *Baltimore Sun* (May 27, 2007), A1; Bethany Sanders, "Retirement Community Tries to Evict Six-Year-Old Girl," *Babble*, http://blogs.babble.com/strollerderby/2009/10/22/retirement-community-tries-to-evict-six-year-old-girl/ (last visited Oct. 22, 2009); About Brookshire, http://www.retireatbrookshire.com/about_brookshire.html (last visited Jan. 28, 2010); Active Adult Living, http://www.activeadultliving.com/new_communities.htm (last visited Jan. 28, 2010); Randa Abdel-Fattah, "Retired Boomers Who Reject Children Live in an Unhealthy World," *The Age* 13 (Melbourne, Australia) (February 23, 2009) (discussing child-excluding gated retirement communities).

See also Carter Dougherty, "Sturm und Drang About Pint-Sized Neighbors," *The New York Times* 6 (Jan. 28, 2009) (discussing a rash of lawsuits in Germany by neighbors of day care centers complaining about noisy children); "Should We Ban Children from Weddings?," *Daily Mail* (London).53 (July 10, 2008) (describing growing phenomenon in England of wedding invitations saying "No children"); Kimberly A. Kennedy, "Get Aways from, Before, Without Kids," *The Boston Globe* M1 (May 18, 2008) (discussing increase in travel agencies and resorts offering child-free vacation environments).

30   Tim Ross, "Report Condemns Discrimination Against Children," Press Association Newsfile (June 9, 2008).

(or superiors!) in law and culture throughout the world, it would be important to develop an account of what relative moral status they have, so that we have a clearer and more definite point of reference for determining what adults' attitudes toward and treatment of children *ought* to be.

It is worth noting here, though, that there certainly are counterexamples to the hypothesis that prevailing social attitudes are disrespectful of children. In some ways, we might appear to be a culture of child worshipers.[31] Consumer spending on goods for children has expanded tremendously in recent decades, politicians routinely pay homage to "the future for our children," and parenting has become generally less authoritarian and more companionate. As noted at the outset, the social status of children does appear to have improved considerably in recent times. I would caution against making too much of such public rhetoric, however, because much of it appeals to individual parents' interest in their own children rather than to an assumed interest of everyone in all children, and practices often do not match rhetoric, suggesting that much of it is disingenuous pandering.[32] Moreover, in some contexts – for example, the school voucher debate – much talk of children's welfare appears to be code for the wishes of parents or other adults (Dwyer 2002). Again, though, it is not my aim to prove the accuracy of any particular description of children's current status in law, public policy, or prevailing attitudes, but rather to develop a theoretical account of what status we adults should assign to children.

A final preliminary question is whether it is sensible to think of humans' moral status as changing over time. One might argue, to the contrary, that we should view all humans or all "persons" as having the same moral status but simply receiving different treatment over the course of their lives.[33] We might think of moral status as pertaining to beings and determined once and for all by characteristics typical of their type, rather than as pertaining to different stages of life. If everyone ultimately is subject

[31] See Margarette Driscoll, "Our Little Emperors," *The Sunday Times* 18 (London) (June 29, 2008) (discussing an incipient backlash against a perception that Western society has become overly child-centered). See also Macnicol (2006), 28–9 (discussing "denial of aging" among advocates for the elderly, attempting to generate a public image of older persons as "forever youthful," to counter a "norm of decrepitude").

[32] See Hodgson (1997). Of course, empty pandering in politics is not limited to child welfare issues; there is plenty of it with respect to civil rights and public assistance for adults as well.

[33] Wood characterizes this as the "unity of the person" view. Wood (2007) 96.

to the same treatment and the same rules over the course of a lifetime, then none can complain that they have been accorded a lesser status than others. The treatment and rules happen to be better later in life, but those who are subordinate now will have their day.

One response to this position is to point out that a certain percentage of individuals do not survive to adulthood, so there is some unfairness in a "hazing" view of childhood in their case. Even if one were to reject the notion that humans' moral status can change over time, then, one might insist that persons' interests receive equal consideration regardless of life stage. That would still allow for different treatment, as noted earlier, but only insofar as necessary to satisfy equally interests of comparable weight. In addition, though, historically and across the globe, common social practice *has* been to view moral status as changing over the course of a human life, most commonly with such status beginning at little or nothing for embryos and increasing throughout gestation and postpartum life, with development of rational and other capacities.[34] Social practice and debates concerning persons in a coma or persistent vegetative state also suggest acceptance of the idea that moral status can change from one point in a human being's life to another. As noted earlier, popular attitudes suggest a demotion in moral status for heinous criminals. If a superior approach to attributing moral status would elevate the status of any being possessing the traits common to human children above that of adults, it would be consistent with this historical and still common treatment of moral status as temporally variable to conclude that moral status is actually higher for humans in their youth and declines over the course of a human life. To reject the possibility of change over time when it might disadvantage adults would smack of unprincipled self-protection.

Last, there is no good argument for ruling out a change of moral status over time per se. In Chapter 4, I consider reasons for concern about attributing different statuses to different groups of humans in general. Among all possible bases for such differentiation, though, there is no reason to think stage of life is more inappropriate or troubling than others, at least if it is a *decrease* from early childhood (a time of powerlessness) to adulthood (a time of maximal political and social power). In fact, there

---

34 See Macnicol (2006) 5 ("in all societies, age 'is one of the bases for the ascription of status and one of the underlying dimension by which social interaction is regulated.'"), (quoting Neugarten, *The Meanings of Age: Selected Papers of Bernice L. Neugarten* (Dail, ed.) (U. of Chicago Press, 1996) 16) ("A recurring theme in social gerontology is that the transition to modernity has brought with it a degradation in the status of old age").

is reason to suppose it is less troubling. Privileging children over adults does not present the concern of unfairness previously raised regarding the opposite practice – that is, because some humans do not reach adulthood. In fact, it offers some compensation for those who miss out on a longer life. And to adults who bemoan their inferior status, one could say simply: "You had your day." In addition, adults' greater power in the public and private spheres makes it likely that law, public policy, and social practice will always give their interests greater weight than is fitting, so recognizing children as occupying a superior moral status might simply result in more even-handed treatment of children and adults rather than a systematic denigration of adults' interests. One might worry that the elderly would incur unduly poor treatment, but the current reality is that the elderly have substantial political power, and because middle-aged adults anticipate they themselves will one day be elderly they enact laws to protect their future interests. Among age-based groups of humans, it is children who are in greatest danger of being treated worse than their moral status should dictate.

2

How Is Moral Status Determined?

Few people ever stop to ask themselves: "Why do I matter morally? Why should anyone else treat me with even the most basic or minimal respect? Why should the government take my interests or wishes into account in its decision making?" We take for granted that we are morally significant beings and that others owe us moral duties – at the least, negative duties to forbear from harming us in various ways. Our moral status seems self-evident, perhaps just because we grew up in a culture that treats all people as morally important, and in fact as the most important type of beings on earth. We might find it quite difficult to articulate exactly *why* we are of any moral significance.

Were we to ask ourselves these questions, one answer that might come to mind is that we all just agree to respect each other. I am owed respect because I respect others, and my interests count because I acknowledge that others' interests count also.[1] On further reflection, though, this contract-invoking answer is likely to prove unsatisfying as an explanation

---

[1] For an example of a contractualist account, see Carruthers (1992). Contractualist political theories typically just presuppose which beings are morally significant members of society and therefore must be taken into account, directly or by representation, in a theory of justice. Elizabeth Anderson offers up a similar position predicating some (but not all) moral rights on "membership in our society," but adopts a somewhat more relaxed requirement for membership, allowing in nonhumans animals who stand in a relationship of reciprocity with humans – specifically, domestic animals and animals in zoos. E. Anderson, "Animal Rights and the Values of Nonhuman Life," in Sunstein and Nussbaum (2004). In part, this resembles the position of environmentalists who base moral status on a being's contributing to a community, and I address that position below. But Anderson's view is narrower. This is in part because she has a cramped view of reciprocity. And it is in part because she supposes, like contractualists, a tit-for-tat view of moral obligation, which, as explained in the text, is not consistent with the ordinary understanding of morality. On contractualism as an approach to morality more generally, see Scanlon (1998) and Gauthier (1987).

of our moral considerability. For one thing, it would seem to imply that any being incapable of giving respect is thereby rendered undeserving of receiving any moral regard. I generally do not place much weight on settled specific intuitions, but I suggest at the outset that any theory of moral status that implies infanticide does no wrong to an infant (who cannot now and might never become able to assent to a moral contract) or that torturing a dog (who will never so assent) does no wrong to the dog would need an exceedingly strong argument in its favor to appear plausible. But the arguments advanced in favor of a contract-based explanation for moral status are quite weak, often fundamentally confused.

Sometimes contractualist arguments rest on a conflation of necessary conditions for being a moral agent and necessary conditions for being an object of moral concern. Those two things are actually quite different, and there is nothing inherent in the concept of a moral object that limits it to beings that are also moral agents. To be a moral agent means to be a being who can and does base decisions on moral reasons. To be a moral object means to be a being who has *some* property that makes it appropriate for moral concern by moral agents, but not necessarily the property of being a moral agent. Thus, a conceptual argument will not make the contractualist case.

More commonly, the contractualist argument rests on the quite shaky normative premises that we never have an obligation to give more than we receive and never deserve more than we give. Such a tit-for-tat view is a quite cramped conception of human moral obligation. We might call it the "Ebeneezer Scrooge Ethic." Though it is true that we expect reciprocation of the respect we show to other moral agents, that expectation hardly constitutes the entirety of our intuitive sense of what makes even autonomous adults deserving of moral regard. For suppose another person were to say: "I absolve you of all responsibility to respect me. You may think of me as equivalent to a piece of dirt. You may treat me however you like, and I will not complain if you try to injure me. I will defend myself, and I will in turn accord you no respect, but I am opting out of this mutual respect agreement." We would likely believe that such a person nevertheless still owes us respect and has substantial moral duties toward us, especially a duty to forbear from injuring us without cause. And we would still not think it proper to treat that person like dirt. We would likely conclude that our moral considerability and that of others derives not contingently from all of us being willing to enter into a mutual respect pact, but rather from properties we possess, from who we are. To answer these questions of mattering morally and proper respect, then, we would need to identify those properties. Philosophers' theorizing about moral status has generally consisted of a search for such properties. Further, we in the developed world who are relatively well off generally believe that we owe moral duties to those in the direst circumstances, to give them some assistance, and this sense of obligation surely does not rest in any part on the expectation that these people will in turn concern themselves with our well-being, that they will reciprocate in any other way, or that they would do the same for us if the tables were turned. Something else about these people must explain our sense of moral obligation to them.

But are we likely to arrive at a truth of the matter about what characteristics are the basis for moral standing? I have spoken of moral status as something we attribute to beings, suggesting that it is merely a feature of contingent social practice. Moral realists might protest that moral status must be something beings possess inherently, infused in them from whatever the source of morality is, which we might discover but not create. For a theist, that source might be a divinity, and in fact many people appeal to the authority of a religious text in discussing the moral status of different beings.[2] Catholic doctrine, for example, holds that God imbues a soul into each human life at the moment of conception, and that the soul is the source of humans' special place in the moral universe. Hindu teachings say that an embryo houses a reincarnated soul.

My approach, though, and that taken by other contemporary theorists addressing the topic of moral status,[3] is nonrealist and intuition-based, appealing ultimately to widespread and deep intuitions about what matters morally and the value of rational consistency in our moral beliefs and attitudes. I bracket metaethical and epistemological questions about the connection between such intuitions and any truth of the matter about

[2] See R. George Wright, "Dignity and Conflicts of Constitutional Values: The Case of Free Speech and Equal Protection," 43 *San Diego Law Review* 527, 537–59 (2006) (discussing classical and modern bases for attributing dignity to persons and other beings). Cf. Franklin (2005) 86–7 (suggesting that the major religions of Western society would have difficulty reconciling their doctrines with attribution of rights to animals).

[3] See, e.g., John Barkdull, "How Green is the Theory of Moral Sentiments?," in Ouderkirk and Hill (2002), 50 (characterizing philosophical views of Adam Smith and of J. Baird Callicott as resting on "widely felt" moral judgments); Bradie (1994), 166. ("We can no longer appeal to an objective world of moral facts or principles independent of human nature to ground our moral deliberations. But we can, and do, appeal to a shared human nature to conclude that our moral deliberations rest on an objective, intersubjective shared human heritage as shaped by the forces of evolution.") See also Wood (2007), 44 (stating that the prevailing style of ethical theory takes such a coherentist approach).

moral status. Thus, while not committed to an antirealist position, I do not appeal to or attempt to establish foundational moral truths or a priori moral knowledge.[4] I treat moral status as something we who are moral agents confer on beings on the basis of our moral intuitions, without asking whether those intuitions match or arise from moral "truths" in any sense. I appeal to widespread intuitions – which theists and moral realists, as much as agnostics and antirealists, are likely to have and to be guided by – concerning the appropriate general bases for our attributing moral status, in order to reason about what moral status we should attribute to children if we aim for consistency between specific cases and such general principles and criteria. Assuming we do have that aim of rational consistency, whether we are moral realists or not, then if some particular views about children prevalent among philosophers and the general public are inconsistent with the best general account of moral status that can be developed from our shared basic intuitions, we must either abandon our deeper and broader convictions about what gives rise to moral status or else revise our moral attitudes toward children.

The weakness of this approach is that it will not persuade anyone who denies that they share the basic intuitions or general principles on which the analysis rests. They can continue to hold to contrary beliefs about the specific case of children without pain of self-contradiction. Thus, someone who truly is unmoved by manifestations of excruciating pain in nonautonomous beings such as human infants or horses, or who truly believes he himself would lose all moral status whatsoever should he become senile, and accordingly denies that sentience and life per se are of any moral relevance, will likely find little in this book that influences his thinking about children. I suspect, though, that few if any people would, on reflection, insist that only current possession and exercise of the higher-order cognitive capacity we call autonomy gives rise to any moral considerability. As explained later in the book, such a narrow view of what makes beings – including one's self – matter morally could give rise to a rather startling set of specific moral precepts (e.g., allowing for

---

4   As such, my approach works like the reflective equilibrium of Rawls and many other moral and political theorists following him, but it eschews the epistemological commitments generally attributed to ethical intuitionism, which are controversial. See, generally, Stratton-Lake, ed. (2002). My aim is simply to show that viewing or treating children as being of inferior moral status relative to adults is incompatible with the best account of our moral-status-ascribing practices, and that in fact there would be greater coherence between our specific beliefs about children's moral status and that best account if we adopted the view that children are of superior moral status.

infanticide, killing adult humans while they sleep, and wanton torturing of nonhuman animals). That does not, on my account, make such narrow intuitions wrong, but rather just unlikely to be encountered.

The strength of this "coherentist" approach to moral reasoning is that it can persuade others who hold a quite different conception of the good from one's own yet share the basic intuitions.[5] It amounts to asking someone: "Regardless of what else you believe, do you believe X (e.g., that others should consider the effects their actions have on you in part because you can feel pain), and if you believe X shouldn't you also believe Y (e.g., that we should consider the effects of our actions on any being that can feel pain)?" We might therefore achieve consensus more readily than if we aim for a comprehensive theory built on moral truths. And this approach should have something to offer even those moral theorists unsatisfied with a coherentist approach to ethics. Even moral realists, religious and nonreligious, might find the analysis that follows illuminating, for some realists might treat the processes of moral psychology that I describe as methods by which we discover rather than confer moral status, and might be moved by my revealing inadequacies and inconsistencies in the conclusions our current moral beliefs and reasoning reflect to adjust their own thinking about the relative moral status of children and adults. The analysis of this book posits that most people do have certain intuitions as to the moral significance of particular characteristics of themselves and other beings, and it challenges anyone who does have at least some such intuitions to achieve consistency between such intuitions and their views about the moral status of children.

How, then, do human moral agents, at a basic intuitive level, generally go about attributing moral status to beings? By what cognitive process do we come to treat some beings as mattering morally and others as not? This is really a question of moral psychology, of how our minds typically work when we contemplate other beings and arrive at conclusions as to how we ought to be disposed toward them – that is, whether I ought to care about them and take them into account for their own sake in making decisions. The philosophical literature suggests two principal ways in which our minds work in this regard, and both seem consistent with common experience and with recent scientific study of human moral psychology – that is, our minds do appear to work in at least these two ways, often at the same time.

5   On the possibility of shared moral concepts across cultures, see Joseph Raz, "Notes on Value and Objectivity," in Leiter (2001) 225–8.

EMPATHY

The first account is associated with eighteenth-century Scottish philosopher David Hume, who maintained that the root of all morality lies in our affective response to other beings that we encounter – specifically, what we would call empathy and what Hume called sympathetic identification. Empathy is "an affective response that stems from understanding another's emotional state, so that one has feelings similar to those of the other person."[6] We perceive in others characteristics that we ourselves possess, which makes us identify with or put ourselves in the shoes of those others, and this causes us to experience what we believe they are experiencing, to share in their thoughts and feelings. We are then moved to render the same positive or negative judgments regarding their experiences that we do regarding our own. Our judgments about our own experiences as well as the experiences of others somehow, by a nonrational cognitive process, get expressed as normative judgments, as assertions of goodness or badness purporting to have objective truth and to constitute warranted claims on others, rather than merely likes and dislikes. Thus, an emotional reaction to other beings becomes transformed into a "moral sentiment," a propositional state attributing moral significance to the experience of those other beings.[7] I instinctively view my pain as not merely undesired by me but rather objectively bad and potentially giving rise to claims against others, that they not cause me pain and perhaps that they help me avoid or alleviate pain. Empathic identification with some other beings leads us vicariously to experience their pain, in somewhat muted fashion, and so to have a gut-level "badness reaction" to their pain as well, a reaction that can lead us to ascribe to ourselves and others moral duties owed to those other beings.

Psychological research on moral belief confirms this account, demonstrating both that empathy is integral to moral concern for others and that most judgments of right and wrong are at base visceral, explained after the fact by reason but ultimately gut-level emotions.[8] The most

---

[6] Jorge Moll, et al., "The Cognitive Neuroscience of Moral Emotions," in Sinnott-Armstrong (2008c), 8.

[7] See Hume (2006). Darwin offered a similar account of the origins of morality as a social practice. Charles R. Darwin, *The Descent of Man and Selection in Relation to Sex* (Princeton, NJ: Princeton University Press), 98–113.

[8] See Prinz (2007) 32, 36, 41; Jonathan Haidt and Fredrik Bjorklund, "Social Intuitionists Answer Six Questions about Moral Psychology," in Sinnott-Armstrong, ed. (2008b) 181–217.

common way in which people override initial self-regarding impulses with countervailing moral intuitions and act out of concern for others is by putting themselves mentally in the other person's place to vicariously feel their emotional responses[9] Indeed, the various criteria philosophers and legal systems cite in discussions of the moral status of other beings appear to be features of those beings that trigger empathy in us, and some theorists claim particular criteria generate moral status precisely because they create a commonality other beings or trigger our empathy. These are typically features that other beings have in common with us and that we are concerned with in our own lives.

For example, some theorists have argued that every living thing – that is, all beings that are "alive" in the way we understand life – has moral status. Our own "aliveness" is of utmost importance to us, and we intuitively react negatively at the thought of any being's life being cut short, even if that being lacks the ability to or never does worry about it, because the prospect of our own life being cut short triggers painful feelings and identifying empathically with the other being gives rise to similar feelings. We imagine the other being has a *telos*, an end or aim toward which it strives, that would be frustrated by destruction, and we identify with that being for that reason, on that basis. Our instinctual negative emotional reaction to that being's destruction gets expressed as a moral claim on that being's behalf. This is the expectation of pro-life advocates who display pictures of fetuses – that we will perceive a commonality with the fetuses as living beings, triggering a gut reaction that the fetus matters morally and cutting off the fetus's life would be wrong, even though the fetus would never suffer or be aware of its loss.

Other theorists emphasize sentience, and argue for the moral status of all beings that experience pleasure or pain (Franklin 2005, 24). As noted earlier, we humans imagine other beings feeling pain and, because of our own experiences of pain, regard pain as a generally bad thing. Thus, if we were to come upon a deer lying on the ground writhing with a bullet wound, we would perceive it to be feeling pain and would experience the deer's pain vicariously to some degree, having the same kind (though not necessarily degree) of emotional reaction to the deer's pain that we would have to our own – namely, that it is bad. Even hunters manifest this reaction; their code dictates that one should put such an animal out of its misery rather than be indifferent to its suffering.

9   Id. at 194.

Still other theorists would require for attribution of moral status that a being have some higher-order cognitive functioning, whether the barest of self-consciousness or highly developed rationality and moral agency. We can make sense of this in Humean terms by explaining that because we imagine other beings having hopes, fears, projects, and beliefs, we can share in what we imagine their experience is by putting ourselves in their position. Any evidence, then, that nonhuman animals partake of high-order cognitive functioning – that is, functioning beyond impulsive reaction to stimuli or acting on instinct, as seems to be true, for instance, of apes – leads us to feel greater commonality with those animals and to view more negatively harms to such animals.

That Hume's account captures at least some aspect of our moral psychology is also borne out by examining common parenting practices. One thing parents routinely do to instill moral regard for others in their children and get them to accept restrictions on their behavior is to point out that other beings have the same experience they have and encourage the children to recall what that experience is like.[10] If my daughter says something unkind about another child, I might ask her how she feels when someone says something unkind about her, and then tell her the other child likely feels the same way. I would encourage my daughter to contemplate that fact, on the assumption that this will trigger some empathic feelings and a negative assessment of her own actions. As further testament to the accuracy of Hume's description, consider the reactions of fear, pain, and happiness we experience while watching a movie or reading a book in which characters are experiencing those emotions.

UNIVERSALIZING BASES FOR SELF-WORTH

An alternative descriptive account of how we come to attribute moral status to other beings points not to affective responses we have to other beings but rather to a formal property of moral reasoning – namely, its entailing a universalizing of individuals' reasons for action or decision or of individuals' self-regarding moral demands. Immanuel Kant and his followers have developed moral theories beginning with an account of the inherent nature of practical reasoning – that is, the thought process rational agents go through in making decisions for themselves – and then

---

[10] See Prinz (2007) 35; Winnie Hu, "Gossip Girls and Boys Get Lessons in Empathy," *The New York Times* (April 5, 2009) (discussing empathy workshops and curricula in schools nationwide).

contending that such reasoning entails generalizing reasons for action to give them an objectively normative quality. Moral reasoning, as a species of practical reasoning, entails generalizing of bases for making normative demands in our own behalf. Implications for moral status that emerge from this Kantian approach to morality arise from attributing normative significance to certain characteristics of ourselves – for Kantians, our being autonomous rational agents – and on that basis making claims on our own behalf, demanding that others respect us, and generalizing such claims and the bases for making them (Wood 2007, 55, 90–3). We recognize that making normative claims for ourselves based on such a characteristic logically entails an acceptance that the characteristic has objective or universal value, and that we must therefore value and assign normative weight to it wherever it is found – not just in ourselves, but also in other beings. Otherwise, our claim amounts to nothing more than grunting of self-regarding preferences. Kant expressed it thus:

> Rational nature exists as an end in itself. This is the way in which a man necessarily conceives his own existence. ... But it is also the way in which every other rational being conceives his existence on the same rational ground which is valid also for me; hence it is at the same time an objective principle. ... The practical imperative will therefore be as follows: Act in such a way that you always treat humanity, whether in your own person or in the person of any other, never simply as a means, but always at the same time as an end.[11]

Thus, when one undertakes to reason *morally* – that is, with reference to objective norms rather than merely personal preferences, one is rationally committed to applying to other, similarly constituted beings the same norms – rights and responsibilities – that one believes should apply to one's self.

There is a large literature debating the soundness of Kant's reasoning insofar as it aimed to establish the truth of specific moral propositions,[12] but wading into that literature is unnecessary for present purposes. What is important here is that the Kantian account described previously does capture the way people generally think at least some of the time. Common parenting practice again supports an assumption that we sometimes

---

[11] See Kant (1956a), 96. A more explicit statement of this line of reasoning is found in Gewirth (1978). See also Korsgaard (1996a) 60; Franklin (2005) 48–50 (distinguishing Gewirth's view from Kant's).

[12] For a succinct summary of some objections to Kantian moral theory, see Korsgaard (1996a) 219–21.

reason morally by generalizing claims we make on our own behalf. If one of my daughters were to ruin a school project the other was working on, I might point out that when the opposite occurred previously she had reacted with moral indignation, contending that all the thought and effort she had invested in the project made the other's interference wrong and punishable, and then I might ask her whether the same kind of reasoning should not also apply to her sister's project. Implicitly, I would be pointing out that she had appealed to certain general principles in stating her own case – namely, that persons who engage in sustained and complex, goal-directed activities warrant respect on that basis, and that such respect entails a duty of noninterference. And I would be pointing out that the same principles must apply equally to other persons. In everyday discourse among adults as well, moral exhortation to others might begin with "Don't you think you deserve …?" or "Wouldn't you be offended if …?". Empirical research shows that most people are receptive to such appeals to reason when strong countervailing intuitions or self-regarding emotions are not in play and that this is a standard form of moral reasoning.[13]

Importantly, however, this mechanism by which we attach normative significance to traits is, despite its association with Kantian moral philosophy, not inherently limited in its application to autonomy or higher-order reasoning capacities. Peter Singer argued in similar fashion for the position that other beings have moral status not (just) insofar as they possess autonomy or moral agency, but simply insofar as they have interests. He contended that because one's practical reasoning about one's own life and aims involves, first and foremost, identifying, valuing, and claiming protection for one's own interests, moral reasoning must involve recognizing that the interests of all beings that have interests also command respect, and therefore must involve balancing the interests of various beings against each other – that is, utilitarian calculation (Singer 1979, 12). Singer identifies our interest in being free to act autonomously as just one of the interests we seek to satisfy, and therefore as *one* of the interests some other beings have that we must take into account in ethical reasoning, but he goes on to make the obvious point that we have other interests as well (Singer 1979, 83–4). I will show below that Singer inadequately defends the supposition that every being's interests matter equally, but I endorse here his mode of reasoning from the implicit presuppositions of a moral agent's self-regarding claims to recognition of other-regarding duties.

[13]   See Haidt and Bjorklund, supra note 8, at 198.

On these two accounts, then, the Humean and the Kantian, moral status arises, at base, from a recognition by moral agents of commonality with other beings. Both point to the essentially social aspect of human moral psychology. For Hume, recognition of commonality triggers an emotional response – empathy, caring – that humans somehow translate into a moral assertion. For Kant, it triggers a rational response – a generalizing of normative claims we assert on our own behalf. The self-serving and species-ist nature of both psychological phenomena is apparent; we humans consciously or unconsciously accord great significance to our own traits, and by one process or another afford moral status to other beings insofar as they resemble us. Arguably, we should make some effort to broaden our moral scope, to try to identify characteristics of beings that other nonhuman organisms value highly, and should think about whether *those* characteristics should be a basis for attributing moral status to beings. But I will not pursue that line of inquiry. I will accept and work within a morality that looks only to what we humans intuitively value. Importantly, however, looking solely to human moral intuition as a *source* of norms does not amount to authorizing self-serving *application* of those norms. We can and should be even-handed in attributing moral status to all beings that possess the traits we view intuitively as giving rise to moral status; such impartiality is a basic feature of moral reasoning. (DeGrazia 1996, 27–31) In addition, I will suggest at some later points that we should pay some attention to what children value and view as normative that might be distinct from what adults generally value.

AWE AND DISGUST

It is not clear, however, that the Humean story of empathy or the universalizing property of moral reasoning that Kant emphasized, or even a combination of the two, fully explains our practice of ascribing moral status. There is reason to believe humans attribute special significance and inherent worth to some entities – for example, God and parts of the natural universe – that seem quite "other" to us, with which we do not necessarily feel or perceive a strong commonality. For example, I believe many people would intuitively regard as morally wrong a governmental proposal to level the Grand Teton mountains in order to facilitate transcontinental travel, or to allow logging of the great Sequoia trees in the California forests. And I believe most people would think these proposals wrong not just because they would deprive humans of the ability to enjoy those natural wonders, but because they regard those things as having a special status of their own, a status not held by a common hill or tree no matter how much enjoyment people get from it, and a status that generates duties owed to them. This moral regard for parts of the natural universe might stem from our evolving to have a "concern with 'cosmic' structure and position, growing out of the need to bring order and meaning to our lives and fostered by our capacity to view ourselves in intertemporal terms."[14] That same concern supports religious belief, and religious belief and esteem for impressive and powerful entities and forces in nature are often connected. Whatever the source, and whether rationally defensible or not, humans do manifest a sense of obligation to parts of the natural world and to supposed nonnatural entities that does not arise from empathy or universalizing of self-regarding claims.

Whether the notion of owing duties to mountains and trees is nonsensical is something I address below, but for now I just note that the many animist traditions the world has known constitute evidence that such intuitions are common. So, too, does much art depicting such natural objects; witness, for example, the spiritual quality of Ansel Adams's photographic landscapes. Intuitions of this sort might be an important part of the explanation for why legislators have passed laws to protect these natural entities. Moral status appears to arise in these instances from a psychological reaction perhaps best characterized as awe, being impressed by something even when – perhaps in part because – it is unlike us, reacting instinctually or intuitively by attributing special importance, even magical qualities, to certain entities. Some theorists speak in terms of reverence, which is a similar reaction of respect to perceiving surpassing greatness (e.g., Woodruff 2001). In some cases, what impresses us might be sheer size, power, or beauty; in other cases, reverence might also arise from gratitude for the benefits natural entities bestow.

In addition to rendering moral status to additional entities, this reaction of awe also seems to elevate the moral status of beings whom we might treat as moral objects through empathy or universalized self-regarding claims. We seem to accord a higher status to, and be more concerned about, beings that inspire awe – for example, eagles, and whales – than to animals that do not inspire such awe but possess the same qualities, such as sentience or cognitive functioning, that humans possess and on which many philosophers have predicated moral status.

[14] Victoria McGeer, "Varieties of Moral Agency: Lessons from Autism (and Psychopathy)," in Sinnott-Armstrong (2008b).

When we first learn that some creature has impressive abilities of which we were previously unaware, we consciously or unconsciously think more highly of them, accord them more respect. Reflect on the reaction you have upon learning that "the dance-communication of honey bees... appears to have no counter-part in the insect world and is exceeded in complexity and information-carrying capacity only by human speech...; it is the most remarkable nonhuman communication system known" (Steiner 2005, 245). Does that enhance the respect one intuitively believes honey bees are owed? If so, is this at least in part because of the awe this phenomenon triggers? Similarly, learning that the cheetah is the fastest land animal, reaching speeds up to seventy miles an hour, causes us to regard that animal with greater respect than we otherwise would, and with greater respect than we feel for a large cat of lesser ability, such as a cougar; as a result, we might regard extinction of cheetahs as a greater moral tragedy than extinction of cougars. And the tragedy would lie not (just) in humans' loss of opportunity to behold the display of speed, but in the wrong done to such a noble creature.

Indeed, even some humans appear to acquire a special moral status, in the sense of owing them greater respect or deference for characteristics we do not possess. For example, many people put star athletes on a pedestal, and think it more tragic when they are harmed than when other people are harmed. This is not because we recall our own great athletic accomplishments (because most of us never had any) and share in the athlete's experience, nor because of claims on our own behalf based on our athletic or other accomplishments, nor because we might have less opportunity to see them perform; it is simply because they are so impressive, so superhuman. The same is true for great artists and musicians. Statements like "Jimi Hendrix is God" are not entirely facetious. Of course, some people disparage hero worship, at least in certain domains of life, but few disparage it across all domains (e.g., those who think adoration of athletes ridiculous might fawn over brilliant pianists), and the practice seems to be pretty universal across cultures. Kant's moral theory was, by his own account, inspired by his awe upon contemplating humans' moral faculty.[15]

---

[15] In the *Critique of Practical Reason*, Kant writes: "Two things fill the mind with ever new and increasing admiration and awe, the oftener and more steadily we reflect upon them: the starry heavens above me and the moral law within me." Kant (1956b), 166. This nonrationalist strain was more prominent in Kant's earlier work; for example, in *Observations on the Feeling of the Beautiful and the Sublime*, Kant wrote that moral principles can be derived from "the feeling of the beauty and dignity of human nature." Kant (1960), 60.

One might also point to religious devotion, which generally entails ascription of higher moral status to a being (a deity) before whom we stand in awe precisely because of ways that it is unlike us, possessing traits we lack, such as the power to create worlds, and/or a far greater degree of certain positive qualities or faculties than we do. Humans' ascription of ultimate moral status to divinity would be difficult to explain only in terms of the Humean or Kantian psychological processes described earlier. Thus, awe, too, appears to be a cause of our attributing moral status, and awe-inspiring qualities that beings have might also be a widely accepted basis for conferring moral status on them.

Conversely, disgust can cause us to ascribe lower status to some entities. Disgust is a visceral, adverse reaction to things we perceive as especially base or vile, as threatening to contaminate us, reduce us to the level of nonhuman animals, or cause our decay (Nussbaum 2004, 87–98). Anthropology, evolutionary theory, empirical psychology, and neurology all treat disgust as "one of the most elementary human feelings," one that historically has played a role "of very considerable importance for the physical, intellectual, moral, and social spheres of life," and many prominent figures in the Western intellectual tradition have viewed disgust as a reaction following especially clear insight or strong intuition (Menninghaus 2003, 2, 9–11). Indifference to use of rats in research laboratories likely reflects in part association of rats with disease and infestation, which triggers a disgust reaction. Dan Kahan argues that disgust is essential to ranking of criminal acts as more or less condemnable.[16]

Disgust also at least partly explains the denigration of some groups of humans historically, groups viewed as animalistic or abnormal, treated as subhuman or as nonpersons.[17] That we now officially reject such denigrating views of *some* such groups suggests that we can and do subject our initial intuitive disgust reactions to reflection and rational scrutiny. This is true, though, not only of disgust reactions but also of our experience or failure to experience awe, empathy, or feelings about our own deservingness. Any of these kinds of reactions might rest on false empirical assumptions or conflict with other intuitions that we have or would have if we thought through the implications of our reactions. I discuss

---

[16] Dan M. Kahan, "The Anatomy of Disgust in Criminal Law," 96 *Michigan Law Review* 1621–57 (1998).

[17] See John Anthony Terrizi, Jr., "Prejudicial Attitudes toward Homosexuals: The Competing Roles of Moral Reasoning and the Moral Emotion of Disgust," Masters Thesis, Dept. of Psychology, College of William & Mary (2007).

further below the possibility of moral progress within a naturalist, non-realist outlook.

The danger that disgust will lead people to disparage certain other beings in a way we now think or some day will think is reprehensible does not, however, obviously lead to the conclusion that we should ignore disgust reactions altogether in ascribing moral status. In some cases, such as autonomous adults who commit heinous crimes, there might be little reason to resist a disgust-based intuition that those humans are of a lesser moral status and hence are owed less consideration in our moral deliberations and social policies. In those cases, we feel anger or indignation for harm done as well as disgust, a combination of feelings that constitutes contempt (Prinz 2007, 74), and it might be that our moral and political reasoning should heed justifiable contempt reactions more than disgust alone. That conclusion seems implicit in much recent philosophical and judicial reasoning about laws prohibiting conduct, such as sodomy, that some view as offensive but that does not appear to harm anyone.[18] We should be more skeptical of disgust reactions to things that have no adverse effect on others beyond the disgust reaction itself. Thus, there is a substantial constituency behind the idea of equal respect for people who are homosexual regardless of how distasteful some people might find homosexuality, but none behind the idea of equal respect for predatory pedophiles and serial killers.

Nussbaum objects to giving effect to disgust reactions in moral and political practice, on three grounds. The first is that disgust is inherently irrational – not simply nonrational, but contrary to reason and evidence. This is so because it "revolves around a wish to be a type of being that one is not, namely nonanimal and immortal." We are disgusted by things that remind us of our corporeality and animality. Yet, Nussbaum implies, we are no different from other animals, so disgust serves only to suppress the truth (Nussbaum 2004, 102). Her objection therefore rests crucially

---

[18] Mill authored the seminal work normatively differentiating conduct that merely offends from conduct that causes harm. See Mill (2003). Joel Feinberg developed a more elaborate and rigorous account of this view. Feinberg (1984). The U.S. Supreme Court's important decision in *Lawrence v. Texas*, invalidating criminal prohibition of homosexual sodomy, rested crucially on this distinction between mere offense and harm. 539 U.S. 558 (2003). As discussed below, Martha Nussbaum argues against reliance on disgust reactions in law or morality, but does not claim that emotional reactions are entirely out of place in moral reasoning or law making; she concedes that anger might be a more reliable emotional basis than disgust for prohibiting or punishing behaviors. Nussbaum (2004), 122.

on a supposition that we are not morally different from other animals, and so it will be unpersuasive for the great majority of people who reject that supposition. If one believes that humans generally possess some capacities that enable them to rise to a higher level of moral importance than other animals, then perhaps one *should* denigrate humans to the extent that they have those capacities but fail to realize them, and disgust reactions are the vehicle by which we do so. Other characteristics of such humans might counteract that denigration, so disgust will not necessarily justify hierarchy. But so long as we hold on to the belief that humans generally matter more morally than other animals, we should acknowledge that such a belief must rest on humans typically having relevantly different properties, and we should not regard as irrational or inherently misguided disgust reactions to people who routinely make choices contrary to the elevating aspects of human nature. Probably all or nearly all humans do this to some degree – that is, have vices – so perhaps only more extreme cases of depravity warrant attribution of a lower moral status. I return to this idea in Chapter 5.

Nussbaum's second reason for jettisoning disgust from our moral practices is that, in contrast with mere anger, it leads us to dismiss or banish people who act immorally rather than try to redeem them:

> Anger at a bad act is compatible with the desire to rehabilitate the offender and with respect for the offender's human dignity. Disgust, because of its core idea of contamination, basically wants to get the person out of sight.... We should distinguish carefully between persons and their acts, blame people for any bad or harmful acts they commit, but retain a respect for them as persons, capable of growth and change. (Nussbaum 2004, 106)

This argument fails for several reasons. It presumes that we want to banish any person who disgusts us at all, but our reactions are in fact likely to differ considerably based on the degree to which someone disgusts us. I might prefer not to sit on a plane next to someone who picks his nose or has terrible body odor, but that does not mean I want him tossed off the plane or executed. Nussbaum's argument also simply begs the moral status question; Nussbaum presupposes that acting immorally does not diminish one's human dignity or the respect one is owed, then contends that reacting in certain ways to depraved people is inconsistent with that dignity and respect. But it is precisely that presupposition that is in question, so Nussbaum's reasoning is circular. Moreover, treating an especially depraved or evil person as an inferior being might itself constitute

an appropriate form of punishment, a form that might be especially effective in deterring depraved or evil choices.[19]

Third, Nussbaum makes a slippery slope argument, that there always
lurks the danger that disgust will lead us to persecute groups of less-
powerful people who are simply different or who get irrationally associated in our minds with immoral people. She cites the rampant anti-Muslim
sentiment following the 9/11 terrorist attacks as an example (Nussbaum
2004, 107). However, that example actually proves that other negative reactions to immorality, including the anger and indignation that
she thinks are better moral guides, present the same danger of irrational
spillover. The anti-Muslim sentiment was at least as much constituted by
anger and indignation as by disgust; Americans lashed out in anger and
indignation at the larger group with which they associated the terrorists.
People develop animosities toward other groups all the time in reaction
to conduct by single members of the group, without being disgusted by
the group's members. Rival gangs and warring family clans do not necessarily view each other as having repugnant physical or mental properties.
Anger might well be a generally stronger emotion, and so more likely
to result in spillover. As to any negative emotion, the preferable course
would seem to be to reflect on our reactions and to inculcate strong sentiments supportive of being careful and rational, limiting our reactions to
their proper targets. Our history of irrational prejudice should make us
cautious, but our history of recognizing and overcoming such prejudices
should give us some confidence.

All this being said, disgust will not play an especially prominent role
in my assessment of how moral status varies with age or youthfulness. It
will, though, play some role – particularly in thinking about how much
weight to give adults' supposedly greater capacity for moral action relative to children if most adults largely fail to exercise that capacity and
are more likely than youths to make moral compromises and engage in
specious rationalizations for selfish and petty behavior.

I have now identified several potential experiential bases for attributing moral status, all of which appear to be commonly used in everyday

[19] This view solves the conundrum identified by Susan Dwyer (no relation), with psychopaths, whom she says "we are tempted to exclude from the moral community,"
but who at the same time we want to hold morally responsible. Susan Dwyer, "What
Psychopaths Can Teach Us," *The Philosophers' Magazine* (2004). We can hold people
morally responsible for doing evil by demoting them in moral status, at which point
there is less constraint on how we treat them, and in the extreme case hardly any
constraint.

moral practice.[20] In light of this, one plausible approach to philosophical analysis of moral status, the approach I will take, is to determine on the basis of all such psychological processes what specific criteria we should use for determining the relative moral status of different beings. We could reflect on what characteristics of beings cause us human moral agents to identify empathically with them, on what characteristics of ourselves we typically invoke when we make moral claims on our own behalf, and on what characteristics of beings typically inspire awe or disgust in us, and then combine all those characteristics to formulate a list of traits that are, prima facie, relevant to moral status.

IS ONE BASIS FOR ATTRIBUTING MORAL STATUS SUPERIOR?

One might object, however, that we should not simply accept as valid, or as equally valid, all of these mechanisms by which we ascribe moral significance to beings. Perhaps one mechanism alone warrants our relying on it or is superior to the others in some way. For example, Kantians might assert that the phenomenon Kant identified is more essentially human or more likely to lead to a truth of the matter about moral status, in that it involves rational reflection rather than mere emotional responses and an irrational leap from "is" to "ought," and is therefore privileged or deserving of greater emphasis.

In response to such an objection, I would first reiterate that I am not purporting to establish a method of arriving at a truth about moral status. Rather, I aim to offer a fairly comprehensive descriptive account of how our moral minds operate to attribute moral significance to other beings, and then to see what happens when we take all the criteria for moral considerability generated by this operation and try to combine them in a coherent test or calculus of moral status. Because this approach is eclectic in the moral psychological sources to which it looks, it should resonate with a broader range of people than a solely empathy-based or solely rationalistic approach would.

---

[20]   Haidt and Bjorklund characterize as the three "'taste buds' of the moral domain," based on a survey of sociological and anthropological literature, "harm/care (a sensitivity to or dislike of signs of pain and suffering in others, particularly the young and vulnerable), fairness/reciprocity ... and authority/respect ..." (Haidt and Bjorklund, supra note 8, at 203).

   These three components of moral sentiment would appear to map fairly well onto the triggers for moral status reactions that I have described.

Second, I would point out that all of the mechanisms I have identified earlier by which human moral agents do ascribe moral significance to beings share essential features that would make prioritizing them difficult. To respond specifically to the anticipated Kantian objection, the reality is that the process of moral reasoning Kant described, just as much as the process Hume described, begins with a nonrational reaction to some perception and proceeds to a moral attitude by way of some unarticulated leap over the is/ought divide. What Kantians fail to provide is an adequate rational justification for any individual making moral claims on his or her own behalf. It appears true as a descriptive matter that we do inevitably treat our will as authoritative with respect to what is good, that our rationality and autonomy do have importance for us, and that we do react negatively to incursions on them, but what warrants our ascribing value in an objective or normative sense to those aspects of ourselves? What warrants our making moral assertions about how others treat us, rather than simply grunting our pleasure or displeasure? There is a large justificatory gap between "I cannot help but value my rational capacities" and "You must respect my rational capacities." I have accepted as accurate the Kantian assumption that *we do* value our rationality and autonomy, and that *we do* express our objection to others' interfering with them in moral terms.[21] But anyone who believes that Kant failed to demonstrate that we are rationally warranted in doing either, as even some modern defenders of Kantian moral theory do (Wood 2007, 93), and who finds unsatisfactory the efforts Kant's expositors today have made to remedy this defect in his attempt to develop a foundational account of morality from the structure of practical reasoning, can agree that the Kantian approach to ascription of moral status described earlier ultimately rests simply on suppositions with gut-level intuitive appeal.[22]

---

[21] Dale Jamieson suggests that we tend, without rational warrant but as a result of how we are constituted psychologically and as a result of acculturation, to objectify our most important desires: "We begin by expressing our desires in terms of what we like or prefer; then it becomes a matter of what we value; and finally, it is a question of what is valuable." Dale Jamieson, "Values in Nature," in Frey and Wellman (2005), 656, 660.

[22] See Donald H. Regan, "The Value of Rational Nature," 112 *Ethics* 267–91 (2002). Korsgaard states that Kant presupposes a conception of ourselves as ends in ourselves, which in turn commits us to a conception of our humanity as a source of value. And she states that such a conception is a prerequisite to our making any decisions or judgments, suggesting that we cannot help but hold that conception of ourselves. Korsgaard (1996a) ix. Even if this is true, however, it does not make the conception rationally justified; it simply makes it a fact about the human cognition. That we cannot help but believe something does not make it true. Arguably, we also cannot help but believe,

Really, then, all the mechanisms I have described begin with a nonrational emotional state that somehow gets expressed in normative terms. In that sense, all are on equal footing.

In addition, the proposition that rationality is the most important feature of humanity or the singular root of true morality is not obviously true and not one that all or even most people hold. As noted earlier, recent empirical work reveals that moral attitudes usually arise initially from nonrational intuitions, with reason at best providing post hoc rationalizations for emotion-based claims, and most people most of the time are comfortable relying on their emotions and intuitions without logical arguments to justify them (Prinz 2007, 34; Greene, in Sinnott-Armstrong 2008b). Because moral practice rests so squarely on emotion, "moral education is a matter of emotional training" (Prinz 2007, 35). Scientific study of human moral psychology reveals that deontological moralizing (emphasizing fundamental rights and duties rather than consequences), in particular, is intuition and emotion driven.[23] Joshua Green explains:

> Deontology, then, is a kind of moral confabulation. We have strong feelings … that some things simply cannot be done and that other things simply must be done. But it is not obvious how to make sense of these feelings, and so we, with the help of some especially creative philosophers, make up a rationally appealing story. (Greene, in Sinnott-Armstrong 2008b, 63)

Nonhuman animals likewise manifest an instinctual sense that some things are not to be done, some because of immediate self-interest (e.g., defecating where one sleeps, harming one's offspring), but also some because of the demands of social life (e.g., violating hierarchies, refusing to join in cooperative behavior). The Kantian ideal of autonomous moral agency and the Kantian pretension that human nature is of a different order than animal nature are thus simply incompatible with what we now know about how humans and other animals operate. As one moral psychologist puts it, "psychological science is in the process of abandoning the view that humans make decisions in the classical sense, as rational decision makers who reason deliberately under full conscious control."[24] Another writes: "What turn-of-the-millenium science is telling us is that

---

when we perceive it, that the suffering of nonhuman animals is objectively bad. There appear to be many things that our brains are hardwired to believe.

[23] See Joshua D. Greene, "The Secret Joke of Kant's Soul," in Sinnott-Armstrong (2008b), 35–79.

[24] Darcia Narvaez, "The Social Intuitionist Model: Some Counter-Intuitions," in Sinnott-Armstrong (2008b), 233.

human moral judgment is not a pristine rational enterprise – that our moral judgments are driven by a hodgepodge of emotional dispositions, which themselves were shaped by a hodgepodge of evolutionary forces, both biological and cultural" (Greene, in Sinnott-Armstrong 2008b, 72).

In his later writings, Kant himself acknowledged some role for moral sentiment, as motivational support of a commitment to act in accordance with duty, and in fact maintained that we have a duty to cultivate emotions such as sympathy that give rise to inclinations consistent with moral duties to others. He wrote that "it is a duty to sympathize actively in others fate; and to this end it is therefore an indirect duty to cultivate the compassionate natural (aesthetic) feelings in us, and to make use of them as so many means to sympathy based on moral principles and the feelings appropriate to them."[25] He just never fully recognized how fundamental and essential a role emotion plays in moral judgment and action. Justin Oakley suggests that empathy and compassion are important to moral practice not only in generating inclinations to be moral, but also in generating knowledge necessary to optimal moral decision making, by enhancing awareness of and providing greater insight into the condition and needs of others, making us more sensitive to situations that call for beneficence (Oakley 1992, 50–2, 82). From another direction, Martha Nussbaum argues forcefully that emotions are not in fact noncognitive impulses, as some Kantians might view them, but rather have an essential rational component to them, so the denigration of emotion on which the Kantian elevation of rationality in part rests turns out to depend on a false empirical premise (Nussbaum 2001).

Kant's early view that "true morality" consists in acting solely out of respect for what reason tells us are our duties to self and others, rather than out of any nonrational inclination such as might arise from fellow feeling, is also inconsistent with popular understanding of morality.[26] Even among moral philosophers, a group of humans likely to be extraordinarily rationalistic, "such a position has engendered scorn

---

[25] See Guyer (2000) 299–303 (citing Immanuel Kant, *Metaphysics of Morals*, § 35).

[26] Mark Timmons contends that it might never have actually been Kant's view that moral agency must be entirely independent of feeling. He suggests that Kant always had in mind that respect for the dignity of humanity in others would trigger a kind of love for them – perhaps something akin to the fellow feeling one sometimes experiences from contemplating shared citizenship, membership in the same club, or biological kinship – and that this love would provide the effective motivation for moral action. Timmons (2002) 15–20. Still, that feeling is not instinctual compassion that Hume described and that most people view as a commendable, moral experience.

and ridicule from the outset" (Guyer 2000, 289). In recent decades, feminists have criticized more broadly the emphasis on rationality and abstract principles in the history of moral philosophy, as reflecting a distinctively male viewpoint, and have suggested that general principles merely have some utility in social interactions where true morality is lacking. By "true morality," these feminists mean caring emotionally about others. Robin West explains:

> Women's concept of value revolves not around the axis of autonomy, individuality, justice and rights, as does men's, but instead around the axis of intimacy, nurturance, community, responsibility and care. For women, the creation of value, and the living of a good life, therefore depend upon relational, contextual, nurturant and affective responses to the needs of those who are dependent and weak, while for men the creation of value, and the living of the good life, depend upon the ability to respect the rights of independent co-equals, and the deductive, cognitive ability to infer from those rights rules for safe living.[27]

These feminist theorists, who sometimes purport to speak for or to describe the experience of women generally, find much more plausible and attractive the Humean account of moral intuition. In addition, as noted previously, empirical research in moral psychology shows that West overstates the role of rationality even in the "male perspective"; even if men are more likely than women to explicitly appeal to rules of conduct deduced from general principles about individual rights, their moral attitudes originate in nonrational intuitions, and rational moral argument generally amounts to post hoc rationalization of their intuitions.

Feminist scholars are surely right in contending that most people – and I would suggest this includes most men – view caring about others, empathically identifying with others, responding affectively to the perceived experience of others, as a quintessentially moral activity.[28] Some moral theorists writing from a nonfeminist perspective have also contended that it is a more authentic form of morality. For example, Schopenhauer wrote:

> It is the everyday phenomenon of compassion, of the immediate participation, independent of all ulterior considerations, primarily in the suffering

---

27 Robin West, "Jurisprudence and Gender," 55 *University of Chicago Law Review* 1 (1988). See also Warren (1997) 138; French (1985); Noddings (1984) 8, 24–6, 28, 35; Gilligan (1982).

28 For an extended argument for the position that an agent's emotions are pertinent to a moral assessment of him or her, see Oakley (1992).

of another, and thus in the prevention or elimination of it; for all satisfaction and all well-being and happiness consist in this. It is simply and solely this compassion that is the real basis of all voluntary justice and genuine loving-kindness. Only insofar as an action has sprung from compassion does it have moral value; and every action resulting from any other motives has none.[29]

Examples are readily at hand of humans who are paragons of morality and who seem to have acted principally on the basis of love and compassion rather than rational principle – for instance, Mother Teresa and Jesus Christ. In some instances, nobility of character is manifest in declining to stand on principle and instead acting out of sympathy. Kant appears to have rested his valorization of acting from principle in part on the fact that this is often difficult, requiring us to struggle against inclination (Wood 2007, 29–30), but acting out of compassion can also be contrary to inclination and quite difficult.

Pointing in this way to what most people believe or to how most people operate in their moral practices does not amount to proving that Kantians would be wrong in insisting that Kant's approach to ascribing moral value is superior in some sense. But it does put the burden on them to make a very convincing case that this is so. It would be an excessive detour in this book to review and assess modern defenses of Kantian philosophy, so I will simply say that few if any philosophers today would claim that Kantians have made a knock-down case for the superiority of their views.[30]

But we should also reject the position, if any theorists in fact advance it, that affective response is all of morality. Acting on principle is also universally regarded as moral action, even when unconnected with emotional concern for the intended beneficiaries of the action, and moral practice sometimes requires consulting general principles and considered judgments rather than simply acting on emotional or intuitive reactions.[31] Sometimes moral deliberation overrides initial intuitions,

[29] Schopenhauer (1965), 144. See also Blum (1980), 9–15, 163–4 (advancing the view that emotions such as sympathy and compassion grounded in the well-being of others are inherently morally valuable); Michael Slote, "Autonomy and Empathy," *Social Philosophy & Policy* 293–309 (2004).

[30] Christine Korsgaard goes so far as to assert that Kantian moral theory is today generally regarded as a failure. See Korsgaard (1996b) 220–1.

[31] See Jonathan Haidt and Fredrik Bjorklund, "Social Intuitionists Reason, in Conversation," in Sinnot-Armstrong (2008b), 250–1. Hauser et al. describe research on persons with damage to the emotion center of the brain, showing that such persons can still make some moral judgments, by reasoning from known moral precepts in clear cases, but

and sometimes the desire to appear or be good results in acting on the conclusions of our rational deliberations rather than on our immediate sympathies. Just as this aspect of morality is not clearly superior to the affective aspect, it is also not clearly inferior. Ordinary language and social practice tell us that compassion *and* principle are important components of morality. Oakley notes that, while they contribute to moral action by supplying awareness, insight, and inclination, "love, sympathy, and compassion can also be misdirected to morally bad objects, unless they are guided by phronesis [capacity for rational deliberation]" (Oakley 1992, 82). From an evolutionary perspective, both fellow feeling and an ability to take an objective view of individual desires and demands have contributed to the formation and success of human societies. That moral attitudes arise from experiences of awe and disgust is also borne out by historical, cross-cultural, and contemporary practices, and there is no clear reason for altogether disregarding those experiences. We would regard as at least abnormal, and perhaps psychopathic, someone unmoved by beholding the Grand Canyon or Lake Louise in Canada's Banff National Park and not outraged by the idea of using either for garbage dumping.

In sum, a pluralistic approach to developing an account of the practice of ascribing moral status, one that draws on these several mental processes, is truer to our moral psychology, and it is therefore also more likely to appear plausible to many people and to generate consensus. I aim for nothing more in this book. Critically, however, even if there is no way to prioritize among the mechanisms, it is not the case that we must collectively accept and give equal weight to every intuition about what characteristics have value or moral significance that arises from any one of these mechanisms. There might be some other basis for critiquing and refusing to rely on or give great weight to any given characteristic that currently causes some people to identify more with other beings, to make demands on their own behalf, or to be in awe of another. Over time, we in Western society have rejected some criteria that previously had been used to assign moral status – for example, race, gender, physical normalcy, and the social class into which one is born – even though they are things that unquestionably have, historically and across cultures, caused people to identify more closely with

they show a deficit in other cases, especially those in which well-established precepts do not clearly dictate right and wrong. Marc D. Hauser, Liane Young, and Fiery Cushman, "On Misreading the Linguistic Analogy: Response to Jesse Prinz and Ron Mallon," in Sinnott-Armstrong (2008b), 177–8.

others and to feel that they are owed greater consideration. We are in the process of doing so with respect to sexual orientation as well.

We have rejected these characteristics as bases for moral status, however, not because those criteria originated in nonrational reactions to others, but because after considerable public discussion and/or especially dramatic events, most people concluded that they did not want to continue using them. Moral psychologists can account for "moral progress" of this sort:

> Levy suggests that the past century did involve a great deal of moral progress driven by good arguments, many produced by moral experts (e.g., philosophers and religious leaders) that filtered through populations and changed consensual views (e.g., about civil rights, women's rights, and human rights). We agree with Levy's analysis. We add only that moral progress was probably driven more by words and images that triggered affectively laden intuitions (such as Martin Luther King's highly metaphorical "I Have a Dream" speech, and the televised images of peaceful marchers being attacked by police dogs) than by well-reasoned arguments that convinced people to care about the violated rights of strangers to whom they had no emotional ties.[32]

As a result of new experience and discourse, intuitions contrary to prevailing attitudes and practices emerge, grow, and ultimately hold sway.

New intuitions arise and spread in part because increased familiarity with disfavored groups triggers greater empathy. Increased familiarity can dispel false empirical assumptions undergirding conventional attitudes (e.g., that women and people of other races have lesser cognitive capacities or present certain dangers) and can increase awareness of commonalities. A process of moral maturation in societies as well as in individuals follows from increased perceptual sophistication. Just as we become better at relative valuing of foods and wines through experience and greater attunement to detail, our assessment of conduct as right and wrong and our assessment of the relative standing of other beings become more nuanced over time through experience and reflection[33]

In addition, rational consideration of attitudes and practices has at times revealed an inconsistency or incoherence between treatment of disfavored groups and general beliefs about what matters most morally,

---

[32] Haidt, J., and Bjorklund, F., "Social Intuitionists Reason, as a Normal Part of Conversation, " In W. Sinnott-Armstrong (2008b), 150.

[33] Darcia Narvaez, "The Social-Intuitionist Model: Some Counter-Intuitions," in Sinnott-Armstrong (2008b) (pp. 233–240) at 236–39.

and the discomfort generated by realization of that inconsistency has moved people to look at the disfavored groups in a new light and to open themselves to having different intuitions about the standing of those people (Prinz 2007, 290–2). The affective responses described earlier are not all-or-nothing phenomena, but rather can be stronger or weaker; some characteristics of other beings trigger strong identification while others have only a very modest effect on us, and some things about ourselves strike us as more compelling bases than others for demanding that others respect us. We have abandoned discriminatory attitudes toward some groups after concluding that we had exaggerated the relative importance of certain characteristics, such as sensory ability (as in the case of persons who are, for example, deaf or blind). My aim in the chapters to follow is to assess whether we adults have been insufficiently attentive to the positive qualities of children, have self-servingly exaggerated or underestimated the significance of certain characteristics in order to elevate our standing above that of children, and have held on to attitudes regarding children that are inconsistent with general intuition-based beliefs about what gives rise to moral status. This book itself thus partakes of the process of moral progress just described, or at least that is my hope.

Last, another objection might be that I have left out of my account of human moral psychology some other source of intuitions about criteria of moral status, some other mechanism by which we come to attribute moral significance to particular characteristics of beings. I concede that this might be the case, and welcome responses that would improve on the account I have given. My own judgment now is that all the criteria one might plausibly propose can be sufficiently well explained as triggering one or more of the affective responses identified earlier, but that judgment might turn out to be flawed.

In sum, my strategy for reassessing the moral status we accord to children relative to adults is, first, to identify the characteristics of beings that trigger in us (a) empathic identification with them, (b) beliefs that we are entitled to respect, (c) awe, or (d) disgust; then to ask whether there are independent reasons to reject any of those characteristics as bases for attributing or denying moral status; and finally to apply whichever characteristics emerge from this process to the case of children relative to adults, taking into account that any given characteristic might be displayed to different degrees in different humans and that the degree of moral status can vary accordingly. This basic approach appears consistent with what people generally do now, unconsciously, in thinking about different groups of humans and nonhuman entities, and the philosophical aim would simply be to do this in a more conscious, explicit, and rigorous way and then use the results of the analysis to suggest a proper attitude for adults to adopt in their relations with and governance of children.

DEFICIENCIES IN EXISTING APPROACHES TO MORAL STATUS

Yet this approach is quite different from how moral status theorizing is generally done. As Chapter 3 will show, the predominant approach among moral theorists to questions of moral status is to focus on one particular characteristic of beings and to argue that all and only beings who have it possess moral status. Theorists' selection of a characteristic is generally driven by an aim of extending moral concern to a particular class of beings, such as nonhuman animals. Simply put, such theorists believe we ought to treat a certain class of beings, such as animals or fetuses or trees, with more respect, and set out to identify what it is about that class of beings that warrants their belief. Other theorists' objections to such single-criterion accounts generally rest on a given account being incompatible with beliefs about other specific cases – for example, that requiring beings to be self-aware in order to have any moral status would mean that newborn human babies and adults in a coma have none and so do not matter for their own sake.

This pervasive and near exclusive reliance on intuitions about specific cases makes the inquiry quite narrow and result driven. At the extreme, this approach can make theorizing about moral status vacuous; it can become an exercise in merely contriving an explanation for the moral beliefs people generally already have. This approach also tends to cause theorists to overlook some important distinctions and questions. Much unsound reasoning in the philosophical literature rests on a failure to appreciate the distinctions between a characteristic being *sufficient*, *necessary*, and *relevant* to moral status. A characteristic might be sufficient for having moral standing but not necessary, because some other characteristic is also sufficient. For example, being sentient might be sufficient to possess moral considerability, but it is conceivable that some nonsentient beings also have moral status, perhaps because they are simply alive or because they are awe-inspiring. On the other hand, a characteristic might be necessary but not sufficient, if some other characteristic is also necessary. For example, many theorists suppose that a being must be capable of having interests in order to have moral status, because morality is about protecting and promoting interests. (I challenge this view below.) But it would not follow from this supposition alone that all beings that have interests, however defined, have moral status; it might well be that we owe moral duties to only a subclass of all beings that have interests. Last, a characteristic might be neither necessary nor sufficient by itself to confer any moral standing, yet still be relevant to moral standing because it enhances the status of those beings who satisfy whatever conditions *are* necessary and sufficient. Thus, for example, one might think that means-ends rationality is not necessary for having moral status, because sentience is a sufficient condition, and one might think that means-ends rationality is also not a sufficient condition for having moral status, because some entities (a computer program, for example) might possess it but be incapable of suffering, yet one might still conclude that beings who do have moral status because of other characteristics have even more, all else being equal, if they possess means-ends rationality.

In addition, most theorists have failed to consider adequately whether the degree of moral status might vary among all beings who have some. Variation might arise from the fact that beings can manifest a particular morally relevant characteristic to different degrees and/or because some beings might manifest only one morally relevant characteristic while others manifest several. This is an important point, because if two beings both have moral status but one has a higher status than the other, then uneven treatment of them might be appropriate even when they have identical interests at stake. For example, a cow and a human infant might have equally strong interests in avoiding N amount of pain, but if a cow has lower moral status than a human infant it might be permissible to inflict that pain on the cow but not on the infant, even if all else is equal. In Chapter 4, I consider objections to moral status hierarchy among human beings, but it will be useful to describe briefly here the argument some theorists have given in favor of a radical egalitarian position, under which beings either have "full" moral status or none. In that view, if a cow and a human child both have any moral status, then they must have equal moral status, in which case it is just as bad to inflict N amount of pain on a cow as on a human child, all else being equal. In pointing out the shortcomings of the argument, I can clarify some concepts and questions that will be in play in Chapter 3.

The radical egalitarian argument, most often advanced by utilitarians, typically takes more or less this form:

1. For a being to have any moral status, it must be a proper object of direct moral consideration – that is, a being to whom moral duties can be owed.
2. For a being to be one to whom duties can be owed, it must have interests.
3. Only beings with characteristic X can have interests.
4. Therefore, X is a necessary condition for having moral status.
5. Among beings that have X, there is no morally nonarbitrary basis for giving some higher moral status than others.
6. Therefore, all beings with characteristic X are of equal moral status.

There is some surface plausibility to this argument. Premises 1 to 4 sound right, because it seems nonsensical or pointless to attribute moral status to any being if we cannot imagine what it would mean to make it better off or worse off. What would it mean to care about a rock? If a being has no interests, I cannot harm it, and so one might think there is no point in my taking it directly into account in my moral deliberations and no point in ascribing moral standing to it. In addition, it seems unfair to accord less respect to any being that has interests on account of their lacking some further feature, if it is not their fault that they lack it. Proponents of the egalitarian position gain further plausibility by conceding that it does not rule out different treatment for different types of beings, because it allows that different beings might have interests of different magnitude, so that it would be proper to protect a being with greater interests at stake to a greater extent than a being with lesser interests (Singer 1990, 19; DeGrazia 1996, 37, 48). As such, the all-or-nothing stance toward moral status does not have to lead to practical prescriptions that would strike us as bizarre. For example, it does not necessarily lead to the conclusion that, if we adopt a system of universal health care, then we must fully include in the system all nonhuman animals that have any interests, for it is plausible to think that most nonhuman animals have lesser interests in general than humans and so less at stake in whether they remain healthy and alive. Humans greater experiential capacities mean they have greater opportunity for satisfactions, pleasures, realization of aims, etc. (DeGrazia 1996, 252; McMahan 2002, 190–1). The egalitarian view might require that a government-subsidized health care system pay for inexpensive, sure-fire lifesaving treatment for cats before it pays for my massage therapy, but that is not such a counterintuitive implication. Some critics of the position that non-human animals have the same moral status as humans have failed to appreciate this point, resting their case for unequal moral status on intuitions that humans generally should receive more protection and public benefits than other species (e.g., Steinbock 1978, 251, 254).

Nevertheless, this radical egalitarian argument has several weaknesses. First, the interpretation of key concepts is debatable. The concept of duty in ordinary usage is not inherently limited to protection and promotion of interests, as statement 2 supposes. Consider, for example, the sense of duty most people feel toward God, even though they likely do not believe they are advancing God's interests by fulfilling duties to God or that they are capable of making God better or worse off. Consider also the sense of duty some cultures have felt toward the natural universe, which was not limited to aspects of the natural world they believed they were capable of damaging or improving. They may have felt a duty to express respect and gratitude because of a sense of awe or appreciation. Those who assume that morality consists entirely of responding to the interests of other beings, and that all our moral duties entail helping or avoiding harm to beings that have moral status, mistakenly conflate being an object of welfarist concern with being an object of moral duty, but the two concepts are distinct and are not coextensive. Utilitarians might think exclusively in terms of interests, but not all of human moral reasoning and practice is utilitarian.

There is also no fixed meaning for "interests," and different theorists of moral status have in fact advanced different conceptions of interests. These theorists generally all recognize that *having interests* at stake is not the same as, and does not depend on, *taking an interest* or *being interested* in something; it means simply having a welfare.[34] But the concept of interests is sufficiently vague that reasonable people could take different views of what it means. Some moral status theorists insist that having interests depends on being sentient, on being capable of experiencing pleasure and pain, and nothing else (Singer 1975, 8–9; 1979, 90–92; Feinberg 1984; DeGrazia 1996, 226). DeGrazia reasons that because "ethics concerns interests," and because having interests depends on being "capable of suffering and enjoyment" or on having "desires, preference, or concerns," any and only sentient or conscious beings are proper subjects of ethics (DeGrazia 1996, 40). Many, though, go farther and require that a being have sufficient self-awareness to care about its life and experience, appealing to an "if they don't care, why should we?"

[34] See, e.g, R.G. Frey, "Rights, Interests, Desires and Beliefs," in Armstong and Botzler (2008), 55.

sort of intuition (Frey 1980; Regan 1983; Rollin 1992, 76–7; Steinbock 1996, 12, 14–15, 17; 2001, 23–5). Bernard Rollin, for example, stipulates that "morality and moral concern take as their focus the effects of action on beings who can be helped or harmed, in ways that matter to them" (Rollin 1992, 103). Others maintain, though, that it is enough to possess interests that a being has a *telos* or a normal way of functioning or being; interfering with achievement of the telos or with normal functioning could be said to be against the entity's interests.[35] Which definition one adopts is likely to dictate what X in statement 3 could possibly be, and the more basic and widespread X is – that is, the more types of beings it allows in – the harder it will be to make an egalitarian position appear plausible.

Efforts to support a favored definition tend to be very superficial and unconvincing. DeGrazia, for example, defends the position that all and only sentient beings, which he defines as beings capable of experiencing "aversive states such as pain, discomfort, distress, fear, anxiety, and suffering," have interests. Though conceding that "common parlance does not unambiguously support the sentience requirement" and that "the sentience requirement does not tidily account for all of our ethical intuitions," he insists that extending the concept of interests to nonsentient beings is untenable. Yet the only explanation he offers for this conclusion appears to be that defining interests as simply "having a good of one's own" would open the door to attributing interests to cars, buildings, and waterfalls. He does not explain why it would be wrong to attribute interests to such inanimate objects. In addition, he does not recognize that opening a door does not mean letting just anything in, because he conflates necessary and sufficient conditions (DeGrazia 1996, 226–9). The view he criticizes maintains that sentience is not a necessary condition and having a good of one's own *is* a *necessary* condition, but DeGrazia treats the view as maintaining that having a good of one's own is a *sufficient* condition, which does not follow from its being necessary. It might be that some beings that can be said to have a good of their own have no moral status, because they lack some other characteristic.

There does not appear to be any basis other than ordinary language for adjudicating among the several possible definitions of "interests," and that basis, as DeGrazia concedes, is not univocal. The more proponents of a sentience test build in a cognitive component, as they are inclined to do in order to exclude plant life, suggesting, for example, that what we

---

[35] See, e.g., id., at 56; Attfield (1991), 168.

do has to "matter" to the being in question, the more difficult they make it to include many animal species or the infant members of any species – including infant humans! The notion that human babies have no interests has no intuitive appeal whatsoever and is flatly inconsistent with the legal rights babies possess today, so an ordinary language argument that leads to that conclusion will have no plausibility.

Further, there is a gap in the line of reasoning outlined earlier between statement 4, that having characteristic X is a *necessary* condition of having moral status, and statement 5, which seems to presuppose that having interests is also a *sufficient* condition for having moral status.[36] It does not follow from the fact that it is *intelligible* to attribute moral status to a being – in other words, that we would not be speaking gibberish to say that a being should be of moral concern – that we should actually do so. It might well be that some characteristic other than X is also necessary for a being to have interests and that something other than just having interests is also necessary to have moral status. Moreover, even if X is both a necessary and a sufficient condition for having some moral status, it does not follow that X is the only characteristic relevant to moral status; among beings with X, there could be status differentiation based on other (not necessary and not sufficient, but relevant) criteria.

Proponents of the all-or-nothing view might respond that any further characteristic on the basis of which we might circumscribe or discriminate within the class of interest-possessing beings who have moral status must be morally arbitrary, as suggested by statement 5 (e.g., Regan 1983, 239–43). However, an assumption that "not chosen" or "not the being's fault for lacking" is equivalent to "morally arbitrary and inappropriate" is not clearly true or consistent with most people's moral intuitions and practices. That assumption underlies much modern Western liberal political theory relating to justice among humans.[37] But there is nothing close

---

[36] An example of this fallacious reasoning can be found in DeGrazia (1996), 40. ("[A] nimals who have desires, preference, or concerns, or who are capable of suffering and enjoyment, have interests.... Since ethics concerns interests, which animals have, it would seem, prima facie, that the treatment of animals is part of the subject matter of ethics.")

[37] Singer cites "the leading figures in contemporary moral philosophy" as authority for the principle that "everyone's" interests should receive equal consideration (Singer 1975, 5). DeGrazia adopts this line of reasoning as well. He infers from the observation that "all serious contenders among ethical theories have this egalitarian feature," that "morally serious people today accept some principle of equality for human beings" (DeGrazia 1996, 52). He then goes on to observe that "most of the great moral philosophers" have not taken seriously the notion of animals having moral status, but rather than infer from this that morally serious people do not accept a principle of equality among all

to a consensus even among political theorists on the necessity or propriety of extending the principle to nonhuman beings, and popular attitudes around the world throughout recorded history have reflected acceptance of a moral hierarchy not only as between humans and other species but also among humans and on the basis of characteristics for which no one is responsible. Gerbils are not at fault for lacking moral autonomy, nor are cars responsible for not being sentient. In short, proponents of this conceptual argument for radical egalitarianism have a lot more explaining to do, especially given that such an egalitarian view is counterintuitive for the great majority of people. Importantly, and as discussed further in the next chapter, arguments to the effect that some characteristic cannot be a necessary condition for having moral status, even when persuasive, will not demonstrate that that characteristic cannot raise the moral status of some being above others – that is, that it is relevant to moral status even if not a necessary condition.[38]

My own approach therefore relies neither on arguments from specific cases nor on conceptual arguments, and I remain open to the conclusion that moral status arises from more than one attribute and that it is a matter of degree and can therefore give rise to a moral hierarchy. In Chapter 3, I describe the several single-criterion views that have been advanced, and I note some objections that have been advanced based on specific cases and conceptual claims, but in developing my own view, I appeal repeatedly to the basic psychological processes underlying moral belief that I have laid out in this chapter. I aim for a more open-ended and comprehensive study of all the characteristics that might give rise to moral status. I assume that if the ultimate foundation for anyone's intuition that a particular characteristic is relevant to moral status is the bare fact that the characteristic triggers one or more of the moral psychological processes described earlier, then there is at least a prima facie case

---

sentient beings, which might put the burden of persuasion on those who would extend the equality principle to all sentient beings, he chalks this up to bias and superficiality and cites that bias as a basis for putting the burden of persuasion on those who would not extend the equality principle to nonhuman sentient creatures (52–3). Later, DeGrazia simply asserts that "the champion of unequal consideration has no clear way to defend the relevance of cognitive criteria" to moral standing (249). This chapter and the next in this book offer a way to defend that relevance, by showing that higher cognitive capacities can trigger empathy, sense of objective self-worth, and awe.

[38] DeGrazia, for example, presents several arguments as to why moral agency is not a necessary condition for having moral status and mistakenly concludes from them that moral agents do not have a higher moral status than sentient beings that are not moral agents – that moral agency does not elevate the moral status of those sentient beings who have it (DeGrazia 1996, 53–71).

for the relevance of *any* characteristic that triggers one or more of those processes. For example, if animal rights advocates rest their position on reasoning like "we objectively value our own sentience and believe it makes us morally considerable, so therefore we must recognize the value and moral relevance of sentience in nonhuman creatures," then they should concede that if there is anything else about ourselves that we view as objectively valuable – such as our life per se or our capacity for having a conception of the good – then those things also presumptively give rise to moral status. Proponents of a single-criterion view of moral status would need to explain why other characteristics that generate empathy, a sense of self-worth, or awe are morally irrelevant and only their preferred criterion is relevant, and they have uniformly failed to do so.

3

Selecting Criteria of Moral Status

Chapter 2's account of how we characteristically attribute moral status to beings provides a basis for generating a list of candidates for criteria of moral status. We can look for evidence that particular traits of other beings cause us to identify empathically with them, that particular traits in ourselves generally form the basis of moral claims we make on our own behalf, and that particular characteristics of entities inspire awe or disgust in us. There are many places one might look for such evidence, including one's own experience and others' expression of their experience in narrative or art. I will focus in the first instance, though, on the philosophical literature relating to moral status, on the assumption that scholars who have explicitly analyzed the topic have identified at least some of the criteria on which human moral agents commonly predicate moral status.

Most philosophical writing that touches on moral status is not directly or ultimately concerned with moral status per se; it does not aim to develop a comprehensive account of the necessary and sufficient conditions for having moral status generally or even to demonstrate the relevance to moral status of a particular property in the abstract. Rather, discussion of grounds for attributing moral status appears most often in tracts advocating (and occasionally opposing) social policies more protective of particular entities – for example, advocating for animal welfare or stronger environmental laws. As noted in Chapter 2, this advocacy context has in nearly all cases produced a rather stunted investigation of the grounds for moral status and a tendency to jump quickly and unjustifiably to a conclusion that only one trait is relevant to moral status and that all beings partaking of that trait are of equal moral status. This book itself has an applied context, and it ultimately urges a particular view about a certain class of beings – namely, human children. However, it undertakes a much more open and thorough investigation of potentially morally relevant characteristics, and it takes seriously the possibility that among all beings with some moral status there could be wide variation in the degree of moral status, as a result of some having more than one relevant characteristic and/or some manifesting a given relevant characteristic to a greater or lesser degree than other beings.

Thus, in this chapter I review arguments for the moral standing of prebirth humans, cognitively impaired humans, and nonhuman beings, such as nonhuman animals, trees, and inanimate objects, even though my focus will ultimately be on the relative standing of postbirth "normal" children and adults. I do this because the vast bulk of the literature on moral status focuses on such other beings, and consideration of those other beings' standing does elucidate intuitions as to whether particular characteristics, such as aliveness or sentience, are themselves independent sources of moral status, rather than just having instrumental value for beings that have moral status solely on other grounds, such as rationality. For example, if it is sufficient to confer some moral status on seemingly nonrational animals such as rabbits that they are sentient, and if rabbits' relatively greater sentience leads us to confer on them a status higher than that of worms, then that suggests that we intuitively regard sentience as an independent source of moral considerability and we might determine the relative standing of children and adults in part by assessing their relative degrees of or capacities for sentience.

The extant literature on moral status includes arguments for recognizing at least the following traits as criteria of moral status, which I have ordered roughly according to demandingness: simply being alive, being depended on by actual or potential moral agents, being an object of concern for moral agents, being sentient, and having higher-order cognitive capacities. (The second and third of these could be viewed as less demanding than the first, but they are usefully lumped together under the heading of "relationship to moral agents," a criterion sometimes invoked to extend moral status to some nonliving things and sometimes invoked to limit moral status to less than all living beings.) I will address each in turn and then consider whether there are other relevant traits overlooked in the philosophical literature.

It might seem unnecessary to the task of establishing the relative moral standing of children and adults to review all these criteria. Clearly all apply to both groups, except perhaps the last on the preceding list – that is, higher-order cognitive capacities, which adults presumably have but children might lack (depending on precisely what cognitive capacities are pertinent). So it might seem sufficient just to consider whether any one of these criteria that is shared by both is a sufficient condition for moral status. However, as I have suggested, moral status is a matter of degree and the degree to which a criterion is manifest can influence the degree of moral status; and so to assess the relative standing of any two groups of beings, it is necessary to have as complete a list of relevant criteria as possible. It is important to know whether, for example, being alive is in and of itself a source of moral status, because if it is, then the degree to which children and adults manifest aliveness could affect their relative moral status. It will also prove fitting to break down some criteria into component parts. On one conception, aliveness is not simply a matter of being not dead but rather comprises the several phenomena that generate an appearance of vivacity, and different beings might display these phenomena to different degrees.

LIFE

A "reverence for life" view attaches moral status to all and only living beings. This view is often said to have originated with Albert Schweitzer, who wrote in 1933:

> The great fault of all ethics hitherto has been that they believed themselves to have to deal only with the relations of man to man. In reality, however, the question is what is his attitude to the world and all life that comes within his reach. A man is ethical only when life, as such, is sacred to him, that of plants and animals as that of his fellow men, and when he devotes himself helpfully to all life that is in need of help. Only the universal ethic of the feeling of responsibility in an ever-widening sphere for all that lives – only that ethic can be founded in thought. The ethic of the relation of man to man is not something apart by itself: it is only a particular relation which results from the universal one. (Schweitzer 1933, 158–9)

The view was inspired by Darwin's evolutionary theory of the prior century, which had the effects both of revealing greater complexity in the lives and development of species other than humans than had previously been appreciated and of revealing humans' greater commonality with other species. A view attributing moral status to life per se has found adherents in more recent decades among environmental ethicists and proponents of animal rights.[1] Politically charged issues relating to destruction of human life – in particular, abortion, embryo research, and euthanasia – have also evoked expressions of the view that life per se is sacred,[2] though likely those who voice it have in mind only human life.

In many articulations of the reverence for life view, one finds language suggestive of a religious or spiritual perspective, in which living things are imbued with significance by a divine creator. Schweitzer couched his outlook in highly metaphysical terms: "Reverence for Life brings us into a spiritual relation with the world which is independent of all knowledge of the universe. Through the dark valley of resignation it leads us by an inward necessity up to the shining heights of ethical acceptance of the world."[3] However, an intuition that beings have moral significance simply by virtue of being alive can also be explained in terms of the psychological processes identified in Chapter 2, and so need not have any connection to a religious or other metaphysical outlook.[4] Indisputably, a perception that another being is living can, in and of itself, induce some sympathetic

---

[1] Examples include Steiner (2005); Gary E. Varner, "Biological Functions and Biological Interests," 28 *Journal of Philosophy* 251–70 (1990); Rolston (1988) 94–126; Taylor (1986) 14–25; Kenneth Goodpaster, "On Being Morally Considerable," 75 *Journal of Philosophy* 308, 308–25 (1978). For a survey of the different types of views constituting environmental ethics today, see Andrew Light, "Environmental Ethics," in Frey and Wellman (2005). One can distinguish advocacy for animal welfare, which does not always rest on an argument for animals having rights, from advocacy for animal rights per se, but I will elide the distinction in discussing advocacy for animals.

[2] A significant recent example is the U.S. Supreme Court's decision in *Gonzales v. Carhart*, upholding a prohibition on partial birth abortion. The majority opinion noted that the prohibition "expresses respect for the dignity of human life." 127 S.Ct. 1610, 1633 (2007).

[3] Schweitzer (1933) 157. See also Richard H. Hiers, "Reverence for Life and Environmental Ethics in Biblical Law and Covenant," 13 *Journal of Law & Religion* 127 (1998); J. William Futrell, Environmental Ethics, Legal Ethics, and Codes of Professional Responsibility, 27 *Loyola L.A. Law Review* 825, 825–7 (1994). ("Albert Schweitzer's appeal for a new ethic embracing the natural world became a tenet of liberal Protestant thought resounding beyond the churches. ... This shift in environmental ethics was a powerful twentieth-century reformulation of the transcendentalist vision of Emerson and Thoreau that had inspired the earlier conservationists of the Progressive Era. Environmentalism and the hopes and expectations of the Earth Day generation cannot be understood without an acknowledgement of this ethical, indeed religious, shift-a shift as fundamental and disturbing to established social relations as earlier changes in thought leading to the end of slavery in the 1860s.")

[4] An alternative argument for the significance of life per se points to the obvious wrongness of killing someone for no reason even if it could be done painlessly, instantaneously, and without the person's awareness. See, e.g., Rollin (1992) 70. This argument fails, though, because a proponent of the view that sentience alone, or rationality alone, gives rise to moral status could maintain that the wrongness of the act would lie in the deprivation of opportunity for pleasure or rational action in the future.

identification in us with that being, and we do concern ourselves with the fate of some other beings simply insofar as they are alive. Most people, I think, would not find terribly strange a passage like this by Schweitzer: "In everything you recognize yourself. The tiny beetle that lies dead in your path – it was a living creature, struggling for existence like yourself."[5] Even with plants, we can perceive a commonality, stemming from their fragility at birth, their growth under proper nurturance, their competition with other life forms, and their eventual decline and death.

True, many people are careless about the impact they have on non-human life forms, but when we are really attentive to them, we perceive activities resembling our own and then our consciences are tweaked, if only slightly. We might not feel any obligation to help an ant in distress, but our acting affirmatively and intentionally to kill an ant for no reason whatso-ever would strike many people as morally unattractive. It does not make us react with the revulsion we would feel if someone wantonly tortured and killed a horse, but we have some negative, morally tinged reaction, because we can see that the ant is, like us, a living creature trying to survive and reproduce. Empathetic identification with plants appears less common, because we typically do not attribute any intentionality to the growth or other changes a plant manifests. But it is not uncommon for moral agents to feel that others have acted wrongly if they destroy certain forms of plant life wantonly. For example, hacking at the trunk of a thriving tree for no reason would strike many people as morally blameworthy, even if we have no reason to believe this interferes with another human's enjoyment of the tree, because we attribute some inherent value to the tree as a flourishing living thing. If one were to go to the National Redwood Forest, hike into the woods with axe in hand, leave the path and make one's way miles into unmarked forest, to a place where no other human is likely ever to go, and prepare to wield the axe against a towering redwood tree, one would, if normally constituted psychologically, no doubt be troubled by feelings of guilt, by a sense that one is committing a wrong *against the tree*.

The Kantian thought process for attributing moral status also supports a conclusion that life per se matters morally. It seems that we attribute objective inherent value to our own life per se, and on that basis demand respect for and protection of our lives. One illustration of this is the aversion many people have to "assisted suicide," even if their lives should become dominated by pain or devoid of rationality. In addition, those who make

---

5   Schweitzer (1993) 24. On the other hand, many might find strange the remainder of the second sentence: "... rejoicing in the sun like you, knowing fear and pain like you."

an advance directive to have life support removed uf they should lose brain functioning do not thereby signal that they believe it would be permissible for a hospital to treat them, or their bodies, in just any way in such circumstances. Rather, they would expect and insist on a respectful approach to terminating their lives, even though they would not be aware of or suffer at all from disrespectful treatment of their bodies. Another illustration is the fact that we would not think it appropriate, should we lose our mental faculties long before we die, that the date we are determined to have lost self-awareness or rational capacities be put on our tombstones, rather than the date of our physical death. Insofar as we view life in ourselves as objectively valuable, and as retaining some of that value when all that is distinctively human about our lives has ceased, we are rationally committed to ascribing some moral value to life per se wherever it exists.

Further, reactions of awe might well arise from the perception that some beings are alive rather than inert. This might best explain the sense many would have that it is morally wrong to hack wantonly at a majestic redwood tree or, on a bigger scale, to destroy huge portions of the Amazon rainforest, or to diminish biodiversity by driving some species to extinction. We feel awe upon contemplating that certain nonhuman environments teem with multiple forms of life, and we are troubled by the idea of humans decimating that life. In addition, we are sometimes awestruck by perceiving that some single entity displays an extraordinary degree of "aliveness" – for example, an animal that works ceaselessly or a plant that grows prodigiously. Courtney Campbell argues for a more respectful and restrained approach to embryo research by invoking the experience of awe humans uncorrupted by career or financial motivations (especially expectant parents, she might have noted) experience when contemplating what an embryo represents:

> The scientific quest to understand the inner workings of life must be mediated by a foundational sentiment that life is a wondrous mystery, albeit a mystery amenable to our discovery. This sense of awe and wonder in the face of mystery can readily be lost by the routines of demystification that occur in biomedical research and clinical practice. ... The journey of an organism of microscopic size through various developmental phases to the flourishing of a human person is a source of amazement and should be an occasion for "pause" and reflection on the remarkable fact that life *is*. This pre-research sentiment is, in my view, necessary to the cultivation of an attitude that ascribes serious moral consideration to the human embryo.[6]

---

6   Courtney S. Campbell, "Source or Resource? Human Embryo Research as an Ethical Issue," in Lauritzen (2001) at 46–47.

One type of objection to a life-based account of moral status is that, despite whatever intuitions observation of life per se in other beings might trigger, life nevertheless cannot be a sufficient condition for having moral status. It is here that the conceptual arguments critiqued at the end of Chapter 2 are most common. As noted there, some proponents of sentience-based and self-awareness–based accounts of moral status have argued that, to have moral status, a being must have interests or a well-being that we could impact by our actions, because morality consists precisely in giving adequate attention and respect to the interests of other beings (Feinberg 1984; Steinbock 1996, 9–12). And they generally deny that being alive is enough to give rise to interests. Who cares if I kill a tree in the middle of a dense forest? Surely not the tree. And if the tree itself does not care, why should any moral agent?

As suggested in Chapter 2, this debate over welfare and interests in connection with moral status essentially transforms a moral question into a conceptual and semantic one. Those rejecting life's moral relevance conceptualize morality solely in terms of respect for interests and then argue that the common meaning of "interests" entails certain assumptions. But morality is not inherently confined to serving interests; many people believe they owe duties to obey God, to respect the natural world, to fulfill promises made to people now deceased, and it is difficult fully to make sense of these duties in terms of promoting interests. Moreover, the concept of "interests" is not inherently limited to feeling pleasure and avoiding pain or to preference-satisfaction, in the way supposed by many who reject the reverence for life view. Environmental ethicists have offered convincing ordinary language arguments for defining interests, welfare, and injury more broadly. It does no violence to ordinary language use to speak of a shrub's having an interest in receiving water and sunlight, of moisture being good for fungus and intense heat being bad for the grass, or of injuring a tree by driving nails into it (Belshaw 2001, 127). Living things naturally tend toward growth and survival, and they can experience health or illness, thriving or decline, just as we do and just as nonhuman animals do (Goodpaster 1978, 319).[7] Moreover, we ourselves

---

[7] Steinbock, after initially making interests depend on a being having "beliefs, aims, goals, concerns," all of which suggest a high level of cognition and self-awareness, later retreats to the position that beings have interests so long as they "experience their treatment as painful or pleasant" (Steinbock 1996, 23). She appears to have no reason for this hedging except discomfort with excluding infants, third-trimester fetuses, severely mentally disabled humans, and nonhuman animals from having any moral status. (To exclude earlier term fetuses, however, Steinbock points out that they "do not have lives that they

have interests other than just experiencing pleasure, having our wishes be effective, and not suffering pain, and our interests can be affected without our being at all aware of it. Belshaw uses the example of undetected slander or betrayal (Belshaw 2001, 127). Undetected theft would be another. Infants can own property, and stealing property from babies would impact their interests even though they could have no understanding of the loss and even if they never experience pain or discomfort as a result. Nussbaum writes of the dignitary interests of Alzheimer patients (Nussbaum 2000). Goodpaster adds that sentience, which some animal rights proponents valorize as the singular basis for moral standing, might itself have value only or principally instrumentally, as "an adaptive characteristic of living organisms that provides them with a better capacity to anticipate, and so avoid, threats to life," so that what is inherently valuable is living rather than sensing (Goodpaster 1978, 316). One might go farther and argue that "sentience" can also be understood more broadly, as any capacity to react to environmental stimuli, in which case all life forms might be sentient. Plants grow toward light. Flowers open and close in reaction to temperature. A cold spring delays the budding of trees. Snails die if we poison their food supply. These reactions to external conditions are not so clearly different in kind from those of basking crocodiles, migrating birds, hibernating bears, and humans living in a persistent vegetative state as to be irrelevant to moral status.

In any event, the ultimate question is not a definitional one. It is rather whether we *can* and *should* view ourselves as owing moral duties to particular beings. As to the "can" part of the question, we should ask: Are we human moral agents psychologically capable of believing that we owe duties to beings such as a giant redwood tree that do not appear to be self aware nor to have a nervous system like ours? *I* can, and I assume others can as well. Is it possible to give coherent content to such duties? Yes – for example, "don't kill it." As to the "should" part of the question, we should ask: Is there a plausible basis for thinking we do have any such duties?

value," which seems like a return to a more demanding cognitive standard, one that newborns likely do not satisfy!) Steinbock also offers no reason for us to believe that a newborn baby "cares about" being burned with a cigarette in a way that is relevantly different from the reaction a tree would have to its trunk being scorched with a blow torch. Still later, she adopts the view that one can be harmed even if one has no adverse sensation whatsoever from another's actions, in order to support the position that we can harm people by conduct we engage in after their death or after they fall into a coma or persistent vegetative state (Steinbock 1996, 25, 29–30). The chameleon character of Steinbock's view of interests is indicative of just how broadly the ordinary language use of "interests" is.

Yes – most compellingly, generalization of the demand we are inclined to make that others respect our life per se. Even if I become entirely lacking in sentience and self-awareness, so long as my body is still alive I believe others will owe me – or my body – a duty not to hack at it with an axe. Aliveness per se also appears sometimes to trigger empathy and awe.

We should also ask whether there are overriding arguments against positing duties to living but nonsentient beings. As explained earlier, the conceptual/definitional argument fails. I address below further objections based on specific cases, but these objections are directed at the claim that all living beings are of equal moral status, which is a much grander claim than the one just defended – that is, that aliveness is simply a sufficient condition for possessing *some* moral status. But first I flesh out a bit what aliveness means as a basis for ascribing moral status.

If merely being alive generates some moral considerability, we would need to ask how we determine that a being is living. Schweitzer seemed to identify life with having a will to live, which ordinarily suggests substantial cognitive capacity, but he employed a very broad understanding of having a will to live. Being driven by anything to survive, even in the absence of consciousness, appeared to suffice. Mary Ann Warren, who has presented the most comprehensive analysis of moral status to date, in assessing the merits and difficulties of the reverence for life view, considers and appears to reject teleological organization, or goal-directedness, as a criterion of life. She points out that beings generally understood to be nonliving can have a teleological organization (e.g., a space exploration vehicle), whereas beings generally understood to be living might have no teleology (e.g., suicidal persons).[8] However, even if Warren's empirical assumptions are true, teleological organization could be an aspect of aliveness. A characteristic can be indicative of life even if it is neither a necessary nor a sufficient condition of being alive. And it seems quite plausible that we are more likely to deem a being alive if it has a teleological organization – that is, is driven to some end – than if it does not have such organization.

Surely, though, there are many things other than a will to survive or teleological structure that we perceive as bases for deeming entities alive. Dictionary definitions of "alive" or "life" include "activity," "alertness,

---

[8] Warren (1997) 29–30, 47–9. Warren's illustration of this latter point is unconvincing. She suggests that suicidal persons have no goals, because they are bent on self-destruction. But self-destruction can be a goal and a telos for an entity. That a being could formulate self-destruction as a plan of action, and then engage in complex activities in furtherance of that aim, would seem pretty good evidence that the being is currently alive.

energy, or briskness," "capacity for metabolism, growth, reaction to stimuli, and reproduction,"[9] "storage and use of energy,"[10] vigor, liveliness, adaptation to environment, dependence on sustenance, and having pursuits.[11] The activity indicative of life would include both externally observable action, such as self-produced mobility, and internal activities other than merely processing food, such as neural activity and flow of bodily fluids. We are more likely to deem other beings alive if we perceive any of these phenomena.

In addition to asking how we distinguish living from nonliving entities, we might also ask whether all living beings are equally alive, or whether instead some manifest more aliveness than others. Many proponents of the reverence for life view write as if life is an all-or-nothing property, that all entities that are alive are so to an equal degree. For example, in support of animal rights advocacy, Richard Garrett writes that "an animal is a living creature; and as such it is, like any form of life, something sacred. In saying this I mean to imply that any living thing simply in virtue of its being a living thing has an inestimable worth, a worth that lies beyond our clear grasp."[12] Schweitzer wrote that "[t]he teaching of reverence for life makes no distinction between higher and lower, more precious and less precious lives" (Schweitzer 1965, 47).

But this is mere assertion. Ordinary discourse suggests, to the contrary, that often when we speak of things being "alive," we presuppose that there are degrees of "aliveness," and we aim to distinguish certain living beings not just from rocks and corpses but also from other living beings that have, so to speak, less life in them. We speak of people or animals as being more or less lively or animated, and of some unquestionably living things as being "half dead" or "having little life left in them." We might draw a sharp line between being truly dead and being alive, but that does not mean that we think of aliveness as having always the same quality or magnitude, just as drawing a sharp line between a light being off or on does not preclude speaking of it being "partially on" or "mostly on" (i.e., if there is a dimmer switch). Thus, plants can be more or less alive depending on whether they are thriving or withering. We talk of ourselves feeling "truly alive," and of living life to the fullest. This everyday conception of relative human vivacity incorporates expressiveness, spiritedness, passion for living, curiosity about the world, activeness, and ambition. These are

---

[9] *The Miriam-Webster Dictionary.*
[10] *Webster's New World College Dictionary* (3rd ed., 1997).
[11] *Oxford English Dictionary.*
[12] Richard Garrett, "Love's Way," in Graham and LaFollette (1989) 124–45, 127.

all things that make us regard a being as "full of life," as more alive than others, and they are things to which we respond emotionally. We identify more with and are more impressed by a puppy than a slug in part because of the enthusiasm and activeness the puppy displays. We might think our own lives are more worthy of protection the more spirited and ambitious we are. And we typically react with greater admiration for highly active people and other animals than we do for indolent creatures.[13]

One deficiency in many articulations of the reverence for life view, then, is the failure to recognize that aliveness is scalar, comes in degrees, and therefore that moral status might vary in degree among living beings, based on the degree to which they manifest the phenomena constitutive of life. A further deficiency lies in asserting without argument or implicitly simply supposing that being alive is all that matters, such that we cannot sensibly differentiate among living beings on the grounds that some (but not all) living beings also have other characteristics that enhance their moral status. Together these two deficiencies allow proponents of the life-based account of moral status to conclude that all living beings are of equal moral status. Correcting the deficiencies makes that conclusion less plausible.

The conclusion that all live beings are of equal moral status has been criticized by others solely on the basis of its unacceptable implications for everyday moral practice. For example, Warren criticizes reverence for life theorists on the grounds that making life the sole criterion for moral status is incompatible with settled convictions about certain specific ethical problems. It would require moral agents to treat all living beings as of equal moral status, with the consequence that we would presumptively act immorally by unjuring even the lowest of life forms and even in failing to come to the aid of the lowest life forms when they are in danger. Such "radical biological egalitarianism," Warren contends, is wholly impractical. On this view, Warren explains, brushing one's teeth would be the equivalent of mass murder of humans, because it entails intentionally killing innumerable microorganisms – that is, very small, but nevertheless living, and therefore morally equal – beings. An even better example

---

[13]   It might be objected that we also empathize strongly with people or other animals when they are dying. In that case, however, I believe what triggers a reaction in us are (a) the belief that they once had a vigorous life and now mourn the end of that life, and (b) a perception that they are suffering, suggesting that their sentience induces identification with them in spite of their relative lack of life. We typically empathize more strongly the younger a dying person is, because the person typically was more alive before the onset of the terminal condition.

might be consumption of other living beings, from which we cannot forbear without perishing. Although some moral theorists would say that we should not reject moral conclusions simply because we do not like the practical implications, they would likely also doubt the soundness of reasoning that leads to moral conclusions we are literally unable to live by, it being an accepted theoretical precondition for moral obligations that it be possible to fulfill them. And we simply cannot, at least if we are to carry on living ourselves, avoid destroying some other living things.

Warren recognizes that one could modify the view to allow killing other organisms in self-defense. She responds (correctly) that this would not be enough to allow for teeth brushing and other daily human activities, because killing microorganisms would be a disproportionate response to their non-life-threatening incursion on us. She might have added that the plants we eat to survive typically do not threaten us at all. Warren's next move, though, is problematic. She justifies killing these other beings by pointing out that we simply *do* put our own hygiene above the life interest of such creatures, and that we cannot (should not?) live our lives feeling guilty about that, particularly given that, on the radical biological egalitarian view, the guilt should be enormous, the same as what we should feel if we killed many humans. It is okay that we are self-centered, Warren writes, because it is our morality after all that we govern our lives by, and our morality necessarily rests on what we care about (Warren 1997, 43).

Warren's critique of the life-only view is deficient in several respects. First, that view has greater capacity to deal with the practical dilemmas she poses than she recognizes. Warren falsely assumes that having equal moral status means two beings must be treated the same. What equal moral status in fact means is that like interests of two beings must receive equal weight in our moral deliberations, so that if one being has far lesser interests at stake in a conflict of interests, we may favor the other. Proponents of the life-only view could respond to Warren's tooth-brushing conundrum by pointing out that microorganisms, though of equal moral status, have micro-interests at stake even in remaining alive, so that our relatively modest (for us) interest in dental health outweighs the combined interest in living that all the microorganisms in our mouths have.

An additional way out of the tooth-brushing dilemma, a way that neither Warren nor the proponents of the "reverence for life" view recognize, is to acknowledge that even a unicriterion view such as the life-only view could allow for a moral hierarchy, and in fact might *compel* us to establish a moral hierarchy. This is so because the single criterion can be present in different degrees. If one returns to the many aspects of life identified previously, it becomes apparent that beings can possess more or fewer of these aspects and can possess any given aspect to a greater or lesser degree. Some beings grow through metabolism but do not reproduce. Some grow a great deal and some very little. Normal adult humans (not coincidentally) appear to possess all the identified aspects of life, and to a degree far surpassing that of many other entities deemed alive, such as plants. An adherent to the life-only view might therefore have to rank humans above most other life forms in moral status on that basis. Thus, even in the life-only view, it might be permissible for us to brush our teeth if it is safe to assume, as seems quite plausible, that we have a fullness of life much greater than that of the microorganisms that attack our teeth.[14] We might justify killing plants by consumption on the same grounds; we possess more life than asparagus.

Warren might respond to this point by stating that even in an understanding of a life-only view that admits of degrees, uncomfortable conclusions could still result. We might have to conclude, for example, that puppies have a higher moral status than human infants and some disabled adults. In this instance, though, we should be more reluctant to rely on moral attitudes toward particular groups of beings rather than on general principles and basic intuitions. Ordinarily moral analysis works the other way around, treating fundamental, general principles as less dispensable than specific beliefs, and reordering the moral hierarchy so that some specific nonhuman animals rank higher than some humans would not lead to the impossibility of fulfillment problem that the radical egalitarian position would. That general principles lead to specific conclusions inconsistent with established assumptions is a reason to reexamine the general principles, to determine whether they rest on an even deeper assumption that is flawed or simply have not been properly applied; but in and of itself, it does not suffice to jettison or amend the general principles. Otherwise, there would be little point to moral theorizing; we could just do a survey of existing moral beliefs about every specific case and treat the majority view as authoritative. Thus, the proper response to a concern that the life-only view might put puppies above human infants in a moral hierarchy is not to conclude immediately that the life-only view must therefore be wrong, but rather to ask why it is that we think human infants have a moral status higher than puppies and whether the reason for our thinking

[14] As noted in Chapter 2, a biocentric egalitarian view of moral status can also deal with dilemmas such as tooth brushing by saying that humans and bacteria are of equal moral status, but that bacteria have negligible interests, so killing them does not require much justification. Our desire to avoid tooth decay or bad breath suffices.

so is principled. The answer might lie in the reality, discussed further later, that we attribute moral status on the basis of several characteristics, not just being alive, including sentience, higher cognitive functioning, and the potential for having those things in the future.

A second problem with Warren's critique of the life-only view is the way by which she resolves tooth-brushing-type dilemmas herself, which is basically to say that we humans simply do favor ourselves in our moral reasoning and that this is okay because it is our morality after all. This raises an important point about appropriate use of the data of our moral psychology. The problem with Warren's reasoning is not that it entails anthropocentrism in some fashion, but rather that Warren allows for anthropocentrism in *applying* general principles or criteria to particular moral decisions as well as in *developing* the general principles or criteria. The life-only view, like other views of moral status, is concededly anthropocentric in the sense of placing great weight on a characteristic of beings – life – because we humans intuitively value it. And that sort of anthropocentrism – that is, in identifying which basic characteristics of beings have moral significance – might be inevitable in any human morality. But Warren's support for the particular conclusion that it is okay to brush one's teeth relies on the permissibility of *applying* anthropocentrically derived moral principles in a self-serving way, which is quite a different matter. She might be correct that we humans will continue to put our own interests before (most) other life forms regardless of what any philosophers conclude, but that does not mean that we are justified in doing so. Perhaps we *should* feel guilty about the harm we cause the lowest life forms and should take steps at least to minimize the harm.

Rather than rely on such a critique of the reverence for life view on grounds of its allegedly untenable implications, I would criticize its proponents for advancing no argument for excluding other criteria. Most focus only on establishing that life per se matters morally, without addressing the possibility that some other characteristic of beings, such as being sentient, might be an additional basis for attributing moral significance to beings and therefore for ranking some living beings higher than others. The few who have considered that possibility have conceded that other characteristics do matter and can support a hierarchy among living beings (Belshaw 2001, 136; Goodpaster 1978, 323). And if we look to the source of our intuitions that life matters, we can readily see that intuitions about other characteristics also arise from that same source.

As explained above, the root of any unicriterion view is that we humans respond in a certain way – empathetic identification, rational recognition that others belong to the same morally relevant category of beings to which we belong, and/or awe – when we perceive the presence of the characteristic that is the basis of the selected criterion. For Schweitzer, the insight that all life is of value arose from contemplating the variety of life forms around him and imputing to them a will to live, a supposed aspect of their existence that triggered in him a recognition of commonality between himself and them. He then reasoned that insofar as he believed other beings ought to respect his will to live he was rationally committed to respecting that in other beings. This reasoning, which resembles the mechanism of moral intuition I characterized above as Kantian, is captured in these passages:

> I must interpret the life around me as I interpret the life that is my own. My life is full of meaning to me. The life around me must be full of significance to itself. If I am to expect others to respect my life, then I must respect the other life I see, however strange it may be to mine. (Schweitzer 1933, 65)[15]

> Ethics thus consists in this, that I experience the necessity of practicing the same reverence for life toward all will-to-live, as toward my own. Therein I have already the needed fundamental principle of morality. It is good to maintain and cherish life; it is evil to destroy and to check life. (Schweitzer 1985, 314)

At other times, Schweitzer appealed by way of justification of the reverence for life view to empathetic identification with nonhuman life:

> The man who has become a thinking being feels a compulsion to give every will-to-live the same reverence for life that he gives to his own. He experiences that other life in his own. (Schweitzer 1985, 315)

> The elemental fact, present in our consciousness every moment of our existences, is: I am life that wills to live. … The mysterious fact of my will to live is that I feel a mandate to behave with sympathetic concern toward all the wills to live which exist side by side with my own.[16]

And at times, Schweitzer's view appears to rest on a kind of awe; he spoke often of the sacredness of life and expressed not simply respect, but a "reverence" for life.[17]

---

[15] See also Schweitzer (1985) 314.

[16] Speech by Albert Schweitzer to the French Academy (1952), in *Reverence for Life* (p. 49) (Harold Robles, ed., 1993). See also id., at 3, 32–3.

[17] Id., at 33 ("I cannot but have reverence for all that is called life."; "Even when I was a child I was like a person in an ecstasy in the presence of Nature …").

It is indisputable, however, that we humans respond in these same ways to other characteristics of other beings apart from just their bare aliveness and supposed will to live. The very multiplicity of unicriterion views supports such an assumption. For example, that we perceive some other living beings to be sentient like us causes us to recognize an even greater similarity with them than that arising simply from their being alive, and so to empathize more strongly and feel greater compassion for them, and also to recognize that, insofar as we demand respect for our own interest in avoiding pain and experiencing pleasure, we must recognize the same claim for other sentient beings. Additionally, we experience reverence for traits other beings possess beyond mere living, such as rationality. The greatest deficiency in the life-only view, therefore, is simply that it appeals ultimately to sources of moral significance in human moral psychology that do not speak in such a univocal manner.

Environmental ethicists might object to adopting a view of moral status that allows for more than one criterion on the grounds that it is unacceptably anthropocentric to adopt additional criteria that favor humans relative to other life forms. As noted earlier, however, our moral practice is necessarily anthropocentric in the sense of needing to appeal to things our human minds can have some basis for valuing, for we have no other source to consult for criteria of moral significance. We have no access to moral beliefs of other living entities; indeed, as far as we know, no other living entities have moral beliefs, though some might engage in behavior we would assume to be motivated by moral beliefs if done by humans.[18] Schweitzer's ethical outlook, as reflected in the passages above, was quite anthropocentric in its focus on what humans value and feel. The sort of anthropocentrism that we can avoid and to which environmental ethicists or animal rights proponents might therefore justifiably object is a refusal to extend to other kinds of living things the elevated moral concern we insist on for ourselves even when they possess the same characteristics that we possess and on the basis of which we demand that other moral agents respect us.

---

[18] Some animal rights advocates assert that animals do engage in moral behavior. See, e.g., Francione (2008) 57–8. But absent access to animals' beliefs, we can only say they manifest behavior that would appear to reflect moral beliefs if engaged in by humans. Paradoxically, some such advocates also maintain that it is presumptuous of us to suppose what animals' conscious experience is like, because they want to counteract claims that animals are of lower moral status as their mental experience is inferior to humans' mental experience in some way. See also id., at 227 (objecting to "speciesist" selection of moral status criteria).

Another objection to allowing for considerations in addition to life per se might be that doing so leads down a slippery slope of supporting dangerous moral distinctions among people. There is no logical necessity in a multicriteria approach's leading to distinctions among humans, but it might well do so. I devote more concerted attention to this concern in Chapter 4, but for now I will reiterate that even if life were the only criterion of moral status, it could generate a moral hierarchy even among humans. Once one extends the human moral compass beyond concern just for other humans, an all-or-nothing approach to moral status becomes very difficult to maintain, whether one insists on a unicriterion account of moral status or accepts a multicriteria view.

RELATIONSHIP

A few moral theorists ground moral status in the extrinsic property of involvement in a relationship with other morally-significant beings. The idea is not that beings have different moral status in the eyes of those with whom they are in a relationship,[19] but rather that the status of any being is enhanced from an objective or universal perspective by being connected in a certain way to other beings that matter morally.

Contribution to a Community

One kind of relationship on which some theorists have focused is one of interdependence. J. Baird Callicott contends that moral status arises from playing a role in a social or biological community, benefiting or being useful to others. Callicott referred explicitly to the Humean account of moral psychology, as well as to a Darwinian account of instinctual emotional response, to explain our intuitive respect for any entities with which we stand in a relationship of interdependence.[20] No doubt for evolutionary reasons, we instinctively feel positively toward and so attribute objective value to beings connected to us in this way. Not just other human beings, as in a family or clan, but also nonhuman species and even plants and nonliving things are related to us in this way. Callicott argues

[19] For defense of the view that a moral agent's partiality toward other individuals with whom the agent is in a relationship – for example, family members – is not incompatible with a general commitment to moral impartiality, see Mendus (2002) 55–63.

[20] Callicott (1989) 78–80, 82–6, 118–25; J. Baird Callicott, "My Reply," in Ouderkirk and Hill (2002) at 292–3.

that recognizing this fact should trigger in us the same kind of affective response (though the strength of the response might vary) when we contemplate those nonhuman entities (Callicott 1989, 124–7). A proper appreciation of our material connection to the earth as a whole should lead us to respond emotionally in such a way that we feel concern for, and intellectually attribute intrinsic and not just instrumental value to, our "biotic community," just as we attribute intrinsic value to our human community or to our family. If we do so, we will thereby come to respect for their own sake all the entities that serve a function in our ecological community, rather than viewing them only instrumentally and protecting them, if at all, just for our own sake. The members of the biotic community acquire moral significance by participating in that collectivity, in a manner analogous to the way in which many religious people believe humans acquire moral status by virtue of their participation in "God's plan." This basis for moral status allows for an extremely broad attribution of moral status, beyond even living things to all of the natural universe, including the soil and water. As such, it is arguably less demanding than the reverence for life view.

This account of moral status has some resonance with common experience. It might not be so much, or only, an experience of sympathetic identification of the sort Hume described, but rather mostly a feeling of reverence or awe.[21] We experience awe when we contemplate the intricate workings of our ecosystem, and all the entities that contribute in a significant way to the functioning of the ecosystem partake of that awe-inspiring quality. We develop a sense of respect for otherwise unremarkable lower life forms when we learn how vital they are to soil aeration, pollination, a food chain, and so on. Gratitude might also play a role. But it is not simply that we value these beings instrumentally, for what they contribute to our welfare, but rather or also that we ascribe inherent worth to them such that we respect them as contribution-making entities even if we are not aware of any personal benefit from their existence. Some cultures have even worshipped nonhuman living and nonliving entities that were vital to sustenance.

We could also justify or explain attribution of moral status on the basis of interdependence and entities' usefulness to other beings on Kantian grounds. It is not uncommon for people's sense of their own

---

[21] There are many explicit references to awe or wonder in the environmental ethics tradition of which Callicott is a part. See, e.g., Callicott (1989) 125 (citing the work of Aldo Leopold that is the starting point for Callicott's views).

worth to rest in large part on their contributions to their community, to the welfare of animals, or to preservation of the natural environment. Elderly persons sometimes express the view that their life is not worth living or preserving, and that they themselves are worthless, because no one needs them anymore. Others respond by pointing out that they do or could contribute a great deal, perhaps just in a way different from how they did earlier in life. If we believe, even unconsciously, that we ourselves are objectively more deserving of respect and protection than others insofar as our existence contributes positively to the world, or insofar as we fulfill an important role in society, then we are rationally committed to recognizing the inherent worth of other entities that do so as well.

Callicott has incurred much criticism of his view, most based on the conflict between his assumption that contribution to the biotic community is the measure of a being's moral worth and the widespread belief that humans are of greater worth than any other beings even if humans on the whole have a less positive impact on the environment and biotic community than other beings. Warren goes further to point out that we feel a sense of obligation to some beings even though they do not appear to contribute positively to the ecosystemic and even though they are not in any sort of social relationship with any humans – that is, that contribution cannot be a necessary condition for moral status. For example, hordes of wild rabbits might threaten to destroy an ecosystem rather than enhance it, and we might therefore feel justified in eradicating much of the rabbit population. But we would still feel obligated to kill the rabbits in a humane way and not to cause them great suffering, suggesting that we attribute some moral status to the rabbits even if they detract from rather than contribute to an ecosystem. Another, human, example might be an unemployed, reclusive sociopath, who contributes nothing positive to the economy, to culture, or to other individuals, but rather detracts from the social good and the welfare of everyone with whom he comes into contact. We believe that person nevertheless has some moral status and that we owe him some duties.

Callicott could respond to such examples by suggesting that they represent anomalous cases within classes of beings that generally do contribute positively to the welfare of other beings that have moral status. We have these intuitions about the rampaging rabbits and the sociopath just because our intuitions about the standard case of rabbit and human are so strong and have become detached in our minds from their origin in an appreciation for how rabbits and other humans generally make our lives better. Callicott might further suggest that we should try to override such intuitions about those rabbits and the sociopath, by reflecting rationally on the situation. We owe no duties, he might say, to beings that do nothing good for others.

To deepen the criticism of Callicott, though, and to better deal with the counterexamples noted, one could point out that the perceived contribution of beings to our social or biological existence is simply not the only characteristic that triggers in us intuitions that other beings have intrinsic value and command moral respect. Our moral psychology is much more complicated, and Callicott offers no argument for concluding that biosocial relationship is the *only* moral status trigger to which we should pay attention. We likely feel a moral duty to the destructive rabbits because of their sentience, and perhaps simply because they are beings pursuing lives, struggling to survive, both of which can trigger empathetic identification in us. We owe some moral duties to the sociopath – for example, not to torture him for sport, because he is a sentient and reasoning being. We might think the rabbits and sociopath have less moral status than they otherwise would, because they are a negative factor in the biotic or social community; we are not oblivious to the fact that they detract from our lives. But we still believe they have some.

Because contribution to the community does appear to be an appropriate, recognized criterion of moral standing, simply not the only one, it is important not to misunderstand the nature of the criterion. An additional criticism Warren makes of Callicott's view appears to rest on a misunderstanding. She points out that the notion that biosocial relationship is all that matters to moral status cannot account for certain well-ingrained specific moral beliefs about duties owed to people independently of how they contribute to our lives. She notes that a theory of moral status resting exclusively on biosocial relationship will generate degrees of status, because some entities will be more vital than others to our lives or to our biological and social communities, and she points out that we believe some duties owed to peripheral members of our communities should outweigh some duties owed to central members of our communities (Warren 1997, 134). For example, a duty we owe to a stranger not to kill him would generally outweigh a duty we owe to our children to provide them with an education, if the two were to conflict (e.g., if the stranger were competing with our children for a place in school, of if we could take the stranger's money and use it to pay for our children's schooling). A "biosocial relationship only" view, Warren asserts, cannot account for this conviction.

This criticism by Warren is off the mark for a couple of reasons. First, Warren here appears to assume that if one being has a moral status higher to that of another, then *every* one of the former's interests must, in our moral deliberations, trump *every* one of the latter's interests. But that is incorrect. As explained in Chapter 1, having a greater moral status means that one's interests will generally count for more than *like* interests of others. This allows for the possibility that a morally inferior being's fundamental interests outweigh less important interests of a morally superior being. For example, if a family of geese crosses the road in front of me when I am driving, the fundamental interest of the geese in remaining alive might outweigh my interest in getting to my destination a minute sooner than I will if I stop to let them pass, even on the assumption that my moral status is much higher than that of the geese. In addition, as noted in Chapter 1, even if one being's interests count for less than like interests of another being, they might still count enough to warrant the same practical treatment as the other receives. Thus, even if a stranger's interest in not being killed properly counted for less in my moral deliberations than my children's interest in not being killed, the stranger's interest in not being killed might still be strong enough to support an absolute moral prohibition against my killing him.

Second Warren misinterprets Callicott as advancing an agent-relative account of moral status, one in which beings have different moral status for different agents, depending on what the beings contribute to a particular agent's well-being. That is not Callicott's view, or at least is not the best rendering of an interdependence view. Callicott seems to have in mind a more universal or agent-independent attribution of moral status, based on a being's contribution to the thriving of any other morally significant beings. Thus, the moral status I attribute to a corn crop, if any, should not depend on whether I eat corn or any animal that feeds on corn, nor on whether I personally benefit in some other way from the existence of the crop, but rather on whether it benefits any morally significant beings in the world. And the moral status I ascribe to other persons should not vary on the basis of whether *I* am in a family relationship with them, but rather on the basis of whether *anyone* is in a family relationship with them. The stranger whom Warren worries about can, in the biosocial relationship theory, have a moral status equal to that of the agent's children for all moral agents. I might owe special duties to my children because of our special relationship, but those special duties arise from the morality of relationships rather from a difference in moral status among persons.

Reciprocity

A different sort of relationship-focused moral theory is that of Nel Noddings, writing from the perspective of care ethics (Noddings 1984). Noddings does not write directly about moral status, but rather offers a phenomenology of human caring about other beings and advances certain normative positions based on an assumption that nonrational caring responses are the source of all morality. Noddings relies heavily on, and in large part simply elaborates on, Hume's moral psychology. Implications for moral status in Noddings's work arise from her positions concerning humans' ability to care for or about particular other kinds of beings. Caring, Noddings writes, entails displacing one's own concerns in one's thinking with the reality of another being, a shift from attending to one's own interests to receiving the other's experience and being motivated to act in the other's behalf (14–16, 30). Noddings's notion of caring therefore appears to be, in part, what we typically do when we perceive that other beings matter for their own sake, which is equivalent to their having moral status for us. If caring were equivalent to, or the only proper reaction to, ascribing moral status (I do not believe it is either), then it might be that beings could have moral status only insofar as they could be objects of care. And in Noddings's account of care, which requires that the cared-for being reciprocate in a certain way, many kinds of entities simply cannot be objects of care, including some living beings (hence making her view more demanding than the reverence for life view).

Noddings's notion of reciprocity is not entirely clear. She writes that it involves the cared-for being's "receiving" the caring. Such receiving can happen in at least two ways. One way involves subjectively recognizing that caring concern has been given and then responding appreciatively (70–1, 151). Clearly this requires a relatively high level of cognition. Another way, though, is simply to benefit from the care per se (as opposed to just the activities that constitute care giving) and to manifest an enhanced ability to pursue aims as a result of that care; "receiving may be accomplished ... by a happy and vigorous pursuit of his own projects" (74, 151). What seems to be required in both cases is that the one caring receive the gratification of seeing that her caring attitude itself has a positive effect on the cared for. Thus, only those beings capable of manifesting recognition of or benefiting from our caring attitude per se, and thereby giving us this gratification, can be an object of care. And beings are more or less appropriate objects of care the more capable they are of responding in this way (159–61). Insofar as Noddings advances or presupposes a view of moral status, rather than offering just a phenomenology of caring, it would therefore seem to be a view under which moral status arises from the capacity to respond to a caring attitude.[22]

There are several problems with Noddings's articulation of this view. First, Noddings does not justify limiting our caring or attributing moral status to only those beings who give us the gratification of responding in the right way. The Humean account of moral psychology to which Noddings appeals would seem to allow for ascription to a broader class of beings; there might be beings with which we sympathetically identify even though they cannot reciprocate in the way Noddings requires. I can identify in a way with an ant struggling to bring a crumb of bread to its lair, and so care enough to refrain from stomping on it, even though the ant seems incapable of sensing my attitude or even of sensing that I have made a decision about it. In addition, this Humean account is not a complete account of our moral practices. There might be beings incapable of reciprocating caring that we nevertheless ascribe moral status to because our desire to be rationally consistent compels us to do so – that is, because we demand respect for ourselves on the basis of some characteristic that those other beings have, or because we react to them with awe (e.g., a divinity).

A further criticism of Noddings's view is that it appears at times to make ethics agent relative. To have moral status on Noddings's view, it seems, a being must not only have the capacity to respond appropriately to caring, but must also actually be the object of moral agents' caring, and then it has moral status only for the persons who actually do care. That would make the ethics of caring vacuous; "I have an obligation to care about what I happen to care about" is not a particularly meaningful moral principle, and it is not consistent with the ethical views of many people. Noddings makes some attempt at expanding the obligation, by suggesting that one has an obligation to care about not just what one happens to care about but also other beings like it. For example, if I care about my cat, I should care about any cat. But that is not much of an improvement, both because she offers no justification for that move and because it leaves moral status agent relative, with no grounds for criticizing someone who does not care about any cat and so tortures any he finds.

[22] Noddings does not appear to hold consistently to such a view, however, for she seems to grant that a person who does not happen to care about any cats would have no obligation to any cats, even though she believes cats have the capacity to respond positively to a caring attitude. Id., at 156.

As with the biosocial view, though, the fix is easy. We might say that being an object of *anyone's* care gives rise to some degree of moral status that all moral agents must recognize and respect, though in most cases it might be only the slightest degree. Thus, we moral agents would all have an obligation to take into account in our moral reasoning the interests or integrity of beings that are actually cared for or about by *some* other beings. Other beings matter objectively insofar as they are important subjectively to some third parties. Again, we can account for special moral duties that a given moral agent might owe to particular members of a class of beings – for example, a moral agent's own children or pets – even if we conclude that all members of the class have equal moral status, by appeal to the morality of relationships rather than to a theory of moral status.

This more plausible version of the view that being cared about enhances moral status is consistent with many common practices. Domestic pets are held in somewhat higher regard than other animals by virtue of their close relationships with humans. For this reason, although I have never had a cat as a pet myself, I accord domestic cats a higher regard, and view their interests as commanding more protection, than I do raccoons, though I might otherwise regard them as moral equals. (Being shown that raccoons have emotional ties with each other might change my intuitions somewhat.) And if reciprocation does matter that dogs in general might occupy a higher moral status than cats do, because in addition to being very important to their owners (and other dogs, if they are allowed such association), they appear on average more capable of manifesting appreciation for care given. I might be mistaken in that empirical assumption, and if it were demonstrated to me that I am mistaken, then I might revise my view of the relative moral standing of cats and dogs.

Even as among humans, it might be that we, consciously or unconsciously, regard persons as more worthy of moral respect the more they are cared about by others and enmeshed in personal relationships. A particularly sad example of this phenomenon is the relative nonchalance many people have about the death of recluses (even very wealthy ones) and solitary vagrants. The occasional story in newspapers about a deceased homeless person who was more connected to others than one might have expected seems intended to bolster the person's humanity and moral standing in our estimation, to make us think he mattered. In contrast, when a parent of young children dies, we need no coaching to find it tragic, because the assumed importance of the parent to the children makes him matter greatly. This intuition is not limited, though, to conscious or even sentient beings, which suggests that reciprocity is not a necessary feature of the phenomenon. Even inanimate things can be objects of intense concern for some moral agents – for example, the Shroud of Turin, tribal burial grounds, and great paintings. Those things thereby acquire a certain aura of importance and inviolability that affects even those who are not among the persons who revere the objects; we ascribe inherent value to those things, in addition to having concern for the feelings of the persons who do revere them.

Peter Singer criticizes the view that moral status turns, in part, on being in relationships and being cared about, on the ground that it would justify racism (Singer 1979, 66–7). If people have higher moral status by virtue of being cared about by others, then would minority groups that are scorned by the majority thereby occupy a lower moral status, and would we have stronger obligations to those with whom we have closer relationships? This might justify white people according higher moral status to white people than to black people. Singer insists that moral obligations should be determined wholly apart from how we feel about particular other beings.

Singer's own sentience-based account of moral status and moral obligation, though, is partly based on affective responses. He writes of sharing in the pain of other creatures, of sympathetically identifying with them. Singer is thus not really opposed to having feelings play a role in morality. A better response to his concern about racism in this context is to remove the agent-relative aspect of the account of moral obligation, as explained previously. We should say that other beings' (including other humans') moral status does not turn for me on how I feel about them, nor on how most people who share some attribute with me (such as my race) feel about them, but that the person's moral status could derive to some extent from his or her being cared about by *anyone*. People of all races are cared about by their families and communities, so in this approach, basing moral status partly on being cared for and being in caring relationships does not support racism.[23]

---

[23] In addition, it does not rule out having special obligations to people with whom one stands in a relatively intimate relationship. It is not inconsistent with attributing equal moral status to all humans, if that were appropriate, to say that we bear extra duties toward, or simply are permitted to favor, any humans who happen to be comembers of a very close association, such as a family. Two members of a perfectly egalitarian society clearly could create special rights and duties with respect to each other by contract, and there is no conceptual obstacle to their doing so also by engaging in intimate association, with the special reciprocity that entails.

In addition, as noted earlier, it is always legitimate to reject on principle particular bases for moral status, even if they have prima facie appeal because they arise by one of the three processes noted at the outset. We have the capacity to interrogate and override our intuitions if they conflict with settled moral principles or if they rest on empirical assumptions that prove unwarranted. For example, we can acknowledge that it is not skin color per se that has sometimes blocked sympathetic identification with others, but rather the association of skin color with some other attribute, such as membership in a group deemed hostile. We can then recognize that this association is false or artificially imposed and reject skin color as a basis for moral status. But the intuition that it matters to moral status whether a being is cared about by other humans or is in relationships with other humans might not conflict with any settled moral principles nor rest on false empirical suppositions.

SENTIENCE

A quite common view among philosophers writing on moral status today is that sentience is a necessary and sufficient condition for having it, and indeed that it is the only characteristic relevant to moral status. The prevalence of this view might reflect the impressive amount of writing on animal rights that philosophers have generated in recent decades, though some theorists writing about abortion and the moral status of fetuses take this view as well. The most common form of the view maintains that being sentient is a necessary condition for having *any* moral status, and sufficient for having *full* moral status, equal to that of any other sentient beings.[24] The standard "argument from marginal cases" reasons inductively that, because prevailing moral beliefs accord moral status even to humans who lack the higher-order cognitive capacities of rationality, language, and self-consciousness, including normal newborns, anencephalic infants, and severely mentally disabled adults, there must be a widely shared general principle that sentience per se gives rise to moral status. From the general principle, animal rights advocates then deduce that sentient nonhuman creatures must also have moral status.

The style of reasoning deployed in this view is coherentist; it says, "if you think mentally disabled humans matter morally for their own

----

[24] See, e.g., Bonnie Steinbock, "Respect for Human Embryos," in Lauritzen (2001).

sake, then to be rationally consistent you should think the same about many nonhuman animals." Pointing out that some nonhuman animals are more sentient and operate at a higher cognitive level than humans in the categories just mentioned lends plausibility to the position that all sentient beings have equal standing, for most people would feel uncomfortable saying that baboons matter more than mentally disabled humans. Conversely, supporters of abortion rights and supporters of research using embryos rest their position in large part on the supposition that preterm fetuses and embryos lack the capacity for experiencing pleasure or pain.

Proponents of the view generally understand sentience as the capacity to experience pleasure and pain, including not just "simple feelings of pain and pleasure," but also "more complex emotions, moods, and passions" (Warren 1997, 55). They typically assume that consciousness is a prerequisite to sentience, or that pleasure and pain are inherently conscious experiences (52, 55), but generally deny that language is a prerequisite to consciousness, so that even human infants can and do have the requisite consciousness for sentience (58, 61). They recognize that feelings of pleasure and pain arise only after or as part of perceptual experience, but deny that affectively neutral perceptual experiences are constitutive of sentience.[25] In other words, on the prevailing sentience-based conception of moral status, the sentience that is relevant is not simply the capacity for any sensation, but rather just the capacity to experience pleasure or pain, because that capacity is supposed to be necessary to have interests. Beings do not have an interest in seeing per se, it is supposed, but rather only in the pleasure or facility in procuring food that seeing might provide.

This understanding of sentience is inconsistent with the standard dictionary definition; Webster defines sentience primarily as the "capacity for feeling or perceiving; consciousness," and secondarily as "mere awareness or sensation that does not involve thought or perception."[26] Merriam-Webster Online defines having sentience as being "responsive to or conscious of sense impressions." More important for our purposes, however, is whether nonaffective sensations are relevant to moral status, and it seems that they should be considered so. Sensory capacities enable an awareness of and interaction with the world that matters to us. I can and do empathize with other beings to a greater extent if I believe they are aware of things happening around them, as I am, and such awareness depends on perceptual abilities. I might empathize with an animal that is suffering even if it has no awareness of me or of the cause of its suffering, but I empathize more if I think it does have such awareness. I can more readily identify with a being that has such awareness, because I can more easily imagine its experience. In addition, I value my own sensation, because it allows me to be cognizant of and to interact with the world, something of great subjective importance to me, and not just because of the pleasures to which such interaction with the world might produce. I demand respect for myself in part because I am engaged thus with the world – not intellectually (though that also matters), but just perceiving it, receiving and processing data, rather than functioning as though encapsulated. Were someone to threaten to put my eyes out, I would object not just because of the pain and loss of pleasure and mobility that this might cause me in the near and long term, but also because the form of connection with the world that my sight allows me is independently important to me. Last, extraordinary perceptual ability can inspire awe in us; for example, it likely enhances dogs' status in our ranking of other beings, even if only very modestly, that they are thought to have especially keen senses of smell and hearing. The same might be said of the visual acuity of hawks and eagles.

An uncomfortable implication of this broadened conception of sentience is that persons with a sensory disability might be viewed as of inferior moral status, all else being equal, relative to those with normal human sensory capacities. And, in fact, in an earlier age, persons who were blind or deaf were viewed in our society as quite unlike those with sight and hearing and were treated as inferior beings.[27] (On the other hand, some cultures have accorded blind people a higher status, on the assumption that they possessed superior abilities of another sort, such as an ability to predict the future or to receive communications from a divinity.)[28] It might be that such a view still operates in many people at an unconscious level, but today we are outwardly committed to rejecting that view. Indeed, law and policy relating to disability today, including a requirement of accommodation and disproportionate spending on

---

[27] See, e.g., Harry Best, *The Deaf: Their Position in Society and the Provision for Their Education in the United States* (2007), ch. 3.

[28] See Moshe Barasch, *Blindness: The History of a Mental Image in Western Thought* (New York: Routledge, 2001) 3, 10.

habilitation of persons with disabilities, could reflect an outward commitment to giving such persons greater moral consideration than is given to nondisabled persons, rather than less.

Why the change? Is it a collective conclusion that sensory ability should be viewed as generally irrelevant to moral status? As noted earlier, we have collectively found reason to deem skin color and gender irrelevant to the moral status of humans (as they have always been, I believe, in our treatment among members of each nonhuman species). Has the same happened with this nonaffective component of sentience? This is an empirical question, and I can only speculate as to the answer, but my sense is that we have not rejected sensory experience altogether as a criterion of moral status. Rather, the transformation of attitudes toward persons who are blind or deaf is the result of people with "normal" sensory abilities becoming more cognizant of the affective experiences of such persons, attributing greater moral significance to affective experience relative to nonaffective perception, and recognizing to a greater extent the commonality we have with such persons despite the difference in sensory ability, on the basis of our similar affective experiences, cognitive abilities, social inclinations, and so on. It might also be, in some part, a belief that persons who have lesser sensory ability of one sort compensate with more acute sensation of another sort (e.g., deaf persons being more visually attuned to their surroundings, blind persons having more acute hearing). And also at work, it seems, is a modern liberal practice of ascribing greater moral claims to disadvantaged humans than to the advantaged. This relationship between disadvantage and moral status is an interesting topic, and I return to it later.

Everyday experience, then, supports the conclusion that sentience, broadly conceived, is relevant to moral status. As noted previously, many theorists take the stronger position that it is *all* that matters, but on the basis of the flawed conceptual/definitional argument rehearsed earlier. Proponents of the sentience-only view generally also maintain that all sentient creatures are of equal moral status, and that we must therefore treat equally the interests of all sentient creatures in avoiding pain and experiencing pleasures. That contention rests, in part, on the mistaken view that nothing but sentience is relevant to moral status, but also on an assumption that variation in degree of sentience does not translate into different degrees of moral status.

Theorists who reject the sentience-only view generally do so principally on the grounds that it leads to unpalatable practical conclusions – for example, that we have no greater obligations to our own children than we have to pigs; the interests of the latter should matter to us (or at least to legislators) as much as the interests of the former.[29] Singer addresses such concerns to some degree by noting that equal consideration of interests is consistent with unequal treatment of different kinds of animals, given that different animals have very different capacities for pleasure and pain, or very different sensitivities. (Singer 1979, 51. See also DeGrazia 1996, 47–8) A mouse might be incapable of suffering to the extent we humans are capable of suffering. A horse might feel a slap much less than a human would. This does not mean, Singer says, that we should treat the interests of these animals as less worthy of consideration than our own. Rather, it means that for those animals the same actions might have a lesser impact on their interests than on ours. A mouse's suffering matters just as much as an equal amount of suffering that we experience, but a mouse might be capable of suffering that is only very modest by our standards, because of its more primitive neurological system and its seemingly lesser awareness of its experience. Thus, we may as a general matter treat humans more favorably than other animals, though there can be situations in which nonhuman animals do have greater interests at stake than humans do (Singer 1979, 53).

Warren is unsatisfied with Singer's effort to conform a sentience-only view with our intuitions about particular cases, for two reasons. Though she agrees that "sentient organisms differ in their *degree* of sentience," and in the "variety and richness" of their experiences (Warren 1997, 155), she points out that we cannot be sure about the relative degrees of other beings' sentience, and it might be that many common practices central to our social existence would be morally objectionable in this view. We cannot, for example, be sure that the gain in utility we humans experience from tilling the soil to grow certain crops outweighs the harm we cause as a result to the animals living in the soil (79–82). Another reason is that some nonhuman animals, like mature pigs, are likely capable of greater pleasure and pain than human infants or impaired human adults, yet the common intuition is that even those humans occupy a moral status superior to that of all animals (88). In addition, we ascribe higher moral status to some nonhuman animals relative to others that are equally sentient, on grounds of our relationship to them (e.g., dogs, cats, horses) or on grounds of their being endangered, and would have to stop that practice if sentience is all that matters (88). Critics who deny that

---

[29]   Id, at 71, 76.

sentience is even a sufficient condition for moral status likewise point to seemingly unacceptable implications as to specific cases and object that a view such as Singer's would force us to rethink our status relative to other animals or otherwise shake up our operating assumptions. (e.g., Cohen and Regan 2001, 62–5).

As noted in connection with the life-only view, objecting to general principles based solely on unpalatable implications is not a particularly satisfying way of doing applied ethics. The most this approach ultimately can accomplish is development of a set of principles that fits with existing practices or specific ethical beliefs, a set of principles that must always be subject to modification when additional specific cases are cited that do not conform to it. This approach cannot tell us which criteria of moral status are well grounded in fundamental or general moral precepts, and it cannot help us to improve our practices and specific beliefs. And again, the better response to any such single-criterion view is to point out that the basic mechanisms by which humans come to ascribe moral status – mechanisms that proponents of the sentience-only view typically invoke – generate many criteria, not just one, and to show that proponents of the view have not presented a sufficient argument for excluding all criteria other than the one on which they focus.

Singer's argument for the significance of sentience begins with an argument for utilitarianism. He first points out that all moral thinking inherently rests on universal principles, a proposition he contends all leading schools of moral theory have implicitly or explicitly assumed to be true (Singer 1979, 10–11). Moral reasoning, he writes, "takes a universal point of view.... [I]n making ethical judgments we go beyond our own likes and dislikes.... Ethics requires us to go beyond 'I' and 'you' to the universal law, the universalizable judgment, the standpoint of the impartial spectator or ideal observer" (11). Singer then notes that in our nonethical, practical reasoning, we naturally base decisions on our own interests, and on all of our interests (12). When we move from practical reasoning to ethical reasoning, the universality requirement kicks in and we must assign equal significance to the interests of everyone else.

> The most obvious reason for valuing the life of a being capable of experiencing pleasure or pain is the pleasure it can experience. If we value our own pleasures ... then the universal aspect of ethical judgments requires us to extend our positive evaluation of our own experiences of these pleasures to the similar experiences of all who can experience them. (85)

As noted in the introduction, this line of reasoning resembles Kant's better-known arguments for the moral importance of autonomy. It differs principally in that Singer focuses on interests rather than (just) autonomy.[30] Other proponents of a sentience-based account of moral status also appeal to the universalization requirement of moral demands (Nagel, 1970; Steinbock 1996, 23–4). The last step for Singer is to make the assertion that "capacity for suffering and enjoying things is a prerequisite for having interests at all" (Singer 1979, 50), the assertion I debunked earlier in connection with the reverence for life view.

In addition to relying on the unsupportable assumption that having interests consists solely in experiencing pleasure and pain, Singer's sentience-only view is undermined by the fact that his starting point – that is, what we think about when we engage in self-regarding practical reasoning – does not support an exclusive focus on sentience. When we think about what we want for ourselves and on what bases we claim respect and protection from others, we take into consideration many aspects of ourselves – not just our pleasures and pains, but also our being alive per se and our self-conception and relationships with others, and so on. In other words, Singer does not show that the source of moral intuition to which he appeals, the psychological mechanism by which we arrive at normative beliefs, is univocal, speaking only of pleasures and pains. It speaks of everything about us to which we assign objective value and that we think others should respect.

Singer might respond to this by noting that we derive pleasure from having satisfied our preferences regarding what matters to us, but he would certainly be wrong to claim that a belief that that is the case is always what we have in mind when we engage in practical reasoning. The mechanism by which we ascribe moral status that I have characterized as Kantian begins with our conscious thinking about what has value for us and then what has value objectively. The aim of receiving pleasure and avoiding pain is not all that enters into our first-order practical reasoning. And it is not the only basis on which we make moral claims on our own behalf; we claim a right to live, even though dying would mean the cessation of pain, and not just because we want to experience more

---

[30] For Kant, there was another step in the reasoning, in which the individual moves from purely practical reasoning about his own situation to moral reasoning about his own situation – that is, ascribing objective value to his own autonomy and making moral demands on others that they respect his autonomy. It is this move beyond personal preference to ascription of objective value that explains or constitutes the universal quality of ethical reasoning. Nagel reasons along these same lines in arguing that we must consider the experience of all other sentient creatures in our moral deliberations. See Nagel (1970).

pleasure. Thus, the line of reasoning by which Singer aims to demonstrate the moral significance of sentience also demonstrates the moral significance of other attributes. Those other attributes might be present in some sentient beings and not others, thereby elevating the moral status of the former over the latter, and might be present in some nonsentient beings.

In addition, Singer fails to recognize or disprove that there is another source of intuition for the moral significance and status of other beings besides just universalizing the conclusions of our own self-regarding practical reasoning. There is also the empathic response to other beings that Hume described. Absent demonstration to the contrary, this mechanism is just as valid as the Kantian mechanism. And it is not obvious that the only perception that triggers an empathic response in us is a perception that other beings experience pain and pleasure. As discussed earlier, a perception simply that another being has a telos, is alive in that minimal sense, can cause us to identify with it. Having a particular kind of telos, such as realization of potential for rational agency, might generate a stronger response. That another being is cared about by others can also cause us to identify with it, insofar as we are the objects of others' concern as well. Because things other than capacity for suffering and pleasure can cause us to identify with, care about, and feel we have duties toward other beings, it is a mistake to assume that capacity for pleasure and pain is the only characteristic that makes a being worthy of moral consideration or that increasing pleasure and ameliorating suffering are the only aims of morality.

The assertion that all beings sentient to any degree are of equal moral status, such that the interests of all sentient beings matter equally and warrant the same protection, also appears inconsistent with our moral psychology. As noted, proponents of the sentience-only view do not assert that all sentient beings must receive the same treatment; they point out that less sentient beings have lesser interests to protect, and so we might justifiably do things to them that we should not do to more sentient beings, because in doing so we adversely affect them to a lesser degree. However, they do generally assert that being sentient at all is sufficient for having "full" moral status. Yet they offer no theoretical basis for that position. Certainly, pointing out simply that Utilitarianism presupposes that every being's interests matter equally is no help; that just begs the moral status question. The way our moral brains generally operate suggests a different position. Generally, the more a being manifests sentience, the more we empathetically identify with it. And our sense of the respect we are owed by others does appear to vary based on our capacities, including our sentience. If we demand greater respect for ourselves based on the degree to which we are sentient, or more readily empathize with other beings the more sentient they are, then it is presumptively appropriate to give greater weight to the interests of more sentient beings relative to similar interests of less sentient beings. In this view, sparing a ten-year-old human child from X amount of pain would be more important morally than sparing a squirrel from X amount of pain. That consequence is much more intuitively appealing than an insistence that we should be indifferent as to whether we inflict the pain on the child or the squirrel, so assertion of a general principle that leads to the latter conclusion ought to have some argument behind it.

Singer does offer an argument against hierarchy in general, when he criticizes the position that inequality among humans could be predicated on relative intelligence, and this might be construed as an argument against adopting any criteria other than sentience that could be a basis for assigning unequal status. Singer's reasoning, though, is deficient. He writes:

> There is no logically compelling reason for assuming that a difference in ability between two people justifies any difference in the amount of consideration we give to their interests. Equality is a basic ethical principle, not an assertion of fact. We can see this if we return to our earlier discussion of the universal aspects of ethical judgments. We saw ... that when I make an ethical judgment I must go beyond a personal or sectional point of view and take into account the interests of all those affected. This means that we weigh up interests, considered simply as interests and not as my interests, or the interests of Australians, or of whites. This provides us with a basic principle of equality: the principle of equal consideration of interests. (Singer 1979, 18–19)

The first sentence in this passage is mere assertion; Singer does not consider any possible reasons for assuming a difference based on intelligence (or any other attributes). The second sentence assumes that a principle of moral equality is already established, and so assumes the conclusion for which he purports to be arguing. The remainder of the passage appeals to the universal feature of ethical reasoning, but Singer fails to appreciate that beings can actually be differentiated under universal principles. Thus, for example, if I believe that I should receive more respect for my interests because of my relatively high intelligence, I would make a claim for myself on the basis of a universal principle that all beings of high intelligence warrant great consideration and all beings of low intelligence warrant less consideration for their interests. This is far different from making a claim for myself based simply on my being me and my caring more about me than about anyone else. A principle based on the value of intelligence *wherever it exists* is no less universal than a principle that all sentient beings warrant greater consideration than nonsentient beings, the principle on which Singer rests his views.

Likewise with any other criteria of moral status that might be generated by any of the three mechanisms identified at the outset. If we empathetically identify with other beings partly on the basis of their apparent rationality or autonomy, or if we demand respect for ourselves-partly based on those attributes, or if rationality and autonomy inspire awe in us, then these are prima facie just as valid as criteria of moral status as sentience, and the universality requirement demands only that we respect them in all beings that possess them.

In short, there are many gaps in the line of reasoning that proceeds from the assumption that all sentient beings have interests to the conclusions that all and only sentient beings have moral status and that they all have it equally. Animal rights advocates are persuasive in arguing that sentience per se is *one* proper and sufficient basis for ascribing moral status, but they fail to demonstrate that sentience must be understood solely in terms of conscious experience of pleasure in pain (and thus their moral scope is underinclusive), and they fail to demonstrate that all beings who are sentient in the way they define it must be viewed as having equal moral status (and thus their assignment of the highest moral status is overinclusive). The latter failing arises both because they fail to accept that moral status might vary based on how sentient an entity is and because they offer no reasons for excluding other potential bases for ascribing moral status.

HIGHER COGNITIVE FUNCTIONING

That reason confers special moral status on humans is a common belief. This has been a basic assumption of many of the great figures and texts in the history of Western philosophy and religion (Steiner 2008, 92–8). It is surely true that we human rational agents naturally or inevitably value our capacity for higher-order thinking, and that we do commonly attribute objective value to that capacity, and so feel logically compelled to extend respect to others who possess that capacity. In addition, it surely helps us to identify more strongly with other humans than we do with members of other species that we impute to (most) other humans cognitive functioning similar to our own. And particularly impressive mental powers can inspire awe in us.

As with proponents of a sentience-based account of moral status, many moral theorists explicitly or implicitly adopt a view that higher cognitive functioning is *all* that matters to moral status, and that all who have it are of equal moral status. Some do so unthinkingly, because their focus is relations among autonomous adults and they simply fail to consider the implications for nonautonomous humans and for nonhuman beings. For example, Martha Nussbaum writes:

> Whatever else we are bound by and pursue, we should recognize, at whatever personal or social cost, that each human being is human and counts as the moral equal of every other.... Human personhood, by which I mean the possession of practical reason and other basic moral capacities, is the source of our moral worth, and this worth is equal. (Nussbaum 2002, 133)

The first and second sentences in this quoted passage, in addition to being mere stipulations without argument, are simply incompatible. If "possession of practical reason and other basic moral capacities" is *the* source of moral worth, then there must be some human beings that have no moral worth. Surely Nussbaum does not believe that.

Theorists of moral status that more deliberatively maintain that cognitive capacities are all that matter to moral standing typically invoke the concept of "personhood," which they understand to be not equivalent to membership in the human species but rather constituted by possession of certain higher-order mental faculties. One such theory, advanced in recent years by Tom Regan, John Harris, Michael Tooley, and others, but traceable to Locke, deems as "persons" any beings that have the capacity for thought and self-awareness. According to this conception, members of many nonhuman species might be persons. Another theory, that of Kant, rests on a more robust conception of personhood, limiting personhood to beings with rational moral agency, which entails the capacity to regulate one's choices and conduct in accordance with general principles. In this conception, many humans would not be persons.

Neither of these theories, however, is consistent with prevailing social usage of the term "person," which presupposes that all persons are human beings (and so is narrower than the class of all beings that have the capacity for thought and self-awareness) but at the same time extends to human beings that are not rational moral agents, and even to human beings that do not manifest self-awareness (e.g., it is common to speak of "persons in a persistent vegetative state," and most people believe a fetus becomes "a person" at some point in his or her development, a point tied to the potential to live outside the womb rather than to self-awareness).[31] And neither is consistent with the meaning of "persons" in the Anglo-American legal system, where the term is limited to human beings and institutions but extends beyond human individuals to business entities and governments.[32] In short, there is no universal or uncontested definition of "person" (Berg 2007, nn.10–13), and use of the term in discussing moral status to connote beings, human or nonhuman, that have particular capacities is thus more likely to confuse and distract than to illuminate. A clearer answer to the question of moral status is more likely to emerge if we focus directly on the characteristics that matter morally without employing the intermediate concept of personhood.

"Person" is also a morally loaded term, so the creation of confusion might not be innocent. Following Kant, many modern moral theorists adopt by stipulation a binary view of the moral universe, divided into persons and things, in which moral agents owe respect equally to all and only persons but not at all to things.[33] For example, Harris presupposes that if a being is a person, it has the highest moral status available.[34] He then further supposes that "normal adult human beings" are paradigmatic persons, and goes on to determine what predicates moral status by asking simply what distinguishes "us" from "other creatures." This stacks the deck too much in favor of normal adult human beings.[35] To

[31] See Gerhold K. Becker, "The Moral Status of Persons: Introduction," in Becker, ed., *The Moral Status of Persons: Perspectives on Bioethics* (p. 3) (Atlanta, GA: Rodopi Press 2000). ("In today's popular usage, 'person' and 'human being' still have largely the same extension; the restriction of moral status to personhood has thus raised more questions than it has answered.").

[32] See Jessica Berg, "Of Elephants and Embryos: A Proposed Framework for Legal Personhood," 59 *Hastings Law Journal* 369 (2007).

[33] Wood (2007) 95 (discussing Kant); Wright, 43 *San Diego Law Review* 542–45 (2007); Francione (2008); Steiner (2008).

[34] See Harris (1985) 18. In a later writing, Harris explains how the traditional conception of person is one matched by human beings only after a process of development and maturation, and then leaps to the inference that personhood "is an idea used to characterize individuals who have the highest moral importance or value." John Harris and Soren Holm, "Abortion," in LaFollette (2003) 117. Some argument would be needed to justify that inference, but Harris offers none. Other writers who rest analysis on a stipulation that persons matter morally and matter equally whereas nonpersons matter not at all include Francione (2008).

[35] In theory, the term "person" need not connote a moral status; it could be used simply as shorthand for a group of humans sharing a particular, morally irrelevant characteristic, to distinguish them from all other humans, including other humans assumed to have equal moral status. Harris takes this tack (Harris 1985, 9–10). But in standard usage "person" carries moral connotations that would be difficult to eradicate. To say that one human is a person and another is not a person is implicitly to make a

accomplish an inquiry less constrained by presuppositions about the relative place of particular groups of beings, it is preferable to speak just
in terms of observable characteristics believed to be morally significant,
rather than in terms of honorific labels, and I will therefore do so in this
section, addressing the moral significance of capacities for self-awareness
and for rational agency.

Being the Subject of a Life

Tom Regan's theory of animal rights rests on an assumption that all and
only beings who are "subjects of a life" have full moral status. Beings
are subjects of lives "if they have beliefs and desires; perception, memory, and a sense of the future, including their own future; an emotional
life together with feelings of pleasure and pain; preference- and welfare-
interests; the ability to initiate action in pursuit of their desires and goals;
a psychophysical identity over time; and an individual welfare in the sense
that their experiential life fares well or ill for them.[36] Regan asserts that
all such beings have "inherent value," a term he never clearly defines, and
that inherent value is a yes-or-no thing rather than admitting of degrees.[37]
John Harris would similarly rest moral status on a being's having the
capacity to value its own life, which entails self-awareness and a sense
of the future (Harris 1985, 16–18). Harris, too, believes all beings who
possess that capacity are of equal moral status; "Once this threshold is
crossed, no individual is more of a person or more valuable than any
other" (18). Michael Tooley contends that "personhood" is marked by
mental states constitutive of conscious personal identity and that only
persons so understood can be morally wronged.[38]

---

moral assertion of profound significance. Thus, if it were to become common practice to
refer to members of a disfavored group, defined let's say by a combination of race and
religion – for example, black Muslims – as nonpersons, it would be no justification that
this is just a shorthand way of referring to individuals who share those two characteristics. Even if those are characteristics that have some relevance for some purpose, so that
it makes sense to speak of those individuals as a defined group, we would say that some
other term should be used. To call someone a nonperson is deprecating, and can even be
threatening.

[36] Regan (1983) 243. This description resembles Joseph Fletcher's definition of "humanity,"
as including "self-awareness, self-control, a sense of the future, a sense of the past, the
capacity to relate to others, concern for others, communication, and curiosity." (cited
in Singer at 75).

[37] Id., at 240–1. See also Franklin (2006), 17–18 (adopting Regan's view).

[38] Michael Tooley, "Personhood," in Kuhse and Singer (1998).

On such a view, human newborn babies might be thought to have no moral status whatsoever, in which case we would not owe them any duties. We might owe duties to their parents not to injure them, or we might adopt a rule prohibiting maltreatment of them for pragmatic or aesthetic reasons, but we would not wrong *them* by killing or torturing them. If this is the sole criterion of moral status and if it admits of degrees – that is, if humans become increasingly self-aware over time during childhood, then humans' moral status might be said to increase with age, from nothing in the first several months of life and some slight status in early infancy. This would be consistent with historical beliefs and philosophical positions that normal adult humans stand at the pinnacle of a moral status hierarchy and that children occupy an inferior status. Some theorists still take this position, explicitly. James Walters argues, for example, that "a developing individual's right to life increases as he or she approaches the threshold of indisputably personal life, the life of the normal adult in any society" (Walters 1997, 63).

Critics of the subjects of a life view have objected both that it is too narrow a criterion, because it cannot account for common intuitions about the wrongness of wanton torture or killing of sentient beings, human and nonhuman, that operate at lower cognitive levels, and that treating all subjects of a life as of equal status conflicts with intuitions we have about differential obligations to humans relative to self-conscious nonhuman creatures. Warren points out, for example, that most people think it is permissible to sacrifice even some higher-functioning animals to preserve ecosystems they threaten or to develop land for human purposes, and that we do not owe such nonhuman animals the same protection we owe to human children to protect them from predators or natural disasters.[39]

Some proponents of the subjects of a life view, such as Regan, do concede that there might be characteristics other than being the subject of a life that give rise to moral status. Regan claims only that being the subject of a life is a sufficient condition, not that it is a necessary condition, for moral status (Regan 1983, 245–6). Harris does not consider explicitly whether valuing one's own life is a necessary condition for moral status, but at one point he states vaguely that "there are good reasons for avoiding subjecting any sentient creatures to pain if this can be avoided" (Harris, 1985, 19). So they might avoid the narrowness objection. Both Regan and Harris do maintain, however, that no moral distinctions can be made among beings satisfying the subjects of a life criterion, which

---

[39] Warren (1997) 111–16.

they view as the pinnacle of morally significant characteristics. Walters likewise contends that absolute equality prevails among those who rise above a "threshold of personhood." (Walters 1997, 63). These theorists are, therefore, still vulnerable to objections based on specific cases in which common intuitions are that two classes of beings, both falling under this conception of personhood (e.g., chimps and humans), are not of equal moral status and so might receive different levels of protection for like interests. Tooley, on the other hand, acknowledges that organisms might have different moral status by virtue of the fact that they possess to different degrees the capacities constitutive of personhood, which he describes as "the ability to remember one's past actions and mental states, and the ability to envisage a future for oneself, and to pursue goals and projects" (Tooley 1998, 121).

Whatever the strength of objections from specific cases, though, a stronger objection would point simply to the internal weaknesses of the view advanced. Regan offers no argument for the moral significance of being the subject of a life other than that he does not like the implications he thinks certain alternative views entail. The class of just moral agents is too narrow for him, the class of all living things too broad, because he perceives in everyday practice an intuition that we have duties to some beings that are not moral agents but not to all living things (Regan 1983, 239–43). In other words, he appears to derive his favored criterion for moral status solely by an inductive method, leaving him open to objections based on conflicting intuitions about specific cases. He has nothing to say in response to a demonstration that most people disagree with his position on the status of any particular living being – for example, a showing that most people believe all nonhuman animals have a status inferior to that of humans. Regan does argue against certain alternative criteria for moral status, such as talents, on the grounds that such attributes are unchosen consequences of a "natural lottery" (234), yet his own criteria of moral status – being the subject of a life – is just as much an unchosen consequence of the natural lottery.

Harris and Tooley do suggest some rationale for making self-awareness a necessary condition for moral status, one similar to the conceptual/definitional argument about the meaning of "morality" and "interests" discussed at the end of Chapter 2. Harris reasons about moral status mostly in terms of permissible killing. At one point, he asserts that the reason it is wrong to kill a person "is that to do so robs that individual of something they value," and points out that "[c]reatures that cannot value their own existence cannot be wronged in this way" (Harris 1985, 18–19). Stated thus, this rationale does not support predicating moral status on just the *capacity* to value one's own life; it only supports predicating moral status on *actually* valuing one's own life. If someone capable of valuing his life in fact intensely disvalues it, killing him would not rob him of something he values. Recognizing this, Harris ultimately rests his position on the capacity to value rather than actually valuing, precisely in order to avoid this implication (17). But that leaves him with no rationale for the criterion of moral status he selects; he does not explain why the mere capacity to value matters. He expressly eschews a strategy of judging whether people *should* value their lives or second-guessing the reasons they happen to have for (or against) valuing their lives:

> The point is this: if we allow that the value of life for each individual consists simply in those reasons, whatever they are, that each person has for finding their own life valuable and for wanting to go on living, then we do not need to know what the reasons are. All we need to know is that particular individuals have their own reasons, or rather, simply, that they value their own lives.... [I]t's wrong to kill them because they do value life. (16–17)

In short, Harris at best offers a rationale for respecting beings because they *do* value their lives and want to continue living, but no rationale for respecting the capacity to value. This might not seem a serious shortcoming of his view, if we assume that all beings do in fact value their lives and do so equally,[40] but observation of human behavior and self-expression suggests that some humans do not and that people vary significantly in terms of how much they value their lives. Many engage in self-destructive behavior, some to the point of committing suicide, whereas others cherish each new day of life.

In fact, though, Harris does not adequately explain why being the subject of a life gives rise to moral status at all. The first quoted passage above suggests some (not very compelling) reason for making it a necessary condition – that is, "Why should we care about a being that does not care about itself?" But it does not follow from this that we must care about a being that does care about itself. And his reasoning in the second quoted passage rests on a highly contestable yet undefended implicit major premise – namely, that we are morally obligated to value in other beings what they themselves value. On the other hand, he does

---

[40] Franklin makes this assumption. Franklin (2006) 18 ("the life of every sentient being is as important to that individual as our life is to us").

not explain why we cannot have moral obligations to a being that does not care whether we fulfill them. "If he doesn't care, then why should I care" is a common and plausible line of reasoning with respect to our actions affecting other competent adults, but it would have no plausibility when said about stealing from or kidnapping a newborn baby. A theorist who believes having interests is a sufficient condition for having moral status might say that Harris wrongly supposes that having one's preferences satisfied is the only sort of interest beings can have.

Additional problems with Harris's attempt at justifying exclusive focus on "personhood" as Harris understands it are, first, that there are other reasons why it is wrong to kill "normal human adults" besides depriving them of something they value and that there are other wrongs one can do to other beings besides killing them. In killing a being, one deprives the being of the opportunity for pleasure, accomplishment of goals, support of others, and other things. Our capacity for these things is part of what makes us think that others owe us duties, and others' capacity for them is part of what causes us to empathize with them and value their lives. In addition, as Harris acknowledges, just inflicting pain can also be a wrong, and many creatures that do not have the mental capacity for the sort of self-awareness and sense of the future that personhood entails for Harris are capable of experiencing pain (the non-humans he treats as persons are just some chimpanzees) (Harris 1985, 19). Thus, Harris, too, fails to justify excluding other potential bases for moral status.

Tooley argues for the position that "personhood" is all that matters by invoking as an example a medical situation that resembles some end-of-life cases. He suggests that we would do wrong by destroying a person's "upper brain," where consciousness resides, but not by destroying the lower brain, which controls physical life processes, after the upper brain is already destroyed. "Many people," he asserts, would say that destruction of a person's entire brain is no worse morally than destruction of just the upper brain (Tooley 1998, 118). It seems unlikely, though, that "many people" would in fact say that one does no wrong to a person in a persistent vegetative state by walking up to them and shooting them in the head. And if humans devoid of self-consciousness are nevertheless capable of pain, it is hard to imagine someone saying there is no wrong done to such humans by burning their skin for sport. Tooley's appeal to intuitions is thus unpersuasive. He tries to make it more appealing by confusing the issue of moral status with ones of personal identity and euthanasia, asking: "Are *you* worse off as a result of" someone destroying your lower brain after they have destroyed your upper brain? (118; emphasis added). We have a hard time seeing ourselves as the person entirely lacking in consciousness. And we might think a life without consciousness is not worth living, in light of what we now enjoy. But we are nevertheless likely to say that some other human who is alive but permanently unconscious has some moral status, so that we owe some duties of forbearance to them – for example, that while they are alive, we not inflict pain gratuitously, steal their money, and so on. The legal system's insistence on strict adherence to advance directives in decision making for unconscious persons, and its recognition that such persons alone have rights with respect to end-of-life decision making,[41] reflects an assumption that we continue to owe duties to such persons despite their lack of consciousness, which in turn presupposes that they retain sufficient moral standing in their own right to have claims against us.

Tooley also appeals to the conceptual argument that morality concerns itself with interests and that only beings that have interests can be proper subjects of moral concern, and, more explicitly than Harris, simply defines interests more narrowly than the sentience camp; he equates having interests in a morally relevant sense with having conscious desires. He notes that "[t]he term 'interest' … can be used in quite different ways," and that under "one sense of the term, anything that contributes to the proper functioning of something is in that thing's interest," but he rejects that sense of "interests" because it "applies to things that have no moral status" (123). But that is simply circular; it presupposes which beings have moral status in order to justify use of a criterion for determining which beings have moral status.

In addition, proponents of an all-or-nothing 'subjects of a life' view offer no cogent argument for the counterintuitive position that all beings having "inherent value" must have equal value, and that therefore no moral hierarchy among beings who have some moral status is possible. Regan simply asserts, with respect to moral agents, that allowing for any ranking among them would be "morally pernicious." Then he reasons that if it is impermissible to ascribe different statuses among groups of moral agents, all of whom have inherent value because they are subjects of a life, then it must also be impermissible to ascribe a different status to "moral patients" – that is, subjects of a life who are not moral agents – relative to moral agents (Regan 1983, 236–40). But it is not as obvious as Regan supposes that assigning different moral statuses to moral agents,

---

[41] See *Cruzan v. Director, Missouri Dept. of Health*, 497 U.S. 261 (1990).

so that the interests of some would count more in moral deliberations than those of others, is morally pernicious. Certainly *some* differentiations, or some ways of treating people on the basis of supposed differentiations, we collectively view today as morally pernicious – Regan cites "chattel slavery, rigid caste systems, and gross disparities in the quality of life" (234). But it does not follow from this that *all* differentiation is ruled out; some forms of differentiation could be quite attractive from some reasonable perspectives.

Moreover, Regan fails to consider that moral agents might have equal moral status inter se, not because they are all subjects of a life, but because they are subjects of a life that are also moral agents, a postulate that is not inconsistent with the position that subjects of a life that are not moral agents also have some (though lesser) moral status. In addition, neither he nor Harris deals with the obvious fact that self-awareness and thinking about one's life vary considerably across species as well as among humans. If any nonhuman species are subjects of a life in Regan's or Harris's view, it is likely that "the consciousness, the imagination, the hopes and fears of a human being are immeasurably richer" (Belshaw 2001, 220).

Harris challenges several possible bases for "grading" persons, including age, but his rejection of each is deficient. With respect to age, he allows that we might permissibly choose to save the life of a twenty-year-old rather than that of a ninety-year-old person if faced with an either/or situation, but on grounds of fairness between two equal persons rather than on the basis of treating one as inherently more worthy of consideration. The latter is ruled out, according to Harris, because "[e]ach person's desire to stay alive should be regarded as of the same importance and as deserving the same respect as that of anyone else, irrespective of the quality of their life or its expected duration." This is so, apparently, because "the value of the unelapsed possible lifespan of each person who wants to go on living is equally valuable," which in turn Harris assumes because of "the extreme difficulty involved in discounting the value of someone's life where we and they disagree about whether or not it is worth living" (Harris 1985, 100–101). But as a matter of fairness, we can prefer the younger person on the grounds that the older has already enjoyed more years of life.

Harris's rejection of grading here rests on two assumptions, one empirical and one normative, both of which are implausible – namely, that all persons who value their lives do so to an equal degree and that nothing matters to moral status other than whether people value their lives. A ninety-year-old might well have the same thirst for life as a twenty-year-old, but common experience suggests that thirst for life diminishes in later life for most people, as quality of life diminishes and new experiences are hard to come by. That ninety–year-olds *can* "see their lives as enterprises they wish to control, bringing delight and events they wish to experience" (103) suggests that it is not age per se that matters morally, but the reality that such desires generally dissipate with age supports "grading" of people even on the personhood view on a morally relevant basis that correlates roughly with age.

Harris also considers the possibility of grading persons on the basis of their importance to other people – for example, saving the lives of parents rather than the lives of the childless in an either/or situation. He first attacks this possibility simply by characterizing it as offensive, without explaining why it is offensive (105, 106). He next attempts to diminish the significance of parents to children. He writes: "I believe that the dependence of children upon adults let alone on parents is usually grossly exaggerated.... So long as children are provided with someone to depend on in the requisite sense, they will survive." Further, "[i]t is not, of course, only children who grieve, but also friends, and I know of no evidence to show that the grief of children is necessarily greater or more deserving of prevention than any other sort" (105–06). Harris is perhaps to be excused for being unaware of the enormous literature on the vital developmental importance for children of attachment and bonding with, and continued relationship with, nurturing parents, given that most of this literature has come out in the past twenty years, after Harris published *The Value of Life*. The parent-child relationship is different from a friendship in several very important ways. But in any event, being in friendships could also enhance one's moral status; all else being equal, persons who are friends to many might warrant greater protection of their interests than the friendless, a possibility that Harris never seriously addresses and that I consider further later.

Last, Harris considers and rejects "moral worth" – that is, one's goodness, as a basis for grading persons. Again, he views the issue exclusively through a "who should we prefer to kill" lens, as do many other theorists. This is too narrow a lens, however, given that there might be reasons not to distinguish among people in choosing whom to kill that do not apply when making less momentous decisions, such as distribution of resources or conferral of political rights. But even with respect to the "whom to sacrifice" question, Harris's answer is inadequate. He reasons that it is not reasonable to prefer noncriminals over convicted murderers in such a dilemma, because doing so "would amount to heaping an extra penalty on top of those already decided as appropriate for their crimes and doing so without any further judicial enquiry" (109). That is nonsensical. If we adopt as a policy that convicted murderers will be sacrificed first and will be last to receive scarce resources such as organ donations, then we will all henceforth understand this to be part of the normal "penalty" inflicted when a person is convicted of murder, not something extra piled on. In addition, it is not clear what further judicial inquiry one would want to have in deciding whether a noncriminal should receive a heart transplant before someone who was convicted of murder with all of the procedural protections currently guaranteed to murder defendants. Many people's intuitions would strongly support a conclusion that persons convicted of heinous crimes have forfeited some of their moral standing and should no longer receive the same consideration of their interests; it is not uncommon to hear people refer to criminals on death row as beasts, monsters, animals, filth, scum, and other terms suggestive of a diminished moral status.

Ultimately, Regan, Harris, and Tooley do usefully highlight a characteristic of beings that has intuitive appeal as a basis for assigning moral status. Certainly it facilitates our identifying sympathetically with other beings that they, like us, have "beliefs and desires; perception, memory, and a sense of the future," an emotional and experiential life, an ability to pursue goals, and a desire to remain alive. That we have those things is also a basis on which we make demands for ourselves. But their highlighting of this characteristic is not grounded in any plausible theory of what, at base, gives rise to moral status, and it comes with no cogent argument for treating as equals all beings possessing the characteristic. As Tooley acknowledges, it is likely that subjects of a life differ in the *degree* to which they are subjects of a life, with some having a greater self-conception and more robust thoughts about their future than others, and moral status could vary based on that degree.

Harry Frankfurt has contended, for example, that human life is different in kind from the life other animal species manifest, because we are capable of standing back from our desires and projects and asking whether they are the sorts of desires and projects we want to have, whether the kind of person and life those desires and projects reflect are the kind of person we want to be and the kind of life we want to live (Frankfurt 1988, 12). Moreover, people can value their lives to dramatically different degrees and their desire to continue living can vary greatly from one person to another and for any given person over the course of a lifetime. In addition, Regan and Harris fail to demonstrate that no other characteristics are morally relevant and could allow for differentiation between some classes of beings within the category of subjects of a life, with consequences that are not so clearly "morally pernicious." Even if being the subject of a life were a necessary condition for being morally considerable, it would not follow that no other characteristic is relevant to a being's moral status.

Rational Moral Agency and Autonomy

Before the modern era, the prevailing view among philosophers was that reason, conscience, and free will distinguish and elevate humans relative to other animals, and such a view still has great popular currency. Kant presented an elaborate and powerful theory of the moral significance of rational moral agency and moral autonomy, and he has many modern defenders and expositors. Kant understood autonomy as including the mental capacity to subordinate nonrational inclination to the guidance of ethical principles – that is, of universal normative rules or laws. This capacity, according to Kant, gives (normal, adult) humans a freedom and self-mastery that nonautonomous creatures do not have, and therefore gives them alone a dignity worthy of moral appreciation. No being can claim dignity for itself if it is merely the passive instrument for the will of others or for nonrational inclinations. Dignity arises only from active agency, from being the source of choices and actions, which is possible only with a rational will, to which external and nonrational forces are subordinate.[42] Autonomy also includes stepping back from received norms and values to assess independently what sort of life one will lead, what one's "conception of the good" is. This too, is a faculty assumed to be unique to humans and so also conferring special dignity.

In the Kantian view, man's special dignity calls for a kind of moral regard owed to no other being, one that precludes mere instrumental treatment. Thus, in one of his formulations of the Categorical Imperative, the Formula of the End in Itself, Kant wrote that we must treat every rational moral agent as an end in itself, rather than as merely a means for use by others. By treating beings as ends in themselves, Kant meant

[42] Kant, (1956a), 400, 435–6. See also Wood (2007) 85–95; Paul Guyer, "Kant on the Theory and Practice of Autonomy," in Paul, Miller, and Paul (2003), 83–9; Jonathan Jacobs, "Some Tensions Between Autonomy and Self-Governance," in Paul, Miller, and Paul (2003) 222–6; Rollin (1992) 39–40; Frankfurt (1988) (emphasizing the capacity to have and act on the basis of second-order desires).

treating them as having dignity and inherent value and according significance to their particular ends.[43] In contrast, Kant suggested that beings who are not rational agents are not ends in themselves and are owed *no* moral obligations; at best, they might be beneficiaries of "indirect duties" – that is, duties moral agents are under to treat other creatures well not for their own sake but because doing so cultivates the proper virtues in or serves to protect moral agents. Thus, beings other than rational moral agents have no moral status; *only* the characteristic of rational moral agency gives rise to moral status.[44]

Few contemporary theorists explicitly maintain that only rational moral agents have any moral status. As noted earlier, there are theorists who unthinkingly suggest it simply because they are only interested in questions of justice among autonomous adults. In addition, there are a few philosophers who offer defenses of the view that humans acquire moral considerability only after a certain stage of cognitive development, so that human infants have none, and nonhuman animals can never possess any moral status. For example, Luc Ferry has argued that the distinctively human capacity for freedom and self-improvement gives those who possess it a value and dignity that should not be compromised for the sake of any other beings.[45] But that is a decidedly minority position.

The objection most moral status theorists have made to the Kantian position is, unsurprisingly, that it conflicts with strong intuitions about specific cases, because it excludes too many beings from the category of the morally significant.[46] In this case, this type of objection is arguably more persuasive than in the case of the other single-criterion views discussed earlier, because a rational-moral-agency-only view *so* constricts the class of beings with moral status that its results would conflict with intuitions about a very large class of cases and intuitions that are so deeply held as to shift the burden against any general principles that conflict with them. In particular, a view that possessing the faculty of rational moral agency is all that matters to moral status would likely

---

[43] Kant (2005) 90. Kant's moral theory emanates from numerous, complex works. My aim here is not to determine precisely what Kant thought, but rather to consider a Kantian argument for the exclusive moral relevance of rational moral agency. I therefore rely principally on modern Kant scholars' interpretations of Kant, understanding that the theory I describe might be as much that of certain neo-Kantians as it is Kant's own.

[44] See Kant (1997)239 ("Animals are ... merely as means to an end. That end is man."). See also Jacobs (2005); Korsgaard (1996b) 156; Rollin (1992) 42; Warren (2005), 440.

[45] Ferry (1995). See also Steinbock (1978) 254

[46] See, e.g., id., 101–04; Warnock 1971, 151; DeGrazia 1996, 70.

mean that various groups of human beings – babies, severely mentally disabled humans, persons in a coma – have no moral status whatsoever and therefore no moral rights, not even a right not to be tortured and killed. Marina Oshana suggests that Taliban women are not autonomous, because they were denied throughout their lives the experiences needed to develop that capacity, and she goes on to argue that if Kantians would attribute personhood, and therefore moral status, only to autonomous beings, such women would seem to be nonpersons and of no moral status (Oshana 2003, 104–05). The same might be said of persons raised in other authoritarian subcultures that affirmatively endeavor to stifle development of autonomy, which might include the Amish, some fundamentalist Christians, reclusive religious cults, and some other groups (Dwyer 1998, ch.1). If a robust form of rational agency is prerequisite to dignity and moral considerability, and if some otherwise normal adults do not possess it, then apparently, in the Kantian view, we would owe no moral duties whatsoever to such humans. That implication is so far out of step with widely shared views of the moral standing and moral rights of infants and other humans that are not viewed as autonomous as to make such a view facially implausible and in need of strenuous defense.

Many Kantians avoid that implication regarding infants by stipulating that the *potential* for rational moral agency and autonomy can give rise to moral status.[47] This amendment to the Kantian account of value appears ad hoc, not following from any premises inherent to that account. Those who offer it typically just assert it without attempting much of a defense, or else they offer a defense that ends up treating rational agency per se, rather than the individuals who might come to possess it, as what has moral worth (that is, they posit an obligation to protect the potential for more of this supremely good thing to come into existence), which is not responsive to intuitions that babies matter morally in their own right.[48] Kant himself rejected the notion that we have an

[47] See, e.g., Wood (2007) 96–7; Thomas E. Hill, Jr., *Respect, Pluralism, and Justice* (Oxford: Oxford University Press, 2000) 102; Allen W. Wood, *Kant's Ethical Thought* (New York: Cambridge University Press, 1999) 144; Allen W. Wood, "Kant on Duties Regarding Nonrational Nature, 72 *Proceedings of the Aristotelian Society Supplement* 198–9 (1998).

[48] See, for example, Wood (2007) 96–8. Wood's noble attempt to salvage Kantian suppositions ultimately descends into incoherence. Wood says autonomous adults are "persons in a strict sense," and children are "persons in an extended sense," and that "in order to respect rational nature" we must treat children "exactly as if they were persons in the strict sense" and grant them a moral status "exactly like that of beings that are persons in the strict sense." But then, he says: "Persons in the extended sense do not have

obligation to bring rational agency into existence in others, suggesting that no duties are owed to beings by virtue of their potential for rationality. Moral status arose for Kant, it seems, only from current possession of rational moral agency, and he thought we moral agents have a duty to ourselves to work on strengthening our moral capacities but not to help others become moral agents (Korsgaard 1996a, 125). I will offer reasons later for concluding that potential does in fact matter, but that does not appear to have been Kant's view, and present-day Kantians have generally not offered reasons for adopting such a view other than the need to fit theory with convictions about infants.

Once again, though, we can improve on the critique of the single-criterion view by looking to the ultimate source of the view – in this case, to Kant's underlying theory of moral value. Several aspects of Kant's thinking support his treatment of rational moral agency as the highest moral good. One is his account of practical reasoning. In this account, it is inherent in making any choices that we view the objects of our choices as good, and so, Kant inferred, we must view our rational agency as value-conferring, and this in turn entails viewing rational agency generally, which Kant viewed as synonymous with "humanity," as inherently good, valuable, and important (Korsgaard 1996a, ix–x, 16–17, 122–3). Thus, Kant believed that "the value of humanity itself is implicit in every human choice" (Korsgaard 1996b, 122). Kant purported to establish thereby that, as an inevitable outgrowth of practical reasoning, we ascribe intrinsic moral value to rational agency. And because "value" in a moral sense is necessarily objective and universal, valuing our own rational agency rationally commits us to ascribing intrinsic moral value to the rational agency of other persons (Korsgaard 1996b, 132–43; Korsgaard 1996a, 17).

Another Kantian tack to the conclusion that rational moral agency gives rise to moral status begins with an assumption that the only unconditionally good thing is a good will, by which Kant meant a will that acts solely out of duty rather than out of nonrational inclination, impulse, or desire (Korsgaard 1996a, 12–13, 117, 123). Kant contended that there must be some unconditionally valuable thing that is the source of all value, and that this could only be a good will (Korsgaard 1996a, 16). And only rational moral agents can have a good will; indeed, good will

---

precisely the same moral status as persons in the strict sense." Yet "they do not have a lesser status." To add to this confusion, Wood goes on to deny the status of "persons in the extended sense" to fetuses, even though they, too, have the potential to become rational agents, not because of something else inherent to fetuses, but rather because doing so would violate the rights of pregnant women.

and rational moral agency are synonymous, insofar as having a good will consists in acting solely on reason and not on our animal nature (Korsgaard 1996a, 17).

In addition, Kant spoke of regarding rational moral agency with a kind of reverence; as noted in Chapter 2, he explains his belief that moral agency gives mankind a special status in part by remarking: "Two things fill the mind with ever new and increasing admiration and awe, the oftener and more steadily we reflect upon them: the starry heavens above me and the moral law within me" (Kant 1956a, 166). Kant placed much emphasis on what distinguishes (competent adult) humans from other creatures, apparently supposing that any distinguishing characteristic must have moral significance, and rational moral agency is the one characteristic he deemed distinctively human (Korsgaard 1996a, 110–11). Many contemporary moral theorists likewise emphasize the higher order and morality-related cognition of which human adults are capable – in particular, to regulate conduct on the basis of reason and duty, rather than being driven unreflectively by brute desires – as a basis for distinguishing humans morally from other creatures.[49]

Kant's moral theory has been subjected to many serious challenges. Among the objections has been one to the assumption that when we make any choices we must be ascribing *objective* goodness to the objects of our choice. Many of our choices we recognize to reflect simply our personal preferences, and in theory one could view all one's choices as such. In addition, most people do not view their reason as value conferring in a moral sense; most people believe their minds aim to perceive moral truth rather than creating it, and many are frustrated by the apparent limits of the human mind to do this. In short, it does not appear that most people are in awe of human rational capacities in the way that Kant was.

But it does seem accurate to say that people generally believe they are morally entitled to some respect as rational agents, particularly in the form of protected freedom, and voice moral objections when they believe the government or other entity with the power to do so prevents them from making effective choices for themselves. Moreover, Kant was surely right that such moral claims are inherently objective or universalistic in nature – that is, they implicitly assert that anyone similarly situated ought to have a moral right to freedom, and so rationally commit those who make them to recognizing that other rational agents likewise have moral

---

[49] See, e.g., Frankfurt (1988) 12. ("No animal other than man appears to have the capacity for reflective self-evaluation that is manifested in the form of second-order desires.")

standing and moral claims by virtue of their rational moral agency. Thus, though Kant might have been unsuccessful in showing that engaging in practical reasoning of any sort *compels* us to acknowledge the ultimate goodness of human reason, a Kantian argument can be made successfully that our common moral practices happen to entail a belief that rational moral agency has objective moral worth and gives rise to moral status.

Even if we took Kant's arguments at face value, however, they would not establish that rational moral agency is the *only* attribute that can give rise to moral status. This is so not for the reason Korsgaard presents, however. Korsgaard contends that as rational agents we necessarily value our larger human identity, including our animal nature and our sentience, and so therefore must ascribe intrinsic value to nonhuman animals and carry moral obligations toward them.[50] The idea seems to be that our physical self, including our sentience, is prerequisite to our exercising our rational moral agency, and so we must inevitably also ascribe value to being alive and being sentient. The problem with this contention is that it does not show life per se or sentience to be inherently valuable, or necessarily viewed as such by us; we might view life per se and sentience as merely instrumentally valuable, and only so in the possession of rational moral agents. Similarly, we must view food as valuable, because we need it to remain moral agents, but that does not require us to say that food is inherently valuable. Thus, Korsgaard's contention does not establish that we must assign moral status to beings other than rational agents.

A real problem with Kant's theory is that he does not demonstrate why inevitability matters morally – that is, what special significance there is to the fact (if it is such) that we cannot help but value our rational moral agency. Implicit in this assertion is the proposition that things we value only contingently do not also matter. There is no argument in Kant's writings for the proposition that things most of us do regard as intrinsically valuable are not truly so if we *could* conceivably not view them as intrinsically valuable. If reason has value-conferring status, and if our reason happens to tell us that many things other than rational moral agency are intrinsically valuable and give rise to moral status, then should we not also regard those dictates of reason as valid, even if we could imagine ourselves not believing these things?

---

[50] Korsgaard (1996b) 152–3. Gewirth presents a similar argument. See Alan Gewirth, *Reason and Morality* (Chicago: University of Chicago Press, 1978). I use "intrinsic" and "inherent" as synonyms, following common usage and standard dictionary definitions, although some philosophical writing treats them as distinct concepts.

In other words, it does not follow from the supposition that we must believe our reason has inherent value that we cannot or should not intuitively believe that other aspects of humans and other beings have inherent value. We might, for example, regard certain forms of beauty, such as towering mountains, symphonic music, or the human physical form, as intrinsically valuable. Certainly these things, too, inspire awe in people. We also view certain pleasures – for example, being loved by others – as intrinsically valuable experiences, and view pain as intrinsically bad.[51] Everyone's self-conception as human and sense of others as like beings includes reference to an emotional self as well as a rational self (consider the nonhumanness of the hyperrational, nonemotional Dr. Spock in Star Trek). We could perhaps have evolved differently so that we did not have these beliefs and conceptions, but we could also have evolved so that we did not possess rational agency. The fact is that we ascribe objective value to many things about ourselves, and we make demands that others respect us on the basis of many things about ourselves – our being alive, our experiencing pleasure and pain, our having emotions and concerns, our being in certain relationships, *and* our being rational agents with life projects. The universality requirement Kant believed fundamental to morality would therefore require us to treat those things as bases of moral consideration for all beings that possess them, at least unless we are prepared to cease valuing those things, but Kant gives us no reason to take that step.

In addition, while Kant might be correct in assuming that a good will is unconditionally good, he did not demonstrate that it is the *only* thing that is unconditionally good. Compassion – that is, caring about other beings and sharing in their experience – seems also to be a good

---

[51] Korsgaard argues that pain is not intrinsically bad, but the argument is muddled. She points out that sometimes we welcome the sensations ordinarily associated with pain. Korsgaard (1996b) 154. For example, I might welcome the burn in my legs that comes with climbing a steep hill on my bicycle. But she herself defines pain not as a physical sensation but as an objection to a sensation. Id., at 145. If I truly and thoroughly enjoy the burn in my legs, then it is not pain under her definition of pain. Korsgaard also notes that sometimes we welcome what is ordinarily viewed as pain because it is cathartic. For example, she writes, no one would prefer not to feel grief at the death of a loved one. Id., at 154. But that does not demonstrate that grief is not intrinsically bad; it simply shows that we might wish to experience something intrinsically bad because that is the price we have to pay for some larger payoff – in this case, for solace or necessary adjustment of one's view of the world or respect for one's self. Similarly, the fact that we sometimes want to turn off our rational agency – namely, when we want to sleep – does not mean that rational agency is not intrinsically good. Intrinsic bads can be welcomed, or at least accepted, and intrinsic goods can be forgone, in order to achieve a greater good.

candidate for an unconditional good or a phenomenon that is unconditionally valuable.[52] Kant's view that true moral action is that motivated
solely by a sense of duty is inconsistent with common understandings
of morality. As discussed in Chapter 2, there is an alternative tradition
in moral philosophy, and a substantial, perhaps predominant current in
social morality, that makes love and compassion morally ultimate, rather
than acting on principle. This other viewpoint treats principles as useful guideposts to moral action, but as secondary and subsidiary to what
might be called a good heart.

Further, Kant himself acknowledged that some things might be
valuable, and morally worthy ends, even though not unconditionally so
(Korsgaard 1996a, 117–19). And he gives no reason to think that condi-
tional goods cannot give rise to moral status. Kant specifically identified
happiness as objectively good, and this is a good in which beings other
than rational moral agents might also share. In fact, the kind of condition
that Kant cited as potentially making happiness not good – namely, that
it is experienced by someone with a bad will – might be impossible for
beings that are not rational moral agents, in which case happiness would
always be good and valuable in their case.

Still more, the assumption that whatever is distinctive about human
beings has special moral significance is quite presumptuous. As a major
premise in the argument for the superiority of (normal) humans, it is
unjustifiably narrow and self-serving. A properly generalized major premise would be that any being with a characteristic (or useful capacity?)
distinct from that of other beings is of higher moral status than those
other beings. We might, then, have to say that the distinctive radar ability
of bats elevates them above all other beings. But, of course, given that
every species is by definition distinct in some way from other species, this
major premise would lead to an infinite number of logically incompatible
conclusions. True, we can only value what we can give ourselves reason
for valuing. But it is not clear what the reason would be for valuing
"whatever is distinctive about us" per se. We might find it useful to have
the radar ability that bats have, the underwater communication facility

---

[52]   Accepting this proposition does not entail believing that it is always best or morally
      right to act in the way our compassion inclines us. In some situations, doing the right
      thing might require subordinating our compassion to aims greater than preventing
      another being's suffering. For example, sometimes parents must let their children strug-
      gle with difficulties and figure out a solution for themselves, though their compassionate
      instincts incline them to step in and solve the problems for their children. Their compas-
      sion is nonetheless a good thing.

of dolphins, or the seemingly limitless affection-giving capacity of dogs. Moreover, there might be characteristics distinctive of humanity – for example, our capacity for senseless violence and our capacity to despoil the environment on a massive scale – that we have reason to disvalue, and others that most people do not think morally significant, such as the unique physical form of *Homo sapiens* or of one of our internal organs.

Last, Kant's assertion that there is special moral significance to rational agency rested on highly questionable assumptions about the independence of that agency from the material world. Warren observes that Kant's elevation of rationality was grounded in a "dualistic metaphysics of freedom," a view that moral agency, and moral agency alone, is free of causal determination. She further observes that most philosophers today reject that view (Warren 1997, 100), but one can still find philosophers advancing this account of human agency. Keith Lehrer, for example, writes:

> I choose to do what I think I ought to do because of reasons that I have for thinking that I ought to do it, without desire nudging me to do what I think that I ought to do.... I do not have to wait for a desire to arise in me to drive my sense of obligation to action. I am autonomous in the matter; it is up to me whether I go where reason and obligation direct. I do not, having reflected on what I ought to do and having reached a conclusion, sit by helplessly waiting for some desire to lead me to act.[53]

Research and everyday experience reveal that Lehrer is flatly wrong.[54] To be sure, we sometimes do things contrary to some of our desires, out of a sense of obligation, but that is because we also have a desire to fulfill our obligations and act morally, and that latter desire is strong enough to override others. People lacking the desire to act morally, even though they retain their reason and reach conclusions about moral action, do not do what they know is right. That is what psychopaths are like; moral judgment is present, moral motivation is not[55] Persons who have incurred

---

[53] Keith Lehrer, "Reason and Autonomy," in Paul, Miller, and Paul (2003) 180. Lehrer rests his position on a mysterious distinction between desire and "preference," which he defines as "a disposition to choose given the opportunity, which incorporates higher-order evaluation." Id., at 181. But this definition would serve very well for "second-order desire" as well. He seems to have in mind a sort of mental note about whether, when, and to what extent we will seek to gratify first-order desires, based on a prior deliberation and balancing. But we do not act on such mental notes unless we have a desire to advance our happiness or well being at the moment when action is called for. Without such a desire, such mental notes would be inert curiosities to us.

[54] Joshua D. Greene, "The Secret Joke of Kant's Soul," in Sinnott-Armstrong (2008c), 40–1, 64.

[55] Susan Dwyer, "What Psychopaths Can Teach Us," The Philosophers' Magazine (2004).

damage to the part of the brain where moral emotions reside can still answer questions about right and wrong, and to some extent can still reach the answers other people would reach, but they do not act on such answers.

In general, modern scientific understanding of our moral psychology is clearly contrary to this notion that something in the human mind can rise above all inclinations and desires to regulate choices autonomously and propel action. There is always some nonrational inclination or desire playing a but-for causal role in anything we do, including engaging in moral reasoning. Many people (but not all) are habituated to consult ethical principles in some situations, and so there is a comfort they enjoy, and a satisfaction of a (not necessarily conscious) desire for a self-conception as a moral person, when they think and act rationally and morally. Children, like the young of some other species, are trained to resist impulses and to mediate between conflicting desires. Humans are simply able to do this in a more sophisticated way than other animals. And as discussed further in Chapter 5, most human adults never progress beyond the level of moral development in which a desire to conform to convention constitutes the entirety of their functioning as moral agents.

A quite different argument for the unique significance of human rational agency appeals to the idea of a social contract, a line of reasoning I mentioned at the outset of Chapter 2. According to this argument, we owe moral obligations to other beings only insofar as there is a reciprocal commitment on their part to fulfill like obligations to us, and so any beings that are incapable of so committing are outside the compact and are owed no moral obligation (Narveson 2002, 266; Steinbock 1978, 252). In this view, only humans who have reached a certain level of rational functioning could have moral standing, though that level might be lower than that which inspired Kant with awe.

Peter Singer objects to this contract view on the grounds that it leads to the unacceptable conclusion that we owe moral obligations only to humans who have sufficient cognitive capacity to make a contractual commitment *and* who are in close enough proximity to enter into such an agreement, which would exclude not only nonhuman animals but also, for any given moral agent, most of the human population (because most people will be too far away).[56] He thus shows an inconsistency between the social contract view of moral status and a very large set of specific

---

[56] Singer (1979) 69–71. The proximity condition for contracting might be less an obstacle to a universal contract in the Internet age.

moral beliefs. I would add that it has not been part of our shared conception of moral duties that we must receive some benefit in exchange for holding and fulfilling them; that our sympathetic reactions to other beings are in no way limited to those who have made promises to us; and that we make moral demands for ourselves on bases other than having signed on to a moral compact. Thus, there is no basis for limiting moral status to beings who can recognize our own moral status and who promise to fulfill duties to us. Most social contract theorists, in fact, recognize that we owe some moral duties to nonhuman animals and to humans who are not autonomous (Darwall 2006, 29; Rawls 1971, 512).

In sum, higher-order cognitive functioning, and certain kinds of experiences related to that functioning, do constitute an additional criterion of moral status. This includes mere awareness of oneself as a being existing over time, but also the rarer capacity to set and pursue higher, long-term aims, rather than being driven only by immediate impulse, and to reason morally. In its most rarified form, it can include spiritual longing for meaning and transcendence. But despite a preoccupation with higher-order cognitive functioning among many moral philosophers, it cannot plausibly be viewed as the *only* basis for moral status. Indeed, as discussed in Chapter 5, it is not obviously the most important. Further, it is a multifarious thing and is manifest to substantially different degrees among humans (and in some ways to some degree among some nonhuman animals).[57] Thus, according moral significance to rational agency does not amount to showing that only rational moral agents have moral status nor that all rational moral agents are of equal moral status.

Theorists who argue for the equal moral worth of all humans or of all sentient beings, however, err in supposing that they make their case by undermining the claim that rational agency is a necessary condition for moral status (DeGrazia 1996, 53–72). They would need to show, further, that rational agency is irrelevant to moral status, that its possession does not enhance moral status in beings that do satisfy whatever condition is necessary, and they have not done so. In particular, they would need to address the psychological reality that others' rational agency enhances our empathy with them and that we intuitively believe we are owed greater respect by virtue of our rational agency.

---

[57] See Marina Oshana, "How Much Should We Value Autonomy?," *Social Philosophy & Policy* 99–126 (2003) 102; Bradie (1994) 158; Laura Purdy, "Children's Liberation: A Blueprint for Disaster," in Leahy and Cohn-Sherbok (1996) 149 ("an individual's 'autonomy profile' can consist of many widely varying capacities and tendencies. All of this means that autonomy admits of degrees").

SUMMATION

An approach to identifying criteria of moral status that looks to the normal functioning of our moral psychology supports recognition of several criteria put forward in the existing literature: being alive per se, being an important part of our ecosystem, being cared about by other morally significant beings, having sentience, being the subject of a life, and being a rational moral agent. Each of these traits causes us to care about other beings that possess them and so to regard as bad destruction of such other beings or thwarting of their aims or interests. A fundamental problem with each argument for a view that there is only one criterion is that none justifies exclusive focus on the one trait it emphasizes. At bottom, each relies simply on the fact that we adult humans do value a particular characteristic, respond to it in other beings, demand respect for ourselves on the basis of having it, and/or react with awe when we perceive it. But if our valuing and reacting emotionally and intuitively to a trait is what matters ultimately, then why not incorporate into an analysis of any beings' moral status consideration of *all* the traits that we value and to which we react in the relevant ways? If there is no good answer to that question, then we should adopt a multicriteria view, incorporating, at a minimum, all the criteria emphasized in the existing literature on moral status.

ADDITIONAL CRITERIA

But might there be other criteria as well, criteria that have been overlooked or underappreciated? We might get some sense of this by examining everyday experience and depictions of people in the arts and entertainment, to see whether people are implicitly treated as more worthy of consideration because of particular characteristics. We should not assume at the outset that all bases on which people are esteemed would hold up under rational scrutiny, but we might say that common practices have a prima facie authority or constitute prima facie evidence of legitimate criteria of moral status.

So what are the things about other people or other entities that cause us to identify with them or to be in awe of them? And what things about ourselves cause us to believe that we command respect, that others should take our interests into account in their decision making and moral deliberations – apart, that is, from their or our simply being alive, being in relationship with moral agents, being sentient, or having certain cognitive capacities?

Potentiality

The discussion previously focused principally on beings' present possession of particular traits. I did note, in connection with rational moral
agency, that many Kantians extend the scope of their preferred basis for
attributing moral status to include not only beings that possess rational
moral agency or moral autonomy but also those who are expected to
acquire it in the future. They usually do this simply by stipulation and
principally in order to avoid the counterintuitive conclusion that young
children have no moral status and so have no right themselves against any
form of cruel treatment others might want to inflict (e.g., Rawls 1971,
509; Wood 2007, 95–7). On the one hand, this ad hoc amendment to a
Kantian view of moral status might seem underinclusive, insofar as it still
leaves many mentally disabled adults with no moral status whatsoever.
On the other hand, it might seem overinclusive, insofar as it suggests
sperm have moral status, and this implication has been the basis for much
of the resistance to the position that potential matters morally.

In fact, though, there *is* theoretical justification for conferring moral
status on the basis of potential to become a being that possesses *any* of
the traits relevant to moral status. First, what other theorists of moral
status have failed to appreciate is that *every* attribution of moral status is
based on the potential for being a certain way in the future. It is implicit
in giving consideration to any other beings in our moral deliberation
about how to act that we assume they will be a certain way for some
period of time in the future, during which the actions we contemplate
would have an effect on them. If I am deliberating about whether to
shoot a deer when some friends drag me along on a hunting outing, my
consideration of the deer rests not in the fact that yesterday it was a sentient creature, nor even in the fact that now while I am thinking about it
the deer is a sentient creature, but rather in the fact that it has the potential to be a sentient creature in the next moment, and the next moment
after that, and so on for a considerable time so long as I do not shoot it.
If somehow the deer were not sentient now but would become sentient
in one minute so long as I do not shoot it, my deliberations should not
change. In fact, we might think of a sleeping deer as approximating the
hypothetical case of a currently nonsentient but potentially sentient-very
soon-deer. Similarly, in some view of rational agency, a sleeping human
might not be a rational agent, and one who believes rational agency is the
sole basis of moral status would have to struggle to explain why we do
not lose our moral status when we go to sleep. Recognizing that potential

for being a certain way in the future always matters crucially to moral status, and in fact arguably is *all* that matters, allows us to deal with the sleep conundrum. It also allows us to explain why it would be wrong to kill someone even if we could sneak up on them and do it instantaneously without their having any awareness or suffering.

John Harris argues against the moral relevance of potentiality on two grounds. First, "the bare fact that something will become X ... is not a good reason for treating it now as if it were in fact X." He notes by way of example that every living person will become dead at some point, but that it would be silly therefore to treat currently living persons as if they were dead. Second, he invokes the sperm counterexample, pointing out that, just as with a fertilized egg (and, he might add, just as with a newborn baby), if the right things happen to the sperm it will become a new human being.

Harris's first objection misconstrues what a moral agent is doing when attributing moral significance to potential. When I think that a newborn human baby has moral status in part because of its potential to become an autonomous human adult, I am not thinking that the baby is now an adult, and I would not treat the baby as an adult. I am instead thinking that this being is a human baby with certain current capacities and experiences and the potential to develop other capacities that are morally significant, and both the current attributes and the potential for the future enhance this being's standing in my moral deliberations. Similarly, recognizing that another living adult human will someday die does not commit me to treating him or her as currently dead. It does, though, temporally limit the person's potential for future life, sentience, rational moral agency, and relationship, and that limitation might be morally significant. Confusion often arises from speaking of "potential persons," rather than of currently existing beings whom we expect to become self-aware and rational beings, because the former way of speaking suggests that there is now no being existing that could have moral status. A newborn baby is a being now, just as a human adult in a temporary coma is a being now, and the inherent potentiality for future experiences, cognitions, and so on can be, and in fact typically is, a basis for ascribing moral status in either case.

Harris's second objection is also inadequate to defeat the potentiality argument. The objection rests entirely on an assumption that sperm do not have the moral status of persons; it is a *reduction ad absurdum* argument to the effect that any theory contrary to that assumption is absurd. The objection works, if at all, though, only against a view that leads to the conclusion that sperm have the same moral status as fully formed human adults. It does not work against a view that sperm have some moral status but less than that of a fully formed human adult, a view that could rest on an assumption that potentiality matters. It might be true that what the sperm has the potential to become is the same thing that a newborn baby or a nine-year-old child has the potential to become, but making the sperm's potential morally significant does not mean one must give it the same moral status as a newborn baby or a nine-year-old or an adult. We might – in fact, appear to – discount the moral status of sperm dramatically based on the exceedingly low probability of its becoming a fully formed human.[58] Probability is built into the notion of potential. Steinbock estimates the chances of a given sperm's "developing into a person," even if ejaculated into a woman (which is not true of the vast majority of sperm), as one in two hundred million. Likewise, we discount the value of a woman's unfertilized egg by the somewhat higher but still quite low probability of its becoming a person, and the value of a zygote by the fifty percent likelihood that it will not survive (Steinbock 1996, 63). Analogously, the moral considerability that an adult in a coma commands might well depend on the probabilities of emerging from the coma. It is because the probability of a potential being realized matters that expectant parents' view of a fetus typically changes as time goes on, as the risk of miscarriage diminishes in successive stages of pregnancy.

Truth be told, most people probably do not think about the moral status of sperm and unfertilized eggs, but when any do think or talk about it, they seem to view it in a somewhat different light from other substances of a similar consistency or appearance. People have custody and inheritance battles over sperm, politicians debate the morality of selling sperm or eggs, and the Catholic Church has condemned masturbation in part based on an assumption that reproductive material is sacred. Should someone propose extracting and selling unfertilized human eggs for consumption rather than reproduction, there would be impassioned calls to imprison the person just for voicing the idea. In sum, while sperm and eggs might have precious little moral status, we do appear to accord them some, and the reason is their potential to become fully formed humans.

Note that potential cannot be adequately accounted for in terms of the interests a given being has. To illustrate, imagine we developed the

---

[58] See, e.g., Soren Holm, "The Moral Status of the Pre-Personal Human Being; The Argument from Potential Reconsidered," in Evans and Pickering (1996), 200–01.

technology to bring humans back to life in some cases within ten minutes of all life functions ceasing, and imagine a five-year-old street urchin presented such a case. In the absence of all life, sentience, cognitive functioning, and relationships, the deceased street urchin would appear to have no moral status, so that we owe no moral duties to that being even though she might be said to have great interests in being brought back to life, unless we assume that her potential – in light of the technology – gives rise to moral status.

An additional objection one might make to this treatment of potential is that it suggests we can simply render a deer or human of no moral status by killing one or the other. If I do shoot the deer, then it no longer has the potential to be a sentient creature in the future, and therefore it would no longer have any moral status. However, accepting this implication does not mean that wanton killing is morally permissible. At the moment we choose to kill a living being, it has moral status that is presumptively incompatible with our killing it, a moral status that arises from its inherent potential for future life, sentience, moral agency, and so on, and we commit a wrong by killing it.

As further defense of making potential matter morally, we can note that potentiality does typically trigger the psychological processes discussed in Chapter 2. We can easily think of ourselves as once having been in a state of potentiality with respect to traits we now possess and so sympathetically identify with other beings who have such potentiality. We would likely assent to the proposition that the potentiality we possessed as infants to live full human lives, to become the adults we have become, in and of itself imbued us with a worth that commanded protection, and then we would be rationally committed to extending moral concern to other beings possessing that potentiality. And awe is a common reaction when parents and other adults contemplate that potentiality in beholding a newborn child or even a fetus shown on a sonogram.

Talents and Abilities

Intelligence is an additional characteristic on which some people base their belief that they are owed respect, and our culture in some ways shows greater respect for more intelligent people. Professors enjoy a certain prestige. Geniuses can even be revered. Students cluster around great minds in a doting fashion. So there is an element of awe in the reaction people have to great intelligence. This is true also of reactions to great physical prowess and great artistic ability. Some might bemoan the fact that there is also widespread awe in the presence of persons who are celebrities for no apparent good reason, but we might have to grant that some such persons are celebrities because they have a talent for creating certain (perhaps false) impressions in people – for example, that they are great singers or actors – or simply for becoming popular.

Hinging moral status on talents and abilities is troubling to many people. The idea of treating less intelligent people as ipso facto moral inferiors smacks of an elitism incompatible with modern egalitarian sentiments and commitments. There might well be pragmatic reasons for overriding our instinctual reactions to superior abilities. Egalitarian feelings and commitments can help to foster a sense of community among people, while elitism breeds division, and we might collectively have concluded that social and interpersonal harmony is more important to us than effectuating all of our moral intuitions. Such thinking has not been applied throughout our moral practices; we still make status distinctions among beings on other bases, as explained earlier, but this particular basis, which would result in distinctions not just between humans and nonhumans, or between adults and children, but among adults themselves, we find more troubling than others.

We could, though, instead explain our inclination to treat all minimally competent adults as moral equals as arising from a perception that the differences in ability levels among those persons are simply not that significant, and are outweighed by other criteria as to which all minimally competent adults are equal. We might conclude that the basic fact that human adults are alive and sentient and more rational and intelligent than members of other species counts for so much more than relative degree of intelligence, so that the latter has only a slight impact on moral status, so slight that it is not worth considering. If so, then granting that relative intelligence, strength, or artistic ability is, in theory, relevant to moral status need not commit us to a moral elitism.

Negative reactions to the idea that adults might be morally ranked based on their brain power are especially interesting in considering the status of children, for what has generally been invoked as a basis for ascribing children a lesser status is precisely differences in cognitive capacity – that is, children's lesser rationality or autonomy. If we reject the idea that adults can be given different statuses based on the degree to which they display rationality and autonomy, then how can we justifiably make it a basis for attributing a lesser status to children, or to members of other species? Significantly, intelligence is likely to affect what level of moral development and degree of autonomy an individual achieves.

Most humans never progress beyond a conventional morality, in which they obey laws and other norms simply because they have been trained to abide by the rules. If we believe postconventional morality, in which persons comprehend the moral principles underlying laws and other rules and are able to reflect on and question them, is an advanced stage of moral development, characterized by greater moral autonomy, and likely to be achieved only by persons of high intelligence, and if we believe that moral status should vary based on moral capacities, then we would, in effect, be endorsing different levels of moral status between different groups of human adults based on intelligence. Theorists who contend that sentience or life is all that matters might think this unseemly consequence of making cognitive functioning matter supports their position, but that makes theory too result driven. It is preferable, from a theoretical standpoint, to see where our basic intuitions lead us, and then deal with the outcomes honestly, in light of other moral or pragmatic considerations.

Beauty

Other characteristics that generate reactions of awe in people might be even more contentious. For example, beauty can trigger a feeling of awe, but it is rather inflammatory to suggest that beautiful people, all else being equal, have a higher moral status. In fact, the term "beautiful people" is often used to disparage. There are many kinds of beauty, triggering many kinds of reactions, but many believe that at least one form of beauty – namely, the sexual attractiveness of adolescents and adults – should in and of itself be irrelevant to moral status. Yet popular culture clearly does value, even worship, sexual attractiveness, and the awe we experience at beholding extremely beautiful people – think of your own favorite examples – does lead many to treat beautiful people as special, to act as if their interests warrant greater consideration. This is evident in practices as crude as choosing people to enter a popular night club and seating people in the finest restaurants. Beauty matters, and celebrity, which is sometimes based on nothing more than beauty, matters to people. When we step back and think about it, most would resist the conclusion that people occupy a higher moral status by virtue of their sexual attractiveness. But if "actions speak louder than words," it would seem that widespread prereflective intuitions support predicating moral status to some degree on beauty.

Historically, a reaction to appearance has often been a proxy for reaction to some other quality. Appearance signaled other characteristics that truly were the foundation of attributing moral status. This is true of race and beauty. Race was assumed to signal something about the internal experience of beings and/or about their rationality. Beauty was taken as a signal of reproductive capacity. Social and moral progress has entailed recognizing that empirical assumptions underlying certain associations were false – for example, the association of race with the nature of internal experience and intelligence. Reason helps us clarify which signals work or serve as good proxies and when we should simply look for the underlying characteristic that is the true trigger for moral intuitions. In the case of beauty, we could instead look for the ability and inclination to act as a good parent to children, and assign higher moral status on that basis. In a culture that encourages physically beautiful people to be self-absorbed, beauty could actually be an obstacle to good parenting.

Other kinds of beauty, though, appear to be appreciated for their own sake, rather than serving as a proxy, or might serve as a proxy for something else but we are not troubled by our instinctual response directly to them. The beauty of great mountains and clean, rushing rivers, for example, inspires awe and thereby causes us to ascribe some inherent value to them. The beauty and power of certain animals, such as thoroughbred horses, also causes us to think they matter for their own sake, perhaps more so than a mangy farm horse. Extinction of tigers would cause much more public concern than extinction of wild boars. And certain kinds of human beauty also trigger a reaction in us that makes us think it more tragic if certain people suffer misfortune or death. We say: "What a shame. He was such a beautiful person." "She carried herself with such grace." "He lit up the room when he entered." Two of the most tragic deaths of the last half century, if popular reaction is an indicator, were those of Marilyn Monroe and Princess Diana, perhaps principally because of their awe-inspiring, complex (in different ways) beauty. We do not ordinarily speak explicitly of such persons having a higher moral status, but we act and talk as if they do – not necessarily a *much* higher status, but *somewhat* elevated standing. As with intelligence, some will respond that beauty is unchosen and so nothing morally should turn on it, but, again, all the factors discussed thus far are unchosen characteristics for which the being is not responsible.

Venality, Virtue, and Innocence

One possible moral status factor that might be within the control of some beings – specifically, autonomous human beings, is virtuousness. Some of Kant's writings suggest that he believed autonomy per se gives rise to dignity and moral status; it is possessing the capacity, not how one uses it, that matters.[59] This would suggest that we continue to owe to persons who commit the most heinous crimes the same consideration in our moral deliberations as we give to any other autonomous persons. Thomas Hill writes that Kant "repeatedly implies that a person's humanity remains, and so must be respected, even though he defiles, abases, violates, dishonors, or rejects it."[60] Conversely, we owe no greater duties to the most virtuous persons. The interests of all rational moral agents must receive the same weight regardless of how they have used their rational agency.

Kant might instead say that a person who chooses evil is not acting autonomously, but rather heteronomously, driven by nonrational impulses. Kant equated autonomy with acting from a good will, so exercising one's power of choice between right and wrong in favor of the latter is ipso facto to be less autonomous, less in possession of that one attribute he believed elevated some humans above the rest of creation. Paul Guyer explains that, for Kant, "[t]o choose evil is nothing more, and nothing less, than to give one's inclinations free reign over one's choice of ends, or to surrender one's autonomy to self-love" (Guyer 2000) Nevertheless, presumably so long as a person retained the basic capacity for rational agency and moral reflection – that is, did not become entirely nonautonomous as a result of, for example, mental illness, Kant would insist that the person retains inherent value and therefore the equal dignity all humanity possesses.

Common understanding of moral autonomy today, though, is that it is a capacity for free choice as between doing what is right and what is wrong, a capacity that can be exercised for good or bad. On this view of autonomy, it makes sense to say someone is autonomous but evil. And as previously mentioned, a common attitude is that people sacrifice their human dignity and moral worth by choosing evil.[61] In fact, one

---

59 See R. George Wright, "Dignity and Conflicts of Constitutional Values: The Case of Free Speech and Equal Protection," 43 San Diego Law Review 527, 543–5 (2006)

60 Thomas E. Hill, Jr., "Humanity as an End in Itself," 91 *Ethics* 84 (1980).

61 Many people are uncomfortable with calling any person evil, and prefer to speak of "persons who have committed evil acts." This might be because of faith in the possibility of redemption, a postmodern tendency to dispense with moral judgments in favor of judgments of health or sickness, or simply humility. It seems to me, though, that anyone willing to judge another person as being "a good person," rather than limiting themselves to saying that so-and-so "is a person who happens to do good things," ought to be equally willing to say that another person is evil.

contemporary Kantian has interpreted some of Kant's writings as support-ing the view that criminality diminishes moral status. Colin Bird writes that

> the Kantian view of punishment reflects...its ability to account for the characteristic communicative power of punishment as an expression of (merited) contempt (i.e., disrespect) for those liable to it. In a similar vein sociologists sometimes speak of punishment as involving "status-degradation ceremonies."...The ability to command certain forms of treatment from others in ordinary life is, on the Kantian theory, a privilege that can under certain circumstances be withdrawn. When this happens to a person, their status is changed and they become liable to certain forms of publicly expressed contempt. (Bird 2004, 228)

The widespread intuition that people who are evil should receive less moral consideration than people who are good, and in fact less moral consideration than some nonhuman animals, is more than believing sim-ply that someone who does wrong should incur a punishment. That belief would be consistent with treating such a person as continuing to possess the same moral status as other persons. Rather, there is a sense that one's standing in the moral community can be forfeited to some degree, just as membership in a club can be forfeited or rank in the military can be lost by chronic misconduct. When a member of society, a club, or the military commits a single minor offense, applying a prescribed penalty such as a fine or temporary loss of privileges can, in fact, be seen as reaffirming the person's membership and status, by applying the organization's internal rules that apply only to members. But in many spheres of life, we recog-nize that a person can act so contrary to the norms and basic expectations of the group as to warrant a drop in status or even excommunication.

Thus, it is not uncommon for people to say of heinous criminals that they do not deserve to be treated even as well as a dog (the assump-tion being that we need not have as much regard for dogs as for nonevil humans), and banishment was once a common response to chronic crimi-nality. Such intuitive reactions make a great deal of rational sense. Why, after all, should *possession* of a capacity be status enhancing in and of itself, rather than the exercise of the capacity in a valuable way or an expectation that it will be exercised in a valuable way? To the contrary, misuse or nonuse of a valuable capacity, especially the human moral capacity, seems to diminish our empathy for an individual who displays it, lower our sense of self-worth if we display it, and trigger disgust rather than awe. Consider, by way of analogy, an excellent chef who uses his abilities to make poisoned foods appear appetizing, or who declines to use his abilities at all and instead serves frozen dinners to customers; or a master sommelier who takes to drinking only $5 bottles of wine. We would likely form a worse estimation of them and their worth as human beings than if they did not have those abilities in the first place. Comic book superheroes who, under some spell, suddenly refuse to help those in need or start causing harm plummet in our estimation, and the writers create tension by making us wonder if the characters indeed still have the superior status of superhero.

I therefore take the position that persons have greater moral status not by virtue of *possessing* the capacity for moral reasoning and decision making but rather insofar as they exercise such a capacity to do good or to avoid evil. Correspondingly, routinely acting immorally lowers one's moral status, relative to not having the capacity for moral decision at all. Having the capacity for moral reasoning and decision making but simply not making much use of it, if that is possible – that is, living one's life focused always on one's material needs and wants, giving little or no thought to moral questions, never striving for transcendence or worrying about being principled – would also seem to gain one nothing in the estimation of one's self or others. In fact, Kant would likely find it morally blameworthy and perhaps degrading to waste the opportunity to realize one's humanity in this way, having contended that persons have a moral duty to develop and exercise their autonomy. Thus, failing to exercise this capacity once one acquires it might also lower one's moral status relative to not having it at all. Becoming aware that we have squandered our potential for improvement can certainly make us feel we are less worthy, and perceiving that others have squandered their potential can make us less empathetic toward them.

Conversely, persons of extraordinary virtue trigger feelings of awe, and many people suppose that individuals should receive greater social respect and attention to their interests to the extent they live a morally good life. At the extreme, we refer to people as saints, a concept that entails semi-divine status. Interestingly, the story of the Fall in the first book of the Bible suggests a greater proximity to the divine in the absence of autonomy – that is, in innocence. "The Fall" might be construed as a plummeting in moral status, a distancing from the divine.

We might therefore assess the relative moral status of humans based in part on how moral and rational, how innocent or guilty, they are in practice. They might come up short on this count to the extent that they either live their lives thoughtlessly, at a low level of functioning, pursuing satisfaction of their self-interest, *or* that they choose to do things they know to be wrong. On the other hand, manifesting great virtue, charity, and goodness might elevate one's status, and the moral purity that comes from being incapable of moral wrong might substitute for autonomy as a source of moral standing. We could to some extent subsume this consideration under the "contribution to the community" factor discussed earlier; much of what we consider evil is conduct that harms the community, and much of what we consider virtuous is conduct that promotes community well-being. But there is something distinctive about freely (we suppose) choosing to cause harm and, conversely, exercising rational agency to rise above immediate self-interest to do good, that is salient for our moral psychology. We might ascribe value to ourselves and others insofar as we accidentally or involuntarily contribute to the welfare of other beings (e.g., by breathing or paying taxes), but Kant was certainly right in saying that a good will inspires a special kind of respect. Conversely, though we might regret any negative impact our lives accidentally or inevitably have on other beings (e.g., by creating waste), an evil will provokes a very different kind of response, one of disdain and disgust.

Species Membership?

Last, we should address characteristics that might seem to be bases for moral status but in fact are not. Common experience suggests that we identify with other humans per se, that belonging to the same species makes us identify sympathetically more with others. It seems, though, that humanness is really a proxy for other things to which we react intuitively, and a not very good proxy. Historically many people, though certainly not all, have associated humanness with certain emotional experiences, with vulnerability to suffering and capacity for pleasure, with being an object of concern for other people, and with cognitive capacities that allowed for communication and cooperation. So it is really the underlying experience of emotions and of pain and pleasure and the assumption of being part of social relationships – characteristics subsumed under the criteria already considered – that caused sympathetic identification with others, and species membership was just a marker for those things. Species membership might also be thought to give rise to special obligations, in the same way family membership does, so that we might feel stronger duties to humans relative to nonhuman animals independently of the moral status ascribed to each. There is much more to be said about the appropriateness of our making moral standing turn in part on species membership, but the issue is not pertinent to the relative standing of human children and human adults, so I will not pursue it.

CONCLUSION

In sum, the four criteria emphasized in the philosophical literature all find support in our basic moral psychology, and moral theorists have not given us persuasive arguments for excluding any of them from our moral status calculus. In addition, those four criteria are not the only characteristics of beings that give rise to intuitions about moral status. That they have been the focus of attention might suggest that they are the most important or, in other words, give rise to the strongest intuitions or intuitively matter most. But no theorists have explicitly analyzed the relative weight or importance of these various criteria. As noted earlier, most theorists in fact assume, without good reason, that only one criterion matters, and those theorists would naturally have seen no need to think about the relative importance of different criteria. I have suggested that potentiality is in fact far more important than theorists have generally realized.

In addition to concluding that many general criteria are relevant to moral status, I have shown that some of the relevant criteria actually comprise numerous more specific characteristics – for example, the many indicia of aliveness. And each of the identified criteria can be present in different degrees, allowing for differentiation among beings even on the basis of a single criterion. A complete account of moral status based on our moral psychology thus allows in theory for many fine distinctions among beings. On the other hand, its multifaceted nature might also make this account appear impossible to apply in practice in a coherent, objective fashion. I address that concern in the next chapter.

4

Problems in Applying a Multicriteria Approach

Additional, preliminary theoretical issues warrant consideration before attempting to analyze the relative moral status of humans at different stages of life. One alluded to previously is the concern that a metric for attributing moral status that allows for hierarchies within the category of humans, and that bases moral status in part on such things as degree of sentience or rationality, could justify discriminatory practices toward certain groups of people. The other is a concern that multiplying the criteria of moral status makes it impossible to apply a theory of moral status coherently or objectively, leaving us with either arbitrary, thoroughly subjective judgments or radical indeterminacy.

Before addressing these concerns, I will point out one important virtue of a multicriteria, sliding-scale view of moral status, in addition to just its consistency with our moral psychology. Such a view is much better able than any single-criterion view or any all-or-nothing view to explain many widespread specific convictions about the relative moral standing of different entities and about proper treatment of certain entities. In the human realm, it allows us to explain more satisfactorily why an embryo has some moral status but not necessarily the same as that of a normal, conscious, postbirth individual, so that we should treat an embryo with some respect but might justifiably give priority to the life of a pregnant woman over that of an embryo in her womb. In the broader scheme of relations between humans and other beings, the multicriteria, sliding-scale metric of moral status generates assessments consistent with convictions such as that human infants matter more than pigs, even if the pigs have more going on cognitively.Pigs still matter, so it is not morally permissible to torture a pig, but it is morally permissible to worry more about whether infants are comfortable than about whether pigs are comfortable. Likewise with the conviction that, though mosquitoes have some moral considerability, so that we should not destroy them for no reason, it is okay to kill one that is trying to bite you and perhaps to eradicate them on a large scale if they are spreading disease.

At the same time, this account lends greater plausibility to some moral views that are highly controversial but not considered repulsive. For example, in my account, second-trimester fetuses appear to have a fairly high moral status. Even if not conscious, they have life – indeed, are growing at a prodigious rate – and have enormous potential for future life, sentience, cognitive experience, and relationship. We might justifiably discount the status of fetuses to some degree on the grounds that miscarriage is still a possibility, but they still would appear to have much greater claim to moral respect than is conceded by many pro-choice advocates and some medical researchers, those who speak of previability fetuses as if they were mere things to be used or disposed of.[1] Indeed, the State of Louisiana recently passed legislation declaring even embryos natural persons.[2]

THE INVIDIOUS DISCRIMINATION OBJECTION

One objection to a multicriteria analysis of moral status along the lines I am proposing is that it could generate a moral hierarchy that would justify discriminatory treatment among humans in ways we have come to reject or in new and dangerous ways. Many theorists simply assume that any "grading" of human beings is unjustified and offensive, and so manipulate their theories to avoid any implication that different groups of humans could have different moral status (e.g., Harris 1985, 105–06; Singer 1975, 4–5). Singer, after predicating possession of any moral status on being sentient, then defends equal consideration, in the face of obvious differences in degrees and depths of sentience, on the grounds that facts about beings' characteristics are morally irrelevant: "Equality is a moral idea, not an assertion of fact.... [O]ur concern for others and our readiness to consider

---

[1] See Courtney S. Campbell, "Source or Resource? Human Embryo Research as an Ethical Issue," in Lauritzen (2001) 39 (describing discussion of an NIH advisory panel concerning embryo research, which treated the topic as if "a business decision were needed about whether to initiate or discontinue a product line," using "language of utility, efficiency, and responsiveness to 'consumer' demands," and noting that "the surplus or resource/property understanding of the embryo is so deeply embedded within the ideology of scientific research"). On the other hand, Steinbock notes that "several important official bodies" have adopted the view that embryo research should be regulated so as to "demonstrate 'profound respect' for embryos as a form of human life." Steinbock (1996) 28.

[2] La. Stat. Ann. C.C. Art. 26 (West 2009).

their interests ought not to depend on what they are like or on what abilities they may possess" (Singer 1975, 4–5). He does not explain the source of the "moral idea" of equality nor offer reasons for accepting it. He simply supposes that the burden of proof is on inegalitarians to demonstrate the relevance of factual differences and asserts that they cannot do so.

From historical, anthropological, and sociological perspectives, one might think the burden of proof lies on the egalitarians. Humans, like other mammal species, evolved in a way that favored hierarchy (Prinz 2007 277–9, 305). Despite the enormous spread of egalitarian ideas in law and popular thinking in the past half century, a culture of status and celebrity remains pervasive in Western society. The closest thing Singer offers to an argument for the egalitarian position is to cite Bentham for the proposition that all interests matter regardless of who possesses them, and to deny that there is any argument against the position (Singer 1975, 7–8). But citing Bentham does not amount to an argument, and even if one accepts this assertion that all interests matter, it does not follow that who the possessor of an interest is must be irrelevant to how much weight is given the interest. Singer implicitly supposes the only possibilities are giving equal consideration or giving none, but in fact there is the alternative of giving some consideration to all interests but not necessarily equal consideration. We could give some consideration to a cow's interests but less than we do to like interests of any human.

Frey does no better in defending an egalitarian, sentience-only view. He notes that "pain is a moral-bearing characteristic for us," and then makes two kinds of attempts to establish that the experience of all sentient beings matters equally. First he asserts, vacuously, that "[p]ain is pain" (Frey 1980, 174), which simply begs the question of whether we should care about the pain of nonhuman beings even if it is experientially the same as the pain of human beings. Second, he discredits distinctively human capacities as a criterion of moral status by reasoning as follows:

> Moral standing, I think, has nothing to do with agency on the part of the subject, nothing to do with the capacity to display virtues in the course of one's behaviour or with the capacity to make contracts.... Humans fully in the grip of Alzheimer's disease may cease to be agents, making choices and directing their own lives, but we do not think thereby that they cease being members of the moral community. (174)

Of course, appeal to the inconsistency between a general principle and an intuition about a specific case always invites the rejoinder that we should rethink the specific case. But even granting that adult humans who have lost their agency remain "members of the moral community" – that is, still have moral status and are still owed moral duties, it does not follow that rational agency is irrelevant to moral status. Frey confuses necessary conditions with relevance, and he unjustifiably assumes that equal moral status and complete exclusion from the moral community are the only options. Rational agency might not be a necessary condition for having some moral status, but might still enhance the standing of beings that have it. Alzheimer's patients could, in theory, have a somewhat diminished moral standing, such that their suffering matters somewhat less than the comparable suffering of some other humans.

Egalitarian theorists might argue on consequentialist grounds, though, that we should be ever striving to overcome our biological predisposition to hierarchy and to convince the masses to view all humans as equals, to guard against unwarranted oppression. Certainly, many atrocities have been committed in the name of giving effect to moral hierarchy. Though such atrocities have generally been justified by claims about moral and social standing that we today regard as indefensible, and in fact we regard certain past events as atrocities in part because we find the claimed justifications wholly untenable, there is a danger of overreaction even to defensible conclusions about moral hierarchy – that is, of *inordinately* discounting the interests and rights of any lower-ranked group. In addition, psychological injury to some people might result from any public recognition of their moral inferiority, and such injury might outweigh any benefits arising from the recognition. Korsgaard notes that "people's lives and happiness can be blighted by the suspicion that they are worthless or unlovely specimens of humanity" (Korsgaard 1996b, 11). Certainly that has been true historically for a substantial percentage of people as children.

An immediate theoretical problem for those who find ranking among humans offensive is that it is quite difficult to defend the position that humans are all of equal moral status while allowing that humans are of higher moral status than all nonhuman animals. Singer and some others deny such a hierarchy between humans and animals, but most moral theorists and most nonphilosophers accept it. Yet if one assumes that some beings other than humans have some moral status, and if one supports differentiation in moral standing within the class of all beings that have some moral status, in order to elevate humans above other beings, one would be hard pressed rationally to explain why there should be no differentiation within any subclass of such beings that manifests internal variation on some criteria deemed relevant to moral status, as is the case with the subclass of humans. Conversely, one who insists that all humans are of equal moral status might *have* to take the position that *all* beings that have *any* moral status are of equal moral status, so that their interests matter equally. As suggested earlier, one implication of the latter view might be that abortion is permissible, if at all, only in a very narrow range of circumstances – for example, only in the first trimester and only if the pregnancy endangers the mother's life. (Some arguments for broader abortion rights presuppose that a fetus has moral status equal to that of the woman carrying it, but some others suppose that the fetus has less moral status.)

Other philosophers who have contended that moral status must be an all-or-nothing thing, possessed by any being that has it to the same degree as by any other being that has it, include Tom Regan, who argued that "inherent value" must be a "categorical concept," one not admitting of degrees (Regan 1983, 240–1). The only reason Regan offers for this view, though, has nothing to do with the meaning or intrinsic properties of "moral status," but rather is simply that allowing for moral hierarchy can lead to unattractive consequences. In other words, he attempts to make a theoretical or conceptual point on the basis of practical implications. The only alternative to equal status for all, Regan contends, is a perfectionist theory of justice under which "what individuals are due, as a matter of justice, depends on the degree to which they possess a certain cluster of virtues or excellences," and such a theory provides "the foundation of the most objectionable forms of social, political, and legal discrimination" (233–4). Regan points specifically to the potential for discrimination among humans based on wealth, race, and sex (236–7). Rather than open the door to such discrimination, Regan would confer equal standing on all "subjects of a life," as discussed in Chapter 3. Inherent value is not essentially a categorical concept, then; rather, Regan simply wants it to be treated as such because doing so would be consistent with the social policies he prefers.

The reality, however, is that we do commonly make distinctions in moral status today, and we always have, and it would be quite perplexing to most people if we altered that practice to make all beings that have any moral status equal in their moral standing. This is in part because few people would, on reflection, confine moral status to human beings. Consistent with the multicriteria account of moral status in Chapter 2, we human moral agents pretty universally ascribe some moral status to dogs and horses, such that we owe some moral duties to them, but we do not ascribe to them the same status that we ascribe to humans, and most people are quite comfortable with that. Animal rights theorists might object to a moral hierarchy as between humans and animals, deriding a view that accords full and equal moral status to all humans but a lesser status to dogs and horses, as laying "the foundation of the most objectionable forms of social, political, and legal discrimination." But then they might concede that some nonanimal living beings or even some inanimate objects also have some inherent value, just less than that of animals. Few people are truly uncomfortable with moral hierarchy per se, so Regan's insistence that we treat moral status or inherent value as a "categorical concept" is inconsistent with widespread belief and common moral practice, as well as with ordinary understanding of value as inherently relative and scalar.

In addition, to the extent Regan succeeds in motivating readers to worry about degrees of moral status among humans, it is only by suggesting the possibility of reliance on characteristics that we in Western society once invoked but today reject as bases for moral status. We publicly rejected those characteristics as bases for moral standing, because we perceived the suffering that reliance on them caused and because other characteristics that poor, minority, and female persons possess eventually triggered sympathetic identification and recognition of similarity. We could do the same in the future with other characteristics, but there is no reason to suppose in advance that all criteria are or will come to be seen as illegitimate bases for attribution of moral status, any more than there is reason to suppose that we will one day reject all our beliefs about morally right and wrong action. Western societies have, in the distant past, characterized as morally proper some actions that today we regard as barbarous – for example, burning alive people believed to be witches and inflicting corporal punishment on noncompliant wives. It does not follow from this history that we should stop differentiating between actions on moral grounds. The same is true with respect to differentiation among humans as to moral status. It is rather ironic for a theorist to reject ranking of beings on the basis of the one characteristic that he believes *is* relevant to moral status, solely on the grounds that ranking has been done in the past on the basis of characteristics now deemed morally irrelevant. If Regan truly believes that being the subject of a life and nothing else makes a being morally considerable, then he should be untroubled by a ranking that turns exclusively on that characteristic. It makes no sense to say, in effect, "historically humans have used morally irrelevant traits to rank people, so therefore we should not use a morally relevant trait to rank people."

In addition, as noted in Chapter 1, it is always open to us to reject particular grounds for ranking humans morally, on the basis of rational arguments for the inappropriateness of doing so, and to refuse to treat groups of humans differently as a matter of social practice, on pragmatic or other nonmoral grounds, while still recognizing differences as a theoretical matter or as a matter of moral rights (Prinz 2007, 289–305). Many bases for ranking we have rejected for such reasons; we came to realize the falsity of empirical assumptions underlying attitudes toward certain categories of people, we changed our views of the relative importance of different characteristics, or we simply did not want to offend certain groups by suggesting they were less worthy of consideration. If the results of the analysis below trouble some people, they can try to explain why the results trouble them, and rational arguments might successfully show that the results need revising or should be ignored in social discourse and practice.

In the present context, there is little reason to worry about adults enduring unjust suffering as a result of elevating the moral status of children, even to a position higher than that of adults. Adults will still be making the rules that govern everyone's lives, and they will not allow those rules to become excessively child centered. Significantly, nonelderly adults generally create legal protections for the elderly as well, because they anticipate becoming elderly themselves, so adult self-interest is sufficient to prevent unwarranted disregard for the welfare of the elderly as well. In fact, it might be that the most that could be accomplished as a practical matter by showing that children are of superior moral status is to mitigate the excessively adult-centered policy and law making that is likely to continue indefinitely. Recognizing children's superior moral status, if the best account of moral status yields that conclusion, might simply push government officials to give children's interests more or less equal weight to that of adults and make adult society somewhat more reluctant to disparage and discriminate against children In Chapter 6, I suggest ways that social practice and legal rules might change if we were truly to recognize and give effect to a higher moral status for children, and any objections to those proposals cannot plausibly be predicated on a concern that adults will become an oppressed class.

As discussed in Chapter 3, theoretical arguments among moral philosophers for the equal status of all beings within a broad class defined by a single characteristic, such as all sentient creatures or all moral agents, are unpersuasive. In large part, this is because they fail to recognize that there is more than one criterion for moral status. In recent decades, political theorists have advanced other arguments for the equality of all rational moral agents or all "persons," who are generally the only beings their theories address. Those arguments, too, are unsuccessful.[3] Most prominent among these theorists, perhaps, is John Rawls, who reasoned that all rational moral agents would, behind a veil of ignorance as to their specific traits, adopt principles of equal treatment among themselves in conferral of basic rights and opportunities and of presumptively equal distribution of material goods. He supposed that this "Original Position" heuristic would generate fair outcomes in part because it represented all who are or have the capacity to become "moral persons" as fundamentally moral equals, rather than as having different claims based on how they happen to have fared in "the distribution of natural abilities, and therefore by contingencies that are arbitrary from a moral point of view" (Rawls 1971, 510–11). All who are capable of giving justice, Rawls asserted, are entitled to equal justice and equal moral respect: "[W]hile individuals presumably have varying capacities for a sense of justice, this fact is not a reason for depriving those with a lesser capacity of the full protection of justice. Once a certain minimum is met, a person is entitled to equal liberty on a par with everyone else. A greater capacity for a sense of justice, as shown say in a greater skill and facility in applying the principles of justice and in marshaling arguments in particular cases, is a natural asset like any other ability" (Rawls 1971, 505–06). Recognizing that infants will not have a sense of justice to any degree, Rawls adds as a basis for equal status the potential to become a moral person. His reasons for doing so are, first, that this "seems necessary to match our considered judgments" that "infants and children are thought to have basic rights," and second, because "as far as possible the choice of principles should not be influenced by arbitrary contingencies."

Rawls was not, however, developing a theory of moral status. He was simply describing assumptions built into his heuristic for developing principles of justice conceived as fairness. "[N]one of this," he conceded, "is literally argument." To the extent anything in his discussion of moral status can be counted as argument, it is the suggestion that no one's treatment should turn on the morally arbitrary allotment of abilities and other characteristics in the natural lottery, and this rejection of disfavorable treatment based on misfortune in the natural lottery might entail a rejection of differences in moral status based on natural characteristics. Significantly, Rawls appeared to view pretty much every human attribute as morally arbitrary, including even the inclination to work hard or virtuously; such dispositions are themselves inherited, not earned or deserved.

---

[3]   See, e.g., Warren (1997) 156–7.

The problem with this appeal to the morally arbitrary is that it clearly is also true of any characteristics that differentiate humans from nonhuman animals, and even of any characteristics that differentiate humans from trees. A tree is just an unfortunate loser in the natural lottery for not having moral personhood. Rejecting hierarchy on the basis of any characteristic that is morally arbitrary in the Rawlsian sense would seem to suggest that trees should have equal moral standing and therefore equal consideration in moral and political practice. Rawls himself acknowledged that we owe duties to other animals and might also owe duties to "the rest of nature," and he simply stipulated that he was leaving them out of his account of justice as a complication beyond the scope of his project. Yet, it would not seem too much more difficult to incorporate other animals than to incorporate children into the theory. We could simply shield from our awareness, in reasoning in the original position, knowledge of our species. The original position is not an actual contracting situation, but just a thought experiment, and it is not impossible for us to speculate about what we would want for ourselves if "we" had turned out to be apes or cows, perhaps even squirrels, just as it is not impossible to think about ourselves being humans with much different characteristics than we have ever possessed – for example, having severe mental disabilities or being a coma. That the result of this thought process might be that we would also demand equal liberty for ourselves as apes or cows or squirrels suggests that Rawls's mechanism for developing a social contract view of justice does not reflect or illuminate shared views or intuitions about relative moral status. Ultimately, then, Rawls's assumption of equal moral status for all humans is, like that of moral status theorists, simply unsupported stipulation.

Many theorists gloss over the problem of demonstrating that some broad class of beings has equal moral status by appealing to the notion of "full moral status." Warren, for example, contends that, because all moral agents have full moral status, they must all be equal. After all, how could anyone have more than full moral status? But the notion of full status is itself problematic. There is no receptacle or measuring stick for moral status, such that one can say it is full in a given case, that a being possesses as much moral status as one could possibly have. Moral status is always a relative matter. To speak of full status rules out by fiat the possibility that some characteristic – for example, divinity – might be an even stronger basis for moral status than moral agency or simply an enhancing factor, or that some moral agents could have higher moral status than others because their capacity for moral agency is stronger or they put it to better use or they possess a greater degree of some other morally significant characteristics, such as sentience. If moral agency is relevant to moral status, and if it is found in degrees, why must the degree be irrelevant? Moreover, why should it not matter whether a moral agent uses this capacity to do great humanitarian works or instead consistently makes immoral choices? Should someone's moral status be elevated by virtue of possessing the capacity for moral choice if the person always chooses evil rather than good, or simply acts amorally and on the basis of self-interest? Apart from a blanket opposition to moral hierarchies, an opposition that most people do not share, it is unclear on what basis one could insist that all moral agents have equal moral status. Likewise, it is unclear why anyone should accept the proposition that all sentient beings or all living beings are of equal status, given that some also have higher cognitive functioning and some do not. As discussed in the next section, it might not be feasible to identify fine distinctions or fine tune laws and public policies to reflect them, but this is nothing new or unusual; law and policy routinely gloss over smaller differences in legally relevant criteria and rely on broad categories. A clear example is use of age categories as proxies for various competencies in conferring liberties such as driving and smoking.

THE COMPLEXITY OBJECTION

How, one might wonder, could we human moral agents, individually or collectively, ever operationalize a test of moral status that has a half dozen scalar criteria, the relative weighting of which is uncertain? The calculations would have to be enormously complex; in fact, one might not even be able to determine with any confidence where to begin when assessing the relative standing of, for example, a jaguar and the Mona Lisa, or a human fetus and a person in a persistent vegetative state. Aversion to complexity might partly explain why so many theorists have fixated on a single criterion of moral status and insisted that moral status is an all-or-nothing matter.

It is not clear, though, that avoiding the complex in favor of the implausible and unpersuasive is an improvement. Ignoring all reasons and evidence that more than one characteristic of beings makes them morally considerable, while still insisting that one is theorizing about moral status, is like insisting that one is still playing bridge after dispensing with bidding and trumps to avoid complexity. Still, some might conclude from the complexity that we should simply give up theorizing about moral status and rely on whatever prevailing views about specific cases happen to exist – forget about general principles and instead go with intuitions of the majority about whether all humans are equal, animals have rights, and other issues.

Mary Ann Warren, while advocating a multicriteria approach to moral status, responds directly to a concern that "ethical eclecticism" leads to indeterminacy. She answers that simplicity is not the only virtue a moral theory can have and that a more important virtue of a moral theory is its consistency with common sense judgments.[4] Only a multicriteria basic theory of moral status can, she contends, adequately account for our commonsense judgments about specific moral issues – for example, whether it is permissible for humans to brush their teeth or plow fields.

This response might be too quick, though. A still more important virtue of a moral theory is that reasoning under it be able to get off the ground and be intelligible. And it might well be that reasoning about moral status based on multiple criteria is so complex or so plagued by conceptual problems that it cannot even get started. Consider the problems a multicriteria view confronts.

First, there are problems even a single-criterion view raises that would simply be multiplied in a multicriteria account. For example, if a criterion such as life or sentience or rational agency is not a one-dimensional trait, but rather is itself multifaceted, if a given being can have some facets but not others, and if each facet can be present in different degrees, then how would one rank the numerous beings that share the criterion in some ways and to some degree? In a life-only view, for example, how important is mobility relative to growth? Proponents and critics of the life-only view tend to assume that all beings are either alive or not, and if alive are alive to the same degree, and therefore all have the same moral status, but I showed in Chapter 3 why that assumption is unwarranted.

A multicriteria approach to moral status raises the same kinds of problems at a higher level. Warren offers no guidance as to how the seven criteria she identifies are to be weighted relative to each other, and she manifests no awareness of the ways in which traits can be present to different degrees across beings or within a single being across the course of a lifetime. Yet any reasoning about moral status that is the least bit plausible, that amounts to more than an intuitive guess, might have to be based on some assumptions about relative weight and the significance of change over time. At first glance, it seems a formidable task to justify any particular assumptions of that sort. It might well be that the entire

---

4   Id., at 21.

enterprise of assigning moral status in a rational way is hopeless, at least if we hope to make fine judgments among all types of beings.

Giving up is not really an option, however; we must, as a practical matter, draw distinctions, and if it is possible to make any distinctions in a principled way, we ought to do our best to identify them. It would seem feasible to make at least some gross distinctions, or distinctions between some types of beings, in a rational way with some confidence. Current law and social practice implicitly rest on some gross distinctions, and the best account of moral status should allow us to make such distinctions on a more rational basis. A multicriteria account might allow us to do that more persuasively than any single-criterion view does. Perhaps some beings, such as "normal" humans, possess all or most of the relevant criteria to a large degree, while certain other beings, such as ants or grass, clearly possess fewer of the criteria, and possess none to the same degree as humans, so that we can feel quite confident in ranking the former higher than the latter.

Moreover, the theory might have the resources for making judgments about the relative weight or importance of different criteria and of different factors underlying any given criterion. Presumably, weight would be determined by referring back to the basic psychological mechanisms from which intuitions about moral status emanate, and asking which characteristics tend to produce the strongest of each pertinent kind of moral sentiment. From a Humean standpoint, we would ask which characteristics trigger the strongest feelings of empathy or make us identify more strongly with another being. Following the Kantian line of reasoning described in Chapter 2, we would ask how we rank our own characteristics when we think about the bases for demanding that others respect us – that is, which aspects of our being present themselves to us as most demanding of respect, such that we would assert them before others if asked to explain why we matter morally. And as to characteristics that trigger awe, we would ask simply which are more awe-inspiring than others. This is an inherently subjective exercise, but some set of intuitions might be close to universal. In theory, we could rank all salient characteristics of beings on this basis, at least if the three mechanisms generated the same ranking; it is not clear how one would resolve any inconsistencies among them.

But rather than undertaking that Herculean task, I will, in the next chapter, take a first stab at the less ambitious task of applying the theoretical conclusions reached thus far just to the question of children's moral status relative to adults, making suggestions at appropriate points as to the relative importance of criteria that appear to differentiate those two groups of humans. Ultimately, debates about various beings' relative moral status might properly amount simply to giving competing descriptions of beings' moral status–relevant characteristics, drawing on the best empirical evidence of those characteristics, and trying to persuade others to see some beings in a new light. In Chapter 5, I offer simply a redescription of children in comparison with adults and invite others to respond with their own descriptions.

Finally, moral status egalitarians must recognize that, even in their view, terribly complex empirical questions arise in resolving conflicts of interest among different beings, because the resolution depends on identifying, weighting, and comparing the various interests beings' can have. In doing so, they would have to look to many of the same characteristics that I have identified as bases of moral status (Francione 2008, 216–17).

CONCLUSION

It might be simpler and more comfortable to say simply that children and adults have equal moral status or, in other words, that humans have the same moral status throughout their lives; and if everyone truly integrated that conclusion into their thinking, this might itself be a substantial advance in the correct direction toward appropriate moral regard for children. The egalitarian impulse of modern liberalism causes many to raise red flags at any suggestions of ranking humans. But there are plenty of people today who would deny children even equal status and insist that they have an inferior status, with no qualms about reifying a moral hierarchy. If nothing else, considering seriously the possibility that children actually should be accorded a status more elevated than our own might shake us loose finally from traditional assumptions of children's inferiority.

In addition, establishing a hierarchy among humans that reverses traditional positions, that elevates an historically subordinate and perpetually unempowered group above a superordinate and politically powerful group, is not nearly so worrisome from a theoretical or practical standpoint as is attributing a lower moral status to historically subordinate and unempowered people. We autonomous adults can take care of ourselves, and being made aware of our moral inferiority, if our status is such, might simply make us more embarrassed to be self-serving in establishing public policies and laws, using public resources, and managing children's lives on a daily basis. In other words, the danger would likely always be that the moral hierarchy does *less* work than it should in practice, not that it does too much.

There is no denying, though, that any analysis of the relative moral status of children and adults will be a messy business, in part because of the multitude of criteria and in part because there might be no hard evidence to support an answer to some pertinent empirical questions. But, again, throwing up our hands is not an option. It is necessary to reach a position on the moral status of all entities that the law affects, and we do so now, only without adequately justifying the positions we take in most instances. It is certainly simpler to say, as we now implicitly do, that life and sentience are yes-or-no kinds of things, so that adults and children are equal in those regards, and that just adding autonomy to the list of relevant criteria elevates adults over children, end of story. But the preceding analysis has shown that such a simpler approach would just be wrong, resting on unwarranted assumptions. There are more criteria than just these, each of which can be satisfied to different degrees, and it would be arbitrary and self-serving to refuse to take these facts into account because doing so threatens to put us adults in a worse light.

It would also be self-serving to say that, because a more refined analysis would be very complicated, we should just be pragmatic and stick with the status quo, which seems to work fairly well. The obvious question this stance raises is: "Works for whom?" Moreover, muddling through or allowing for the "natural development" of moral attitudes is not much different from or better than valorizing the status quo. We should, instead, make our best effort to inject greater rationality and consistency into our moral practices. The empirical complexity of the task does mean, though, that any conclusions must be provisional, always subject to revision based on better evidence or more persuasive descriptions, and so I offer the analysis of Chapter 5 as an opening gambit, hoping others will help to improve it.

5

Applying a Multicriteria Moral Status Test to Adults and Children

> Crabbed Age and Youth
> Cannot live together:
> Youth is full of pleasance,
> Age is full of care;
> Youth like summer morn,
> Age like winter weather;
> Youth like summer brave,
> Age like winter bare.
> Youth is full of sport,
> Age's breath is short;
> Youth is nimble, Age is lame;
> Youth is hot and bold,
> Age is weak and cold;
> Youth is wild, and Age is tame.
> Age, I do abhor thee;
> Youth, I do adore thee;
> O, my Love, my Love is young!
> Age, I do defy thee;
> O, sweet shepherd, hie thee!
> For methinks thou stay'st too long.

William Shakespeare (1599)

> Everything is good as it leaves the hands of the Author of things;
> everything degenerates in the hands of man.

Jean-Jacques Rousseau (1762/1979, 37)

Past and present cultural practices suggest it is reasonable to suppose that the moral status of any particular being can change over time. In particular, as noted at the outset, humans have historically been ascribed a lower moral status in their childhood than in their adulthood. As another example, many philosophers accept that a human's moral status can change as a result of losing conscious experience (i.e., by falling into a coma or persistent vegetative state). Based on the account of moral status developed in the preceding chapters, I consider here whether a change in moral status generally occurs between childhood and adulthood, or in the course of losing youthful characteristics, that is actually in a direction opposite to what has historically been supposed – that is, that aging amounts to a decline rather than an ascendance. Is adulthood a perfection of our being, or is it an increasingly decrepit form of humanity? Do we rise in stature in the moral universe as we age, or is it self-deception that makes us think we do?

If it is possible to reach a defensible conclusion about the relative moral status of adults and children using a multicriteria test, it presumably would be done by asking whether and to what degree adults and children possess each accepted criterion for moral status. This has never been done, because those who have addressed the relative moral status of children at all have largely been proponents of single-criterion views, and those few who endorse a multicriteria approach to moral status have not focused on the relative moral status of children. In this chapter, I consider one by one what Chapter 3 showed to be the best candidates for moral status criteria, and then make suggestions about how it might all add up in the end.

At the outset, though, it is useful to explicate the reasoning by which many people have concluded that children are of inferior moral status, a conclusion often expressed in terms of personhood – that is, that children are not persons or are not "full" persons like normal adults. A few have reasoned that because children may justifiably be treated paternalistically, that they therefore are of lower moral status. But this entails a confusion of moral status and treatment. As explained in Chapter 1, those two things are distinct, and two beings of equal moral status might justifiably be treated differently because they have different interests. As the examples of the infant emperor and child goddess showed, paternalistic treatment might be justified even for a being viewed as of superior moral worth.

The less confused line of reasoning maintains that higher-order rational capacities, and in particular the capacities for moral choice and autonomy, are what distinguishes humans from other creatures, that these capacities are therefore the measure of moral worth, and that because children are inferior on this measure, they must occupy an inferior moral status. By this account, there is only one criterion of moral status, the possession of certain cognitive capacities, which happen to be capacities that normal adults think distinguish them from all other life forms in the universe. Those capacities translate into a practical ability of human adults to master the world around them in a way no other beings can, and perhaps because we subconsciously associate power with superiority, there is some intuitive appeal to the belief that we adult humans are the crowning glory of creation, the pinnacle of a moral status pyramid, and the ideal toward which all beings that can should strive. Of course, no one needs much convincing that they are a superior form of life, so some intuitive appeal is sufficient to make such a belief take hold.

Chapter 3 showed, however, that no single-criterion view is tenable. On closer inspection, no such view coheres with our moral psychology and the general beliefs about what matters morally that it generates. Many characteristics of other beings trigger empathy in us, many characteristics of our selves support our belief that we matter morally, and many things inspire awe in us. Thus, a view that children are of inferior moral status would have to rest either on a claim that higher-order rational capacities are a more important criterion than any others and adults so far exceed children in those capacities as to outweigh any advantages youth might have, or on a claim that adults fare better than children even on a more even weighting of all the criteria. I address both such claims here, in the course of applying the various criteria identified in Chapter 3.

Before proceeding, it is necessary to acknowledge the limitations of this essentially empirical analysis. First, as noted in the Introduction, because humans go through many life stages, especially in the first two decades of life, and vary considerably from one stage to another, manageability requires limiting the age spans addressed within the categories of child and adult. I will principally be comparing preadolescent, school-aged children (roughly aged 6 to 12) with middle-aged adults (roughly aged 40 to 59). These might be the cohorts within each category that are likely to come out highest on the moral status scale; these children are more capable in many ways than infants but arguably more genuine and innocent than adolescents, and these adults are generally thought to be "in their prime," at the highest points in their careers, hobbies, and personal lives. So the selection does not appear to stack the deck one way or the other. I will note at some points, though, ways in which infants and adolescents might outscore preadolescent school-aged children and ways in which younger and older adults might outscore middle-aged adults on some criteria.

Second, as to many aspects of the criteria I will apply, there has been little empirical study of the extent to which the constitutive characteristics are manifest in different age groups. To do the analysis at all, then, requires relying to a substantial degree on unscientific observations, which will always be subject to challenge and refutation. This is true of any reasoning about moral status, though; at present, we must proceed without much strong empirical data. Thus, throughout the literature on animals rights, environmental ethics, and other ethical topics that raise the moral status question, one finds substantial reliance on authors' subjective impressions and understandings of what other beings are like and of what it is like to be some other being, and on generalities that gloss over variation within categories of beings (though increasingly animal rights advocates have been able to point to empirical studies of animals' experience and subjectivity). As with any ethical analysis, we must work with whatever source of empirical evidence we have at hand, and on many factual questions there will be nothing better at hand than each person's subjective impressions. The analysis will point up aspects of human experience as to which more research would be useful. We might actually have more confidence about our comparisons of children and adults, though, than we have of comparisons between humans and nonhuman animals, simply because adults have actually been both human children and human adults, and because there is, between these two categories of beings, a shared language that we understand and through which individual members of the two groups have communicated their personal experiences. To some extent, I look to such personal expressions, in narrative and artistic form.

Importantly, though, I make no pretense of advancing a knock-down case for children's superiority. My aim here is simply to see whether a *plausible* case can be made for such a conclusion. If it can be, this might at least have the effect of banishing once and for all the notion that children are inferior beings in the moral universe, and that would be a significant accomplishment. Beyond that, it might induce others to enter into a discussion of the relative strengths and weaknesses of children and adults on the various factors relevant to moral status. I will not even, myself, conclude that the case for children's superiority is strong and persuasive unless and until the analysis to follow withstands scrutiny by other theorists and by experts in the various areas of human development.

Third, I would caution the reader (and myself!) against the very common mistake among scholars of assuming that they themselves are representative of people generally. This mistake is quite common in debates about parental rights to control children's education; philosophers and legal scholars appear to assume that all parents are as competent as they are in identifying good forms of education and share the same aim of preparing children to attend the best universities. This might be because if and when they think about "other parents," they have in mind their colleagues, friends, and family members, who are likely also to be highly educated professionals. The plain reality, though, is that nonacademics are on average less competent than academics at assessing the relative merits of schools for children, that a substantial percentage of parents are in fact clueless about what makes for a good education, and that a significant percentage of parents place little value on a liberal education or attending good universities (indeed, many do not want their daughters to attend college at all).[1] The present inquiry about criteria of moral status can quite easily produce the same sort of mistake – that is, readers contemplating what middle-aged adults are like might be inclined to assume that all middle-aged adults are like what they are, have been, or expect to be as middle-aged adults in terms of such things as health, adventurousness, intellectual curiosity, sensory appreciation, ethical behavior, and so forth. Again, the reality is more likely that anyone inclined to read a book of moral theory such as this one is atypical in many respects that are relevant to moral status. To put it very simply, you, the reader, might be more youthful in many respects than most people your age. You should not extrapolate from your own life to draw conclusions about your age cohort generally.

The same thing is true, though, with respect to our children, for those of us who are parents. There is a danger that we will assume all or most children are like ours in their level of physical activity, intellectual curiosity, ethical sensitivity and honesty, self-discipline, and beauty. The reality is more likely that our children are also somewhat atypical, having inherited genes from and been raised by atypical people. I realize that my daughters are truly exceptional (of course!), and so try to avoid extrapolating from my observations of them to conclusions about all children.

Of course, these two mistakes might cancel each other out in a sense – that is, comparing atypical middle-aged adults and atypical children might yield a conclusion similar to what a comparison of average middle-aged adults and average children would produce. My point here is just that we should be aware of how limited personal experience can skew observations about what most people are like in certain large groups to which we belong. As it happens, I have worked directly with children of all ability levels and all socioeconomic levels since I was a teenager, I am

[1] See Dwyer (1998) ch. 1.

very involved at my daughters' very diverse public school, and I consume a great deal of empirical literature on children's development. So I have much to draw on beyond just my experience as a parent. Again, though, I would want feedback on the analysis to follow from real experts in human development.

A further complicating fact is that pre-adolescent school–aged children manifest a mix of traits that might be thought "natural" or intrinsic to their stage of life and also behaviors, dispositions, and attitudes imposed on them by parents and other adults. Should we assess their status on the basis of how they are or would be, for better or for worse, in the absence of adult influence (were that possible)? Or should we assess them as we find them, manifesting this mix of endogenous and exogenous characteristics? The former approach would avoid the appearance of allowing adults to diminish children's moral status by "corrupting" them, but even-handedness might then require that we try to abstract from the positive attributes adults instill. I will therefore mostly take the latter approach, but will note instances in which children manifest or fail to manifest traits that diminish or elevate moral status and in which things could be otherwise if adults refrained from imposing particular attitudes and dispositions on children.

As a last preliminary qualification, I would point out that the evidence and observations I invoke in this chapter are mostly specific to Western, and especially American, culture. One might find children and adults acting and thinking quite differently in some other cultures, in ways that connect with the criteria of moral status that Chapter 4 generated. If so, the relative moral status of children and adults could conceivably vary from one culture to another. But I will not investigate that possibility further in this chapter.

LIFE

Because I limit my analysis to the relative moral status of current children and adults, we are concerned here only with beings that are now alive. Both children and adults pass the initial threshold of life, and for theorists who think life is all that matters and that life is an either/or thing, children and adults would have equal moral status (along with all other living things, such as snails and flowers). As explained in Chapter 3, however, that empirical view is too simplistic. Aliveness is actually multifaceted and each facet can be present to different degrees in different beings, or at different stages of a single being's life. Beyond merely both being not dead, current children and adults might manifest aliveness in different ways and amounts, and that can affect the degree to which we empathize with others, view ourselves as morally considerable, or react to others or ourselves with awe or disgust.

Now is a good point to emphasize, as hinted in the Introduction, that the "we" whose empathetic reactions, self-estimation, and awe or disgust is the reference point for assessing moral status cannot be just adults. The starting points for my theoretical approach to moral status were an assumption that moral status is something moral agents attribute to beings and an assumption that moral agents' perspective on what is relevant to moral considerability is inevitably the main, perhaps singular, authority for identifying and weighting criteria of moral status. And as discussed further later in connection with the cognitive capacity criterion, people become moral agents well before adulthood. Pre-adolescent school children might be unlikely to display the kind of moral autonomy that Kant treated as the only inherently good aspect of humanity, but then adults are not much more likely to display it, so consulting only the perspective of humans who display moral autonomy in the rarified Kantian sense would be extremely exclusionary and difficult to justify. In a less demanding conception of moral agency, one that would include all normal adults in the moral community, preadolescent school-aged children are also moral agents and their perspective matters just as much. They generally occupy the conventional morality stage, past which most humans never progress. And everyday experience reveals that what makes children identify empathetically with others and what children value about themselves can differ in some respects from what causes adults to have such experiences. There is considerable overlap, but some divergence.

Recalling, then, the specific attributes of aliveness identified in Chapter 3, we should consider the degrees to which preadolescent children and middle-aged adults respectively manifest growth through metabolism, reproduction, adaptation to the environment, ingestion of food, self-produced mobility, expressiveness, spiritedness, animation, reactiveness to stimuli, goal directedness, a will to live, and ambition. It seems indisputable that on most of these attributes constitutive of aliveness, young children outdo adults, and in dramatic fashion.

First, children grow physically at a much greater rate than adults.[2] Moreover, the kind of growth children typically undergo is healthy,

---

[2]   In fact, if children were to continue growing at the rate of prenatal growth, they would reach adult size by the age of three; in the first year of life, children grow approximately ten inches. Paul Kaplowitz and Jeffrey Baron, *The Normal Pattern of Growth: What*

conducive to survival rather than hastening death. Adults often express awe at the rapidity and degree of children's growth. Most adults, on the other hand, go to significant efforts to avoid physical growth, because the only kind of physical growing we are likely to do is unhealthy growth likely to trigger disgust rather than awe. Obesity is certainly a problem with children, too, to an extent that has alarmed the medical community for many years. However, the alarm stems in part from the fact that obesity is seen as unfitting for children in a way it is not for adults; obesity is more prevalent among adults, yet this triggers less concern. In addition, major causes of this modern phenomenon of childhood obesity are changes in the diet and lifestyle of children that adults have promoted and purchased for them. Before the emergence of large corporations that could reap enormous profits from selling junk food and junk entertainment to undiscriminating, indifferent, or preoccupied parents, children ate more natural foods and had more active lifestyles, and obesity was much less common among them.[3] Children are not naturally inclined to sit on a couch for five hours a day. If children, on average, manifest less aliveness in this respect than they used to, it is because of deadening inputs from adults. It seems, too, that even obesity and lethargy in children do not make us feel disgust the way that they do in adults. In fact, children rarely trigger disgust, even when they are infants and have little control over bodily functions, perhaps because incontinence is cute or expected in infants but in adults is associated with morbidity. In addition to generally getting fatter, middle-aged adults also begin to get shorter. On the whole, then, the growth indicia of aliveness is much more positive for children than for adults.

Children also appear to grow intellectually at a rate far exceeding that of adults. The expression "can't teach an old dog new tricks" is telling. It is really too late for me to become a great guitar or piano player, even if I had a native talent for music, whereas a young child is at the prime age for beginning musical instrument lessons. They are also at a prime age for second language acquisition. If exposed early enough, children can become fluent in three or four languages.[4] But how many middle-aged adults could now undertake to learn a completely

Causes Children to Grow? (2006), available at http://www.enotalone.com/article/11399.html.

3 See Linn (2004).

4 Beverly A. Clark, *First- and Second-Language Acquisition in Early Childhood*, The Clearinghouse on Early Education and Parenting of the University of Illinois, available at http://ceep.crc.uiuc.edu/pubs/katzsym/clark-b.pdf.

new language and become fluent? Adults do possess some advantages in learning. They already have a large foundation of knowledge on which to build – for example, mastery of their first language. And they might be more capable of approaching a learning task in a systematic, efficient way. But children's minds have a pliability and absorption rate that far exceeds that of adults. Whereas adults must *learn* a new language, and think carefully about its use, children can *acquire* a new language, deploy it non-self-consciously, and become as fluent as native speakers. Children also appear to absorb science concepts and cues about interpersonal dynamics and moral attitudes more readily than middle-aged adults.[5] After a certain point in their children's schooling, when the children are learning concepts and operations that the parents never learned or have forgotten, many parents find themselves unable to help their children with school work, because they cannot master the material at all or as quickly as the children.

Children are also generally more active than adults. They are typically (again, if parents do not provide a television to hypnotize them) in constant motion when not sleeping. Even the television is not a sure way of hypnotizing children, as many have too much energy to sit before it for very long. Children tend to have more short-term rather than long-term goals, but they are constantly forming goals and pursuing them doggedly, and they view themselves as having a more open future than adults generally do. Elementary school children talk often about what they want to be and do later in life. In contrast, we are likely to react doubtfully to a middle-aged adult who speaks of taking an entirely new direction in life. Moreover, though children have less conception of what it means not to be alive, they generally manifest a thirst for life and a desire to explore the world around them or to be socially engaged that is greater than that of middle-aged adults. In fact, children tend to be so alive as to leave middle-aged parents, and even young-adult babysitters, exhausted trying to keep up with them.

---

[5] Because children do not have existing value structures to be challenged, they are more likely than adults to be influenced by the moral values of their surroundings and to incorporate those values into their own moral schemas. Daniel Pekarsky, *The Role of Culture in Moral Development*, Parenthood in America, University of Wisconsin-Madison, available at http://parenthood.library.wisc.edu/Pekarsky/Pekarsky.html. This is not to say that children indiscriminately choose their moral sources; they carefully choose who to follow and what to believe. Rachel Thomson and Janet Holland, *Young People, Social Change and the Negotiation of Moral Authority* (2002), John Wiley & Sons. Also see *Science Daily, Young Children Don't Believe Everything They Hear*, Nov. 17, 2006, http://www.sciencedaily.com/releases/2006/11/061116114522.htm.

At this point, it merits mention that many attributes of children that could be viewed in a positive light, as in the preceding paragraphs, adults often view in a negative way, which might be so simply because we adults no longer possess those attributes and in fact now suffer from certain incapacities. For example, parents often criticize their children for being boisterous and having many projects going on at once, thereby creating what the adults view as noise and disorder. In part, parents' negative reaction has to do with the fact that children's projects tend to be short-term and their attention span more limited, and it is difficult for us to see much positive value in seemingly superficial and momentary pursuits. Yet one could view such situations as involving simply different preferences for the level of noise and scatteredness and different capacities or inclinations for exploration. We adults are simply less able than we used to be to tolerate, let alone revel in, what we now call noise and clutter and whimsy, and we make a moral principle of our current preferences arising from that incapacity. It is objectively bad, we assert, to have many voices speaking loudly at once and many activities in process at the same time. Children must be trained not to do those things, and to the extent they resist such training they are blameworthy and to be punished. To some degree or in some ways, then, typical parenting practices constitute another instance in our culture of a group in power imposing what are really simply its preferences as moral truth on a less powerful group. (This is not to suggest, of course, that every belief or rule of conduct parents impose on their children is mere self-serving preference.) Again, it is important to bear in mind that you, the reader, might have a different experience within your own family, but what is pertinent here is what most parents and children are like.

Another indication of children's aliveness is their emotional intensity. Children often emote in ways that seem highly exaggerated to adults, and they generally show much greater spirit and enthusiasm for life. Children react strongly both to disappointments and to positive surprises and opportunities. Their spirit and enthusiasm is sometimes shown through effusiveness in love and affection for friends and caregivers – effusiveness that adults tend to downplay in their interactions with each other. Most children are very open to trying new activities, testing different skills, and undertaking adventures, at least so long as they are in an environment that is comfortable for them.

Statistically children are, of course, much farther from death than are adults. The disengagement or ennui that many adults increasingly display as they age might, in fact, be an adaptive characteristic, insofar as it prepares them for their inevitable death by lowering their perceived cost of exiting this life. Anthropologists tell us that one of the two principal triggers for disgust among humans is death, and phenomena we closely associate with death (e.g., recall the first time you visited a nursing home or intensive care unit at a hospital) induce dread and distaste.[6]

Some criteria for life, though, might not so clearly favor children. Adults generally consume more food than children in absolute terms, though not necessarily more relative to body size. Adolescent boys might best everyone else on this measure. The relative adaptability of children and adults is a complex matter, but seems to depend on the type of change confronted. Children appear more able to change their patterns of thought and physical activities than adults, because their minds and bodies are in an earlier, more pliable stage of development.[7] On the other hand, children might typically be more upset by certain changes, such as a residential relocation, than middle-aged adults are. Adults tend to have a broader worldview, more experience with forming new relationships and otherwise negotiating major transitions, and a greater ability to anticipate and prepare for changes. Many lose that broad perspective and flexibility in old age, and many middle-aged adults are "stuck in their ways," but on average middle-aged adults might be somewhat more accepting of changes in environment and lifestyle. A deeper analysis might question *why* adults can more readily let go of places and people to relocate (less engagement and attachment?), but I will forgo that inquiry. Last, relative reproduction activity or capacity is relatively clear; preadolescents generally cannot reproduce. On the other hand, they have their reproductive lives ahead of them, and whereas adult males can reproduce until they die, adult females lose their reproductive capacity at some point in middle age.

Based just on consideration of the criterion of life, then, one gets a sense of how difficult making fine distinctions of moral status can be. How does the foregoing account all add up? Simply counting the attributes, children would come out ahead, but then we would have to ask whether I have identified all the relevant aspects of aliveness, whether an aspect I have named could be broken down into many, and whether indicia of aliveness should have different weights. I am not certain how

---

6   See Nussbaum (2004); Macnicol (2006) 9.

7   Children's brains are growing and forming new pathways at an extraordinary rate, which gives their minds a greater openness to possibilities. Neuroscience for Kids: *Brain Plasticity: What Is It?*, prepared by Erin Hoiland, available at http://faculty.washington.edu/chudler/plast.html.

to resolve this difficulty. I can say that, having considered the attributes identified here, my subjective, intuitive judgment of whether my daughters, aged eleven and twelve, and other children I know who are their age are more "alive" than I am, would be that they clearly are so, *much* more so, even though I am healthier and more active than the vast majority of people my age.

In addition to comparing ourselves today with current children, we might compare our current selves with our earlier selves. Personally, I would say that I was more alive as a boy than I am now in my mid-forties, based on the dimensions of aliveness listed earlier, taken as a whole. A broad survey of adults on this matter might be revealing.[8] And I have a pretty good idea what the results would be if children were surveyed, asking *them* whether they believe children or adults are more alive. We might also look to literature and the arts for depictions of adult life relative to childhood, where we would certainly find many adults expressing feelings of lost life, disengagement, weariness, being closer to death, and so on. To cite just one example, consider T.S. Elliot's "Lovesong of J. Alfred Prufrock": "I grow old, I grow old, I shall wear the bottoms of my trousers rolled." "I have measured out my life in coffee spoons." "I have heard the mermaids singing, each to each. I do not think they will sing to me."

RELATIONSHIP

The criterion of being *depended on* by others is a big plus for adult humans. Middle age is the period of greatest economic productivity, with middle-aged adults financially supporting both the young and the old. Children are very dependent on their parents, not just for material comforts, but also for the emotional nurturance necessary for healthy psychological, emotional, and spiritual development. Adults also take on the task of societal governance, which is prerequisite to providing children and the elderly with a comfortable life.

Though adults might exceed children in ecosystemic importance, it is not that the young do not display the characteristic at all. Children satisfy important needs for the rest of society. They obviously satisfy an emotional and spiritual need in parents, as most adults place great

---

[8] See, e.g., Herbert L. Abrams, "How it Feels to Get Old," *Stanford Magazine* (Jul./Aug. 2004) 53, available at http://www.stanfordalumni.org/news/magazine/2004/julaug/features/abrams.html (discussing the chronic fatigue and lack of efficiency that seems to accompany aging).

importance on having them. Courts characterize child rearing as a fundamental interest *for parents* and sometimes characterize termination of parental rights in maltreatment cases as equivalent to the death penalty. In addition, children give society as a whole a sense of hope, of the future, and confidence that our human society will continue. They also enliven and enrich our culture, making life seem more worth living. If we imagine a society without children, perhaps because people stopped reproducing two decades ago, it seems a more dreadful place even than a *Lord of the Flies* version of a society with only children. So if this aspect of the relationship criteria cuts in favor of adults, it does so only modestly.

On the other hand, with respect to Noddings's notion of being an object of others' concern, it seems pretty clear that a graph of the relative strength over the course of a human life postbirth would *start out* at its highest point – that is, the apex would be at birth. Offspring do become objects of and responsive to nurturance in utero, so this criterion supports attribution of some moral status to fetuses as well, perhaps even to embryos. But emergence from the womb, becoming able to be seen, heard, and held, is a watershed moment in terms of care. No humans evoke caring in others so intensely as newborn babies, and infant attachment and bonding are the most profound responses to caring that humans ever display. The caring remains quite high throughout childhood, with not just parents but also grandparents and other relatives wanting to spend time with young children and shower love on them. Children reward that caring with affection and devotion, and by thriving as a result of it. Children also become involved in close friendships, typically seeing their friends on an almost daily basis if they go to the same school. Family attention typically wanes somewhat in adolescence, but then attention from peers becomes more pronounced, and is added to parents' continuing concern, with creation of intimate partnerships and lifelong friendships.

By contrast, adulthood is generally marked by a decline in others' caring about us. Parents still love their adult offspring, but as young adults create their own lives that their parents are not as much a part of, parents turn back to their own lives and/or transfer their attention to grandchildren. Life partnerships turn out to be seven- or ten-year partnerships, with nearly half of marriages dissolving and many others becoming merely functional or dysfunctional. Second marriages are generally less emotionally intense and dissolve at a rate approaching two thirds. ("The first cut is the deepest.") Children care about their parents, but not as much as parents care about their children, and the need for nurturance diminishes as their children grow, reducing parents' importance in the eyes of others. At the same time, parenthood tends to corrode older friendships and/ or friendships with people who do not live in the same town, because it is so consuming, and parents' new relationships with other adults tend to amount to cooperative parenting rather than true friendships. Thus, consideration of which class of humans is the object of greater caring by others also strongly supports the conclusion that youth confers a higher moral status.

In sum, middle-age adulthood seems characterized by a diminution of relational lives: Those who have not yet married become justifiably pessimistic about ever getting married. Those who have married but not had children might have closer relationships with their spouses than those with children, but they likely have fewer friendships outside the marriage than when they were younger, because friends who have children are less available. Those who marry and have children find that the children still need them even after becoming more self-sufficient, but as the children age the intensity of parenting declines and children turn their attention more to peers. For nearly half of couples who marry, the marriage falls apart, and many others continue in dysfunctional and/or emotionally empty marriages.

SENTIENCE

As explained in Chapter 3, the sentience that is relevant to moral status is not just the internal experience of pleasure and pain, as animal rights advocates seem to suppose, but also a being's connectedness to the world outside it through sensory experience. Aging is, of course, associated with loss of sensory capacities, and this might be something adults can do little to change. We can try to muster greater energy and enthusiasm for life, but we cannot reverse the death of our taste buds, the weakening of our hearing, or the loss of sensitivity in our skin. With most of our senses, the most we can do is try to slow the deterioration or compensate for it with prosthetics and drugs. A limited exception today is sight, with some restoration of lost visual acuity possible for some through surgery. On the whole, then, children appear to outdo adults considerably in terms of basic sensory capacity.

There is, however, a question of the depth or complexity of the internal experience of sensations. In addition to having organs that transmit experiential data, we have a brain that receives, interprets, and creates affective reactions to the data. A cognitive processing or refinement of sensory input can sort out the multiple sensations that make up a typical sensory experience, producing a subtler, more nuanced appreciation of positive sensory experiences. And the capacity for such processing appears to be generally much greater in adults than in children. Haute cuisine provides a good example. It is lost on most elementary school children. In fact, the complexity can turn them off. They prefer simple tastes. In this respect, adults arguably have a deeper connection with the outside world.

It might well be, though, that whereas adults have a greater capacity for processing sensory input in complex ways, allowing their experience of food, art, and other things to be qualitatively richer, their sense organs are less able than those of children to receive input and they can be attentive to fewer things. Children's processing of sensory experience might be simpler or more primitive, but they might be receiving more data from any given source and taking in data from a greater number of sources at any given time. Children's shorter attention span is explicable in part by their sensitivity to more things in their environment, soaking up input from multiple sources. We often say they are like sponges. As they get older, their focus becomes more concentrated and they increasingly block out potential sensory inputs (e.g., their parents' voices), at the same time that their processing of input and their attentiveness to subtle qualities of things they perceive increases. On the whole, then, it is difficult to say that either middle-aged adults or preadolescent school-aged children have greater sensory capacities than the other on average.

Experiences of pleasure and pain are, of course, causally connected to sensory experience. They are affective reactions to sensory input, to stimuli. There are many kinds of pleasures and pains, including corporal, emotional, psychological, and spiritual. As with perceptual experience, there is reason to believe that children's affective experience is generally more intense. For children and adolescents and even young adults, discovering new sights, sounds, tastes, and cultures is an awesome experience, one that rarely is replicated later in life. Emotional sensibilities appear more pronounced in childhood as well. Many preadolescents "fall in love" for the first time, a quite intense experience; the incidence of falling in love seems to peak in adolescence and then trail off, occurring rarely in middle age. Middle-age adulthood appears more often to be characterized by the dominance of reason, passionlessness, and emotional fatigue. This may be one explanation for the proliferation of romance novels. While adolescents live the romance, adults observe it wistfully from a distance in literary characters. There are many examples in literature of older adults mourning the loss of their youthful passions and dwelling on their memories of the loves they had in their youth. In contrast, one rarely finds anyone other than monks and Kantian philosophers celebrating freedom from emotion.

As with sensory experience, though, it might be that adults' affective experience, though less intense, is more nuanced or complex. If this is so, it might in part be because unfamiliarity the first time we have a given pleasure or pain makes it more pronounced, whereas reiterations of the same affective experience are more muted as the novelty is gone but this allows the brain to process it more. I think, for example, of the first time I ate sushi. It was as if it opened a door to a new pleasure room in my brain and rushed in to fill it, a nearly overwhelming experience. The pleasure has never again been that intense, but my enjoyment of sushi today is more nuanced; I am more attentive to and feel small pleasures from each dimension of the sensations – the flesh and fat of the fish, different for each kind, the wasabi-infused soy sauce, the tingle of the ginger, the bitter-sweetness of the Japanese beer. But I digress. The point is that adults appear to have fewer "WOW" experiences than younger people when it comes to pleasure, but they might be more attuned to and appreciative of subtleties. Another example might be the enjoyment of discovering new places, geographical and intellectual. Traveling for middle-aged adults tends to be a matter of mere curiosity; it is no longer the sort of eye-opening or transformative experience that it is for young people. But adults might understand and appreciate another culture in a deeper way. New ideas are interesting to some of us adults, and we might dissect them more carefully, but they are more likely to trigger an OMG reaction in children. (Translation for old people: OMG is text message shorthand for Oh My God. The idea of creating a new language is also more exciting for children than it is for adults.)

In addition to considering the intensity and subtlety of pleasures, we might ask whether children or adults generally have a better balance of pleasures and pains, if that might affect the degree to which people react empathetically to others or think themselves worthy of moral consideration. We might also ask whether some kinds of pleasures are more significant for moral status purposes than others. Proponents of the sentience-only view never consider the former question. They just speak bluntly of capacity for pleasure and pain. Does it matter to moral status if a person has greater capacity for pain than for pleasure or vice versa? It certainly matters to the value of a person's life – that is, to what they would stand to lose were they to die now. For it to matter to moral status would mean that we would worry more about providing pleasure and avoiding pain in the case of one person than another, based on their respective balance of pain/pleasure potential. I am inclined to think it does matter, because it is more difficult for me to identify with or respect a sad-sack, doom-and-gloom whiner than it is to identify with and respect someone who is generally happy. Whether one can empathize with another might depend to some degree on how happy one is oneself; one sad-sack might more easily empathize with another sad-sack than with a very happy person. But certainly we are unlikely to think we ourselves are deserving of moral regard on account of our having an enormous capacity for misery; rather, we are more inclined to think we have great worth if we have a great capacity for good things in our lives, including pleasure. And an extraordinary capacity for pleasures – especially, for joy, good humor, and refined aesthetic experiences – is much more likely to trigger awe than an extraordinary capacity for suffering. Chronic misery is more likely to trigger disgust.

One moral theorist has suggested that animals in some way have greater capacity for pleasure and less capacity for suffering than humans do, and this might also apply to children relative to adults. Sapontzis writes that "humans are notorious for not getting full enjoyment from present pleasures because they have fixated on past sorrows or are fretting about future difficulties, while animals, like dogs playing on the beach, do not seem to have their present enjoyment thus diluted."[9] This statement would seem equally true if "adults" were substituted for "humans" and "children" for "animals." Many middle-aged adults carry emotional and psychological baggage that interferes with their ability to experience happiness. Other animal rights theorists have suggested that humans sometimes suffer more because they can anticipate and worry about future pain, as well as living through it when it arrives, though in other instances they can mitigate their pain in a way most animals cannot, because they can understand what is happening and know that it will soon end (if that is the case). Like animals, children have less experience and understanding regarding suffering, which sometimes helps them and sometimes hurts them.

Last, there is the question of whether children and adults, as a general matter, experience different types of pleasures and pains and, if so, whether some are more important for moral status purposes. John Stuart Mill famously differentiated "higher" and "lower" pleasures, and suggested that the former have greater utility, so much as to be different in

---

[9]　Sapontzis (1987) 220.

kind not just in degree. In this view, there is more utility to the life of a dissatisfied philosopher, who suffers in many respects but experiences intellectual pleasures, than to the life of a satisfied pig. I dare say most people might empathize more readily with the pig, but if asked why we ourselves have moral worth, we are more likely to cite a capacity for distinctively human satisfactions rather than a capacity for brute indulgences, and the former capacity is also more likely to inspire awe rather than disgust. Whether adults are more philosophical than children, or vice versa, is something I consider in the next section. As for experience of other higher pleasures, such as the arts and literature, my sense is that some adults manifest a capacity for subtle appreciation that a ten-year-old cannot match, but that the vast majority of adults today have little or no appreciation for fine art and high-quality literature. In contrast, most school children enjoy reading great literature or having it read to them, because it opens their minds to new worlds and ways of seeing the world. They also enjoy doing and talking about art, at least as an alternative to other things they might be required to do in school. Both school children and middle-aged adults consume a lot of popular music, with the latter more likely to choose music that reflects impressive musicianship.

Other pleasures are more social. Both children and adults enjoy family life, in different roles but likely to a similar degree. As noted in the prior section, friendships appear more constitutive of children's lives than adults' lives; careers and family life take up so much of adults' time that friends drift to the fringes of our social world. In which category sex belongs, I will leave for others to decide. I will just observe that children generally do not experience it until they enter adolescence, whereas it is a preoccupation for many middle-aged adults, perhaps one of few pleasures they have, and the quality of the sensual experience increases during this period for women but declines for men. Some might say sex per se is a lower pleasure but "lovemaking" is a higher pleasure. It is doubtful that any children experience lovemaking. I am not aware of any studies showing which of these is more common for middle-aged couples, but presumably lovemaking is uncommon for the majority of couples who are either headed for divorce or coasting along in dysfunctional or emotionless relationships.

Sentience, then, is also a complex, multifaceted phenomenon for humans, and ranking children and adults on this criterion is more difficult than it was with aliveness. On the whole, the sentient experience of children appears to be different in significant respects from that of adults – sensorially more acute, affectively more intense, and on the whole more positive (in a nurturing environment, at least). Adult sensory and affective experiences, though, appear to be more nuanced. Many people associate "higher pleasures" with adulthood, "lower pleasures" with childhood, but probably there is at most a weak correlation; everyday experience suggests a substantial percentage of adults aspire to and attain nothing higher than happy pigdom, whereas almost any child will respond positively to a good teacher's attempts to interest them in high culture. Which form of sentient existence triggers a stronger moral status response is not so clear and, importantly, might vary from one moral agent to another. My own sense, as a middle-aged adult, is that acuteness and intensity induce a stronger sense that a being matters, that its life and interests warrant protection, than does subtlety. I presume younger people would share that view. Significantly, older humans are generally aware that something is missing, that they are receiving less sensory input and that they no longer have WOW experiences, and this is cause for regret, whereas children do not feel any lack from having less nuanced processing mechanisms, subtler sentient experiences. Intense feeling signals that we really care about things – what happens in the world and in our lives, our place and life course – so adults' relatively passionless existence might signal that at some level they do not value their own lives as much as they used to.

SUBJECT OF A LIFE

Proponents of this criterion as a necessary condition for moral status have a relatively undemanding notion in mind, some basic awareness of one's self as a distinct being that continues over time. Preadolescent school-aged children and middle-aged adults both, of course, satisfy any such minimal conception of "personhood." A more demanding notion of being the subject of a life might differentiate the two groups, but it is not clear that that is true or that any difference would affect our sense of the moral worth of individuals in the two groups. Adults have more past life to reflect on and have spent more time thinking about the meaning of their lives. Children have more future life to contemplate and are more intensely involved in creating a life course. Both frames of mind lead us to attribute value to people and their lives.

HIGHER COGNITIVE FUNCTIONING

Now we come to the one criterion of moral status that has formed the basis for philosophical arguments that children, along with nonhuman animals, occupy an inferior status relative to adult humans – namely, higher cognitive functioning, encompassing rationality, autonomy, and moral agency. In applying this criterion, I will address several questions: What exactly is the cognition-related characteristic that triggers empathy, a sense of self-worth, or awe? To what extent do children and adults manifest that characteristic? How weighty is that characteristic relative to others in our moral psychological responses?

On a preliminary note, I would mention that the concern about reader bias previously discussed is especially pronounced in connection with this criterion of moral status, and particularly in answering the second and third of the preceding questions. If there is one morally relevant characteristic that academics and consumers of moral theory are likely to manifest and esteem to an atypical degree, it is higher-order cognitive functioning. That this book is likely to have a miniscule readership compared to that of trashy romance novels and simplistic self-help books might be partly explained by its being a poor example of its kind, but certainly it is also owing to the reality that only a tiny percentage of the adult population has the ability or inclination to engage in intellectual study or discourse or sustained moral reasoning.

As to the first question, higher cognitive functioning includes at least means-ends rationality, self-regulation, self-determination, moral reasoning, and moral decision making. For Kant, self-determination and moral agency were one in the same, for he understood autonomy as the mental capacity to subordinate nonrational inclination to the guidance of ethical principles. Moral autonomy, in his view, elevates humans above other animals, making us agents rather than merely passive creatures driven by impulses, and so gives us a sense of having special significance and inspires awe.

As to the second, central question of to what relative degree children and adults manifest rationality and autonomy, developmental research shows that most humans reach the highest level of cognitive and moral functioning that they are ever going to reach by adolescence. During the elementary school years, children do generally operate at a somewhat lower level of reasoning in some respects, particularly analytical reasoning – that is, breaking down complex issues into component parts – and thinking through consequences of actions in many steps. But they approach their ultimate level during the middle school years, when the difference between children and adults is not great, and younger children are certainly reasoning persons.[10] Even first-graders can catch a parent in

[10] See, e.g., *ScienceDaily*, *Mental-state Reasoning Is Universal Milestone In Child Development*, July 29, 2005, available at http://www.sciencedaily.com/releases/2005/07/050729070346.htm (showing that from age three to age five children develop the ability to determine the approximate mental state of another person).

logical inconsistencies. In terms of means-ends rationality, children are constantly engaged in instrumental reasoning, in figuring out how to get what they want from their parents, from their peers, or on their own.[11] They show substantial adeptness is doing so, including finding subtle ways of manipulating their parents. Young siblings might even work in concert to persuade or work around parents.

Children are also more capable of abstract thought and theoretical deliberation than is generally supposed. A "philosophy of childhood" inspired by Jean-Jacques Rousseau's *Emile* has developed an account of children's minds as manifesting a *different* philosophical perspective on life and the world, rather than as being entirely prephilosophical or unreasoning. Garrett Matthews and Michael Pritchard, in particular, have done important work showing that children are surprisingly adept philosophers when presented with questions that interest them and given the opportunity to deliberate about them, even though the vocabulary and concepts they employ are less sophisticated than or simply different from those that adults might use.[12] The Institute for the Advancement of Philosophy for Children develops philosophy curricula that are used in thousands of elementary schools in the United States and elsewhere. Use would no doubt be more widespread if not for opposition on the part of a significant percentage of parents to any instruction that encourages children to think critically, especially about matters of value, and if not for the standardized testing mania.

In addition, children have very active and creative minds, manifesting greater imagination than do most adults. The main character of the book *A Little Princess*, a girl who at seven years of age weaves fantastical stories that enthrall her classmates, might be extraordinary, but most elementary school students enjoy writing stories and their play typically entails fabricating elaborate plots in the lives of dolls and stuffed animals, scripting and putting on shows, and developing scenarios for adventures in the woods or backyard.[13] Relatively few adults manifest such imagination and creativity.

---

[11]   As children play and explore, they develop, as early as age four, causal reasoning that is crucial to life as adults. Deborah Halber, "Child's Play is Serious Study of Cause and Effect," *MIT News*, March 28, 2007, available at http://web.mit.edu/newsoffice/2007/soapbox-schulz.html.

[12]   See Garrett Matthews, *The Philosophy of Childhood* (Harvard University Press 1994); Michael Pritchard *Reasonable Children: Moral Education and Moral Learning* (University Press of Kansas 1996).

[13]   See Doris Bergen, "The Role of Pretend Play in Children's Cognitive Development," *ECRP* 4(1) (Spring 2002), available at http://ecrp.uiuc.edu/v4n1/bergen.html, for a discussion of how imagination and pretend play aid in cognitive development.

The degree to which elementary school children are autonomous is a complex matter. Much depends on the particular definition of autonomy one adopts. Outside the moral realm, we might understand it to be a capacity to act independently of, and even against, immediate desires and impulses – that is, a capacity for instrumental reasoning and rational self-regulation to maximize long-term personal utility, choose long-term ends and reason about how to accomplish those ends, and regulate one's conduct so as to undertake the means identified to accomplish those ends. It might also entail a freedom and flexibility of mind, an ability to change one's mind in response to changing conditions, including the needs and requests of other.

In this understanding, elementary school children are autonomous, just less so than adults. The ability to delay gratification is present even in some very young children. The Stanford Marshmallow Study showed that about a third of four-year-olds tested were able to resist the temptation of a marshmallow in front of them for the promise of an additional marshmallow later.[14] The ability to choose shorter-term ends is greater the more one is able to contemplate alternative ends and to reason about which are more worthy of being chosen, and adults generally have greater experience of life from which to draw possible ends and more practice with reasoning about which ends to choose and what means are best for pursuing chosen ends. But school children are not entirely devoid of life experience or of practice in weighing choices. One can have greater or lesser ability to refrain from acting on impulse and to commit oneself to a course of action, and adults on average are better able to do this, in part because their desires are weaker and in part because they are more accustomed to reflecting before acting. But school children are capable of reflecting on their desires and actions and of resisting impulses; in fact, this is partly constitutive of their readiness for school. They might simply need prompts to do so. They are also able to carry out relatively long-range projects – for example, a drawing that might take weeks to complete in art class or a science project that develops over the course of several months.

Children also manifest some capacity for reflectively and independently choosing long-term goals and pursuing them in a self-controlled and rational manner. Children are often asked, for example, what they

---

[14] *The Stanford Marshmallow Study: Delayed Gratification (Self-discipline) the Key to Long Term Success*, accessed June 11, 2008, at http://www.sybervision.com/Discipline/marshmallow.htm.

want to be when they grow up, and even first-graders can give a thoughtful response to that question. A child might volunteer, with no coaching by parents or anyone else: "I want to be an author of children's books, because I love to write and I make up good stories and children would like my stories and be happy." An adult author's answer to the question "Why did you become an author?" might be no more sophisticated. A first-grader can also recognize that to become an author of children's books she needs to practice writing and drawing and spelling, and if told about opportunities for developing these skills more, like art or creative writing classes for children, she can make a decision to take those classes instead of playing at home, and she can get herself ready for the class every week. What is different about the child's capacity for such a choice might be principally the lesser knowledge with which she operates – for example, a lack of knowledge about a broader range of possible careers and lesser knowledge about the obstacles that lie in the way of making a living as an author – and a lesser capacity to incorporate a lot of information into her reasoning. Children's greatest familiarity is with the careers of the main adults in their lives – parents and teachers – and so they are more likely to express a desire to pursue one of those careers (or to avoid one that they perceive negatively). But the more they learn about other types of careers, the more likely they are to imagine themselves pursuing something else.

Though we are focused here on preadolescent children, it is useful to consider adolescents for a moment, because with respect to this criterion, they provide a good example of how adults sometimes mistake difference for deficiency. It is generally supposed that adolescents have lesser rational capacities and are less autonomous than adults, but that appears actually not to be the case. What adolescents lack, relative to adults, is mainly impulse control sufficient to match their increasingly strong, hormonally driven impulses. This apparent deficiency does not necessarily stem entirely from any lesser mental capacities relative to adults. The portion of the brain responsible for executive functions does appear to continue developing during adolescence. But teens' greater propensity to act on impulse might also be partly explained by their simply having stronger impulses than adults have, being in a period of heightened internal physical activity, and having less experience than adults and therefore fewer aversive impulses to counteract their immediate desires. Adults' desires are less intense (supporting a conclusion that the young are more sentient) and adults have memories of bad outcomes from acting on impulses, memories that trigger aversive feelings strong enough to override impulses and dictate behavior. So adults' rational capacity for self-regulation might not be dramatically greater than that of adolescents or even preadolescents. Rather, the observed behavioral differences might in part reflect the different experiential inputs on which that capacity operates, such that it is simply easier for adult to avoid bad outcomes because the benefits they get from acting on impulse are less and they are more aware of the costs.

Returning to consideration of preadolescent school-aged children, though their reasoning capacities are somewhat less developed than those of adults, they might be similarly capable of self-regulation. Not yet beset with the intense impulses of adolescence, elementary and middle-school students act out less and generally have fewer behavioral problems than high-school students. At the same time, the average adult is not necessarily a paragon of rational self-regulation. If rates of adultery and domestic violence are indicative, adult behavior is driven by nonrational impulses and desires to a considerable degree. Arguably, some nonhuman species are superior in this regard, generally exercising greater caution and less likely to get into avoidable trouble. Children are also quite capable of collective self-regulation when given real control over their lives.[15] The *Lord of the Flies* fear does not pan out in the real world. Children will impose rules on themselves for the sake of order and preservation of future opportunities, though perhaps only because they have learned the importance of this from their parents and teachers. In meting out punishments on peers, youths often prove more punitive than adults would be, as experiments with teen courts have shown. Leaving young adults to their own devices, unconstrained by law or other societal restrictions, is a scarier proposition.

Children also manifest great flexibility in social settings in ways tied to cognitive functioning, arguably greater flexibility than most adults demonstrate – for example, in adapting to new rules and to the preferences of peers and in getting past wrongs that have been done to them.[16] They might emote more in response to slights and minor attacks than adults do, but they typically do not hold grudges the way adults do. Indeed, if adults were as good about adapting to the way others like to live and in moving on after conflict, the divorce rate might be much lower than it is. Of course, children can also be inflexible and annoyingly tenacious in some ways, though this is typically more in their desires than in their thinking.

[15] One well-known example is the Summerhill School in Suffolk, England. See Sam Swope, "Free for All," *Teacher Magazine* (May 2004).
[16] See id., supra note 7.

Children often have difficulty letting go of the desire for a certain toy or for something they want to eat, and they are sometimes irrationally insistent on recognition that they were right about something and another child or an adult was wrong. The need for recognition, though, might reflect more a child's greater sensitivity to fairness, thereby demonstrating higher moral expectations than adults have, or less willingness to sacrifice what they think is right to expedience, rather than inflexibility.

With respect to moral autonomy, we should ask to what extent children and adults, respectively, consult general principles to reason independently toward moral decisions and choose to do what they conclude is right even when it conflicts with self-interest. This mental activity requires a somewhat global perspective, involving contemplation of a complex social environment and understanding of the notion of the rule of law. Doing this well entails having a fairly robust knowledge base and the ability to comprehend and deploy abstract concepts. One might suppose – in fact, probably most people do suppose – that such higher-order, paradigmatically human rational activity is the province of adults, not children.

Psychological studies show, however, that only a very small percentage of adults manifest this capacity for moral reasoning and decision making (Prinz 2007, 33). The vast majority never progress beyond the conventional stage of morality, in which they simply accept rules as rules and apply them mechanically to govern their own conduct and judge others. They do not advance to higher levels of moral development in which they can stand back from conventional rules and consider their merits based on fundamental, abstract moral principles. Most reach the conventional stage in preadolescence and remain there for the rest of their lives, adhering to the written laws and the norms of popular morality, because that is just what people are supposed to do.[17] In short, most adults are not morally autonomous in the strong sense that philosophers generally suppose.

What about the moral capacities of preadolescent children? They are much greater than is generally supposed. Susan Dwyer contends that children are born with a "Universal Moral Grammar" comparable to the innate capacity for language acquisition, and begin very early to acquire moral concepts, through observation as well as instruction, and to make

---

[17] On the moral developmental achievements of adolescents, see Nipkow and Schweitzer, "Adolescents Justifications for Faith or Doubt in God: A Study of Fulfilled and Unfulfilled Expectations," 52 *New Directions for Child Development* 91–100 (1991).

moral judgments. As early as three years of age they can distinguish moral rules from merely conventional ones (e.g., do not hit versus drive on the right side of the road).[18] By the time they enter elementary school, children are able to discuss logically the morality of laws, the associated punishment, and when they should be followed.[19] Elementary school students are familiar with interpersonal and intergroup conflicts, and they comprehend abstract ideas such as fairness and the need for consistent application of rules in connection with such conflicts.[20] Children often assess their surroundings and point out situations when adults disproportionately punish or reward certain behaviors. Weary adults sometimes respond that "life isn't fair." Children come to understand early that in making claims on their own behalf they need to think in terms of general rules. They often act in quite self-centered ways, not thinking beyond their immediate wants, but they will take a broader view with some prodding or independently, in certain environments such as a school, where they are more cognizant of the requirement to take others' needs and interests into account. Even without prodding, children will complain of unfairness that works in their own favor, defending their less fortunate peers.

Preadolescent children therefore operate at or not far below the same level of moral development at which the average adult operates, and children might have a greater potential for being pushed beyond to a higher level. Children are generally very open minded, if parents have not instilled in them fear of questioning what they have been taught. They have not yet organized complex lives around empirical and normative assumptions to the degree that adults have, so in this sense there is less cost to them in considering whether things might be other than they have supposed. One might say their sunk costs in a life plan that conforms to inherited norms is lower. Were schooling today more oriented toward encouraging independent thinking and less toward rote learning, the next generation of adults might have a much higher percentage of morally autonomous members. If children have a potential for development toward moral autonomy that adults lack, this might elevate their

[18]   Susan Dwyer, "What Psychopaths Can Teach Us," The Philosophers' Magazine (2004).
[19]   Charles C. Helwig and Urszula Jasiobedzka, "The Relation between Law and Morality: Children's Reasoning about Socially Beneficial and Unjust Laws," *Child Development*, 72(5) 1382–93 (Sept.–Oct. 2001).
[20]   For discussion on children's insistence on fairness, see Rachel Thomson and Janet Holland, *Young People, Social Change and the Negotiation of Moral Authority* (2002), John Wiley & Sons.

moral status even if the potential is unlikely to be realized in the current cultural environment.

In addition, as discussed in Chapter 2, moral reasoning based on abstract principles is not the only type or ingredient of morality. With due respect to Kant, most people regard empathy and caring as an important component of morality. Research shows that children become capable of empathy as early as age two,[21] and observers of children's reactions to others' suffering have contended that children react empathetically more readily than adults do and are more likely to act on their empathetic feelings (Nussbaum 2002, 143). Whereas killing a spider gives me some, but not much, pause, I know better than to do it when my eleven-year-old, Maggie, is around because she would be extremely upset. Even toddlers will help other children, with no evident selfish motivation; they perceive a need or a struggle, and they react. When it comes to morality, simplicity is sometimes superior, allowing straight-forward reaction to the needs or suffering of others out of compassion or love, without the interference of deliberations and rationalizations (e.g., saving one's wife from drowning because of love, not because of a rational conclusion that one has a duty to her or that overall utility will be increased by doing so).[22]

There is another dimension to autonomy, or to higher-order cognitive functioning more broadly, that is often overlooked but is also relevant to moral status, and in fact it might have been what Kant had principally in mind. It is a kind of transcendence, the will rising above man's animal nature and quotidian life, setting higher aims for oneself, creating meaning for one's life. It is moral and spiritual activity, not mere instrumental and analytical thinking. This kind of mental activity does not appear to be much present in children *or* middle-aged adults. Adolescents and young adults are, perhaps, the humans most engaged in forming higher aims and creating meaning, devoting more thought and passion to it than older adults, whose life course and values are typically already determined. Certainly some middle-aged adults engage in this activity to some degree, but so do some children in the later grades of elementary school or in middle school.[23] Children and middle-aged adults might have equal

---

[21] Jonathan Haidt and Fredrik Bjorklund, "Social Intuitionists Answer Six Questions about Moral Psychology," in Sinnott-Armstrong, ed. (2008b) 204, 206; Prinz 2008, 36),

[22] This example, familiar to moral theorists today, is generally attributed to Bernard Williams. See Williams, "Persons, Character and Morality," in *Moral Luck: Philosophical Essays 1973–1980* (pp. 1–19) (Cambridge: Cambridge University Press, 1981).

[23] See Robert Coles (1990).

capacities for transcendence, and might be equally likely to experience it in their futures – for middle-aged adults, when they approach death, and for children, in adolescence, young adulthood, and old age.

In short, rational capacities and autonomy exist in degrees, and on the whole likely exist in moderately greater degrees in adults than in children, but not dramatically greater. Insofar as possessing rationality and autonomy per se is a basis for attributing moral status, then, it might count in favor of assigning adults a slightly higher moral status relative to children.

But recall the point made earlier that it is not possessing capacities per se that gives rise to moral status, but rather using capacities to good ends. The pertinent question in assessing the relative moral status of school-aged children and middle-aged adults is therefore not, or not just, whether either or both possess the capacities for rational moral agency and transcendence, but rather to what use they put whatever moral capacities they have. One will not find empirical studies helpful to answering this question, so we must rely provisionally on what our own experiences tell us about the typical child and the typical middle-aged adult.

My own sense is that most middle-aged adults manifest little in the way of moral decision making and even less in the way of spiritual transcendence. Most appear to act most of the time on the basis of routine and their own wants or the wants of their immediate circle of family and friends, operating within limits imposed by law because conditioned to do so and averse to the costs of rule breaking, but not giving much thought to their moral underpinnings. Most are, of course, kind to those with whom they stand in reciprocal relationships and courteous to strangers. But the inclination to sacrifice significantly for a higher good seems to peak in late adolescence for any individuals who ever have it and to drop off precipitously in young adulthood. College students are perhaps most likely to display idealism and a determination to make a positive contribution to the world, and the most likely to expect principled action from peers and persons in authority. Young adults are stereotypically the most liberal and the most socially active. Peace Corps and other volunteer organizations gather the majority of their workers from recent college graduates.[24] Older adults, by and large, at best donate small sums

---

[24] See, e.g, Beth Walton, "Volunteer Rates His Record Level," *USA Today* July 7, 2006, available at http://www.usatoday.com/news/nation/2006-07-06-volunteers_x.htm. Middle-aged adults volunteer at higher rates than younger people if one includes as volunteering unpaid efforts they make for their children's organizations and their social organizations; younger people are more likely to engage in volunteer work for strangers.

and organize charity events as a social function, whereas young adults and even teenagers have a greater tendency to volunteer their time and effort, making altruism more central to their lives.

The moral world of most middle-aged adults shrinks to their immediate relationships. Those relationships can take up a great deal of altruistic energy, but the reality seems to be that we simply have less altruistic predilection as we age. We are more self-absorbed, more indifferent to the plight of others, and too ready to rationalize moral compromises.[25] Our behavior and our conversations seem to reflect a persistent, perhaps unconscious, decision not to do all that our consciences believe we ought to do to be moral persons, to correct wrongs in the world. Intellectually, we might know that the starvation and murder of thousands or millions in the Third World, in places like Somalia and the Sudan, or the deprivation children experience in pockets of poverty and dysfunction in our own countries, should matter to us, and indeed would have us pretty upset if we were forced to stare directly at it for a while. But we half-consciously decide to go on pursuing our own self-regarding aims in life, our relatively luxurious satisfactions. Perhaps most adults unconsciously choose not to allow into their minds, let alone to seek out, information about the plight of persons outside their immediate social circle. We accept a rather permanent condition of willful amorality, even immorality. Many more consciously conclude that they owe nothing to less fortunate people, that their moral responsibilities are exhausted by the demands of providing for their family. Many are simply cynical; I recall a law firm partner at an interview lunch relating the aphorism: "If you don't want to save the world when you are eighteen, you have no heart, but if you still want to save the world when you are forty, you have no brain."

This is true of collective, societal behavior as well as individual behavior. We can view state and community decision making as a mechanism by which we adults make choices about particular aspects of life or particular ways of dealing with parts of our lives, and significantly in this realm there is almost a principle of acting *selfishly*. Consider the foreign

---

See Bureau of Labor Statistics, *Volunteering in the U.S.* (2008), available at http://www.bls.gov/news.release/volun.nro.htm.

[25] Cf. Scott Schieman and Karen Van Gundy, "The Personal and Social Links between Age and Self-Reported Empathy," *Social Psychology Quarterly*, 63(2) 152–74 (June 2000) (documenting that after age thirty empathy, concern with social approval, and introspectiveness decline in adults); Peter Muhlberger, "Moral Reasoning Effects on Political Participation," *Political Psychology*, 21(4) 667–95 (Dec. 2000) (documenting adults' tendency to rationalize their failing to become more active in promoting their ideals).

policy decision making of the U.S. government. With most administrations the operating assumption, sometimes made explicit by government officials, sometimes insisted on by members of the public, is that our foreign policy should serve only our own interests, amount to nothing more than the collective self-promotion of Americans. We give significant foreign aid, but nontrivial sums must serve our strategic interests somehow, as by securing an alliance with a nation whose geographical location is militarily important. And we have sometimes supported dictators we knew to be horribly oppressive of their people, in order to secure a strategic advantage for ourselves.

Indeed, some would assert that our government has *no business* acting morally, even though this – federal government action – is the principal mechanism we have chosen for relating to the rest of humanity, to human beings outside of our country. We each have the opportunity, of course, to effectuate our moral beliefs about the suffering of those elsewhere through private charity, and some do that. But for some reason, we view the primary means we have for collective action – that is, the government, which can be more effective than private mechanisms (which is not to suggest that it always or usually is) – as an inherently amoral enterprise. Not immoral, necessarily; few would openly maintain that their country's foreign policy should be unconstrained by moral norms, that we can wantonly destroy any peoples who act contrary to our interests or steal from other peoples, whenever that is in our long-term interest (though most Western nations have done both of those things at times). But we tend to minimize and quickly forget the actions of leaders who do act immorally.

This is true of government action domestically as well as internationally. Few believe government should manifest love and compassion; its aim should be efficiency, eliminating problems such as homelessness at the least possible cost to the rest of us. We view welfare programs either as protection of the interests of the "haves," insofar as they prevent chaos and unsightly squalor, or as a kind of social insurance, something that benefits all of us by giving us a safety net for economic risk taking. Few view public welfare programs as mechanisms for expressing caring about the poor, as aimed at minimizing the suffering of the less fortunate because it has a moral pull on us.

For a substantial percentage of adults, of course, everyday life is not simply morally vapid, but rather consists in significant part of hatred and deceit and illegality. Consider the continued pervasiveness of racism and misogyny, the prevalence of adultery and consumer fraud, and the number of people who cheat on their taxes or engage in violent behavior.

And some of these adults end up in powerful positions in the government. Because we believe adults have a greater ability to act morally, we tend to react to such cruelty, hypocrisy, and selfishness with disgust, in a way we do not with children (Menninghaus 2003, 21).

In contrast, it is a common observation that children are not racist or sexist until adults teach them to think that way.[26] They are guileless until we model deception. Their earliest reaction to being harmed by others is not to strike back, but rather to cry. It would be wrong to paint an idealistic picture of school children. By the elementary school years, many children have absorbed to some degree any hatred or prejudices their parents harbor, though others form friendships with children of other races or religions despite their parents' prejudice. By school age most have learned – from older children or from adults – that lying can sometimes get them out of trouble, and some are given to hitting others when they do not get their way. Children can also be quite self-absorbed or, perhaps more accurately, so focused on their peers that they are oblivious to the interests and wishes of adults. They might be no more likely than adults to choose to sacrifice for the sake of far distant, less fortunate people. So we might conclude that neither children nor adults are paradigms of morality. But children have the advantage here of being at a stage of their development when not a great deal of moral agency can be expected; they are not squandering a capacity for morality in the same way or to the same degree that adults generally are.

In sum, if the normal behavior of most middle-aged adults, those who largely govern our society and set the moral tone of public discourse and social interactions, is at best amoral, despite having a fully developed capacity for moral decision making, it seems unwarranted to claim any moral status advantage for them on the basis of their capacity for moral agency. Contemplation of the way actual adults lead their actual lives suggests that the average adult does not manifest so much greater a capacity for moral action than children, nor so great an inclination to act morally, that philosophers can continue to assert confidently that adults' moral agency elevates them above children in the moral hierarchy of beings.

Even if the criterion of higher cognitive functioning did favor adults over children, we would need to consider how much it should count

---

[26] In fact, witnessing racist acts can create deep fears in children of all races. This fear, if not appropriately counteracted, can lead children to act as the oppressor in future situations where race may be an issue. Patty Wipfler, Hand in Hand, *Inoculating Our Children Against Racism* (2008), available at http://www.handinhandparenting.org/csArticles/articles/000000/000038.htm.

relative to other criteria. Philosophers and others have supposed that this characteristic is of utmost, even singular, importance and value, because it distinguishes us from animals in an important way, serving as the predicate for our being moral beings, capable of rising above our animal, corporeal, instinctual natures and acting on reason and principle. Generally implicit in this supposition is a view of desire as alien to one's human self and, on the other hand, reason or principles perceived by reason as somehow more internal or native to the human self. This view, in turn, appears to rest on an assumption that rationality is constitutive of humanity, of humans' "true self." The metaphysical underpinnings of this aspect of the Kantian view are apparent, and they are highly suspect. They are consistent with a mind-body dualism, and a related disparaging of the flesh, that is prevalent in the Judeo-Christian tradition and in the history of Western philosophical thought. But today such a dualism and conception of action independent of desire or a true self that transcends the material are difficult to defend.

In particular, as noted earlier, empirical work in the field of psychology confirms Hume's view that it is impossible to act independently of desire, that reason by itself is motivationally inert. In fact, research in moral psychology has debunked the philosophical supposition that reason is the foundation of moral judgment; the foundation is actually affective response, and young children (as well as some nonhuman species) manifest the capacity for the relevant sort of emotional response.[27] It turns out that deontological moralizing, especially, originates in and is determined by intuitions, most of which humans are hard-wired at birth or are trained early to have.[28] At our most noble, we act on a desire to appear good, to others and/or to ourselves, or simply to be good, desires that children have at a very early age.[29] Even then, there is always some affective impulse driving action, often unconsciously, including moral

---

[27] See Jonathan Haidt, "Morality," 3 *Perspectives on Psychological Science* 65, 69–70 (2008) (stating that "most of the action in moral judgment is in the automatic, affectively laden intuitions" and that "consistent with research on motivated reasoning and everyday reasoning, people engage in moral reasoning primarily to seek evidence in support of their initial intuition and also to resolve those rare but difficult cases when multiple intuitions conflict," and citing Frans de Waal's finding that "apes show most of the psychological building blocks that humans use to construct moral systems and communities. These building blocks are primarily emotions – such as feelings of sympathy, fear, anger, and affection...").

[28] Joshua D. Greene, "The Secret Joke of Kant's Soul," in Sinnott-Armstrong (2008c).

[29] Kagan characterizes the desire to regard the self as good as a "salient motive [that] presses continually for gratification." Jerome Kagan, "Morality and Its Development," in Sinnott-Armstrong (2008c) 297.

action – a desire for positive regard by self and/or others. The desires at work might be different at a detailed level of content from what any nonhuman animal experiences, but the difference would not appear to be so great as to mark a difference of kind. They are a distinctly human form of social sentiment, but other animals also manifest adherence to instinctual prohibitions and commands, social sentiments that lead them to engage in altruistic behavior, and a desire for positive regard. This empirical reality about moral practice, calling into question the very notion of moral autonomy and the uniqueness of human nature, surely must deflate the importance of rational moral agency to moral status. In any case, as discussed in Chapter 3, there is little plausibility to a major premise that whatever is distinctive about a particular species elevates its moral status above other beings; one would need some independent measure of weight or value to justify treating this particular characteristic as of utmost moral significance.

Moreover, the liberal philosopher's ideal of individual autonomy, independence from others, of the atomistic moral agent, appears to rest on an illusion. Feminist scholars have argued that the human agent is a social product and that normal adult human existence is inherently highly interdependent in many respects central to identity.[30] Dependence changes in nature from childhood to adulthood, but does not disappear. And in the realm of morality, an awful lot of people in Western society do not place much or any value on higher-order thinking and autonomy; a substantial percentage, in fact, believe it a very bad thing to question the ideological beliefs passed down by parents and pastors.

Consistent with the account of moral psychology presented at the outset, we might independently measure the weight of a particular criterion by asking how strong the emotional responses that it generates are relative to other criteria. Until scientific study is done to measure this, we have only our own experience to rely on, so I will relate what mine suggests. First, though perceiving higher cognitive functioning in other beings tends to enhance our empathic response to their experience, and we intuitively feel that our own rational agency enhances our worth, neither of these intuitive or emotional reactions to perceptions of rational agency is clearly stronger than the reactions we have to perceiving that other beings experience pleasure and pain or simply manifest aliveness. Rationality, understood as means-ends reasoning, is useful in life,

[30]　See Martha Albertson Fineman The Autonomy Myth: A Theory of Dependency (New Press, 2004

to be sure, but the fact that another being is reasoning does not seem to trigger empathic reactions as strong as that triggered by another being's vivacity or vulnerability to pain. Indeed, knowing another being has the wherewithal to help itself can diminish our empathic reactions. A deer or dog with a broken leg is likely to trigger more empathy in me than a neighbor with a broken leg, because I know the neighbor can understand his plight and get a doctor to set the leg and provide pain medication.

As a thought experiment, we might imagine two live beings equal in every respect except that one, though capable of instrumental and logical reasoning, has no sensory ability nor capacity for emotion or other feeling of any kind, and another has no or minimal reasoning capacity (sentience might be impossible without some sort of reasoning) but has sensory awareness of the world around it and feels pain and pleasure. We might then ask with which being we identify sympathetically to a greater degree. The first being is actually quite difficult to identify with, because sentience is so fundamental to our experience of our lives, whereas the latter we easily identify with, and in fact there are many living beings that arguably fall within this description and that we care about greatly, including newborn humans. In addition, claims people make on their own behalf seem less often and less compellingly couched in terms of their capacity for instrumental reasoning than on other aspects of their selves. The cries of the oppressed point to their suffering, to their physical needs for safety and comfort, to their emotional needs for self-esteem, a sense of belonging, and the love of family members, and to their striving to make a decent life for themselves. Claims to freedom of thought and respect for intellectual integrity also have much purchase, but we understand that the interest asserted is rather rarified, ulterior rather than basic, so the claims have less purchase than claims to basic sustenance and freedom from physical violence. If Hitler had done nothing more to Jewish people than deny them freedom of expression, his anti-Semitism would receive little attention in history books. Today there is little outcry against a Singaporean government that denies many civil liberties, because quality of life for most citizens is otherwise quite good. All else being equal, then, greater power of instrumental reasoning does elevate one being over another in moral status, but not by much and not enough to outweigh a significant difference in degree of aliveness or sentience or being the object of others' care.

The dimensions of higher cognitive abilities that do seem fairly weighty in the moral psychology of many people (or at least intellectuals) are the capacities for true moral autonomy and transcendence. This might be, in part, because both are manifestations of a kind of aliveness, a spiritual aliveness, and our strongest reactions are to signs of life and teleological directedness. It might also be because these capacities are suggestive of another, semidivine component to the self; they make a self seem larger, superhuman, rising above not only our animal nature but also above every-day human existence, to create something of larger meaning and power. It was this, not mere instrumental reasoning, that Kant viewed as constitut-ing the humanity that inspires awe and on the basis of which we demand respect for ourselves. When we observe other people doing these things, we esteem them more and think they are more worthy of protection. We can also be awed by extraordinarily moral behavior or spirituality. This is part of the reason we viewed Mother Theresa, despite her old age and failing senses, as living on a greatly elevated moral plateau – on a higher plateau, though, because the vast majority of adults live their lives in a way that does not even faintly resemble hers. Thus, although the capacity for the highest sorts of moral experience might be quite important to moral status, this does not count much in favor of middle-aged adults, because few exer-cise it and children have the potential to develop the capacity.

OTHER CRITERIA

I suggested in Chapter 3 that the existing literature might have over-looked some characteristics of beings that trigger moral status–related intuitions – that is, traits that increase the likelihood of our identifying sympathetically with others, add to our sense that we are owed respect by others, or inspire awe.

One particular characteristic that seems to trigger empathy and a sense of self-deservingness is potential for future life and development. This cri-terion, which is much more important than moral theorists have realized, obviously favors children to a great degree. Certainly the death of a child is generally more tragic than the death of an adult, because we imagine all the life that was never realized. This is only in part for reasons to which egalitar-ian utilitarians would point – that is, that the child had greater interests at stake, having a whole life of pleasures yet to experience. It is also because the potentiality of youth is a beautiful and awesome thing. It is easier to see the relevance of potentiality to moral status per se if we imagine two youths of the same age, one of whom seems destined for a very ordinary life and the other of whom manifests the potential for an extraordinary life, perhaps because of talents (so potential can overlap with talents as a criterion) or perhaps because of inner drive or circumstances. We are drawn into the fate of the latter in a way we are not with the former. We might also discern the independent significance of potential by imagining a situation in which a child and an adult have equal interests at stake – for example, an interest in not suffering a disappointment, injury, or unfairness of comparable magnitude. I am inclined to be more concerned about the experience of the child, and this is partly because the "coming of age" stage of life has a powerful aura that commands our attention.

The aging process in midlife, on the other hand, is characterized not only by an increasing proximity to death, but also by a narrowing of possibilities for the direction one's life can take and a loss of opportunity to develop oneself in different ways. The luster of possibility fades. What the middle-aged person is going to be has already been determined; no surprises await. We can even feel an embarrassment when talking with a young person who is full of ideas about her future, recognizing that we are, by contrast, such a known quantity.

Last, Chapter 4 identified characteristics likely to produce just awe rather than either of the other moral psychological processes. With respect to forms of beauty other than sexual attractiveness, these characteristics seem more often found in children than in adults. Middle-aged adults who radiate an inner beauty are few and far between, and if there is any aspect of physical beauty in adults that is distinct from sexual attractiveness, it too fades with age. In contrast, we run out of superlatives to describe the beauty of a newborn baby, and still in elementary school, children radiate a charm and purity that make it almost impossible for an attentive observer not to smile. Sociobiologists explain these reactions in terms of our being hard-wired to react with caring for the young, at least for our own biological offspring, which only serves to support an observation that children possess a kind of beauty that triggers concern for interests and that adults generally do not possess.

We also react with awe to great sexual beauty and physical abilities. Like altruism, these might be characteristics that neither children nor middle-aged adults display very much. Middle-aged adults certainly can be extremely beautiful (a handful of movie stars in their forties or fifties come to mind) and are generally stronger than children, but in America at least most do little to preserve or develop either of these characteristics, and as a result are more likely to induce disgust than awe (depending on who is beholding, of course). On the other hand, agility seems to peak at a point in life closer to childhood than to middle age. Olympic champions in gymnastics and ice skating, for example, are typically teenagers. Professional or Olympic athletes in their forties and fifties are rare. In any event, the connection between physical ability and moral status does not appear a very close one, at least in modern times when physical ability is increasingly less important to everyday life and survival. And some children possess a potential that adults generally do not for great sexual beauty in the future.

These additional criteria, then, on the whole also weigh in favor of children, with children far exceeding adults on measures of potential and nonsexual beauty. No doubt other relevant characteristics could be identified. It is important to keep in mind, though, that not everything positive that can be said about being an adult or a child is necessarily relevant to moral status. For example, it might be that adults tend to be more content with their lives and less subject to complaint than children are. But common experience does not suggest that we react empathically to others when we perceive contentment, or that we demand respect from others on the grounds that we are content, or that contentment inspires awe. Perhaps it is a good thing for us that we are relatively content (thought perhaps it is not), but that does not mean it elevates our moral status.

CONCLUSION

I have considered numerous possible bases for attributing moral status. On several, such as rationality, autonomy, processing of sensory experience, and contribution to a social community, middle-aged adults appear to come out ahead of preadolescent school-aged children, but only by a small measure. On all other criteria – aliveness, being objects of care, sentience (in terms of sensory acuity and intensity of experience), innocence, beauty, and potential for future life and eventually realizing any advantages of adult life – children come out substantially ahead. If we were to give equal weight to each just-listed basis for moral status, children would appear to come out far ahead. They are on average much more alive in so many ways, living more intensely, more dear to others, more prepared to advance in their moral development, more innocent, more beautiful, more full of potential, and on the whole simply more empathy provoking and awesome than adults. But simply tallying the number of criteria on each side is unsatisfactory, for characteristics could be grouped differently and, in any event, we cannot simply assume that each criterion is equally important to an overall assessment of moral status.

It might help in arriving at a final conclusion to reconsider once again the one basis on which many people have predicated claims for the superior status of adults – higher cognitive functioning. This is the principal way in which we adults can claim to be superior to children, in the more advanced development of our brains and our correspondingly greater ability to consider a variety of ends and figure out how to pursue them. These cognitive capacities are the principal way in which we can differentiate ourselves from other species. No wonder, then, that historically we have deemed them so important. Is there a way, though, to think more objectively about the relative importance of moral autonomy to moral status?

We might first ask what concrete difference rationality and autonomy make in our lives. The reality is that our higher cognitive function does make a great difference to our existence. In fact, it has enabled us to control nearly all other species, and to control the lives of children, and that control in turn enables us to satisfy our own interests better. It thus seems clearly preferable to have strong powers of instrumental reasoning and to be autonomous. So this is not an entirely arbitrary basis for distinguishing ourselves from other species; it is a good thing to have, at least from an instrumental, self-serving perspective.

Does the self-serving value of instrumental reasoning and autonomy make them strong bases for attributing moral status? If the essence of moral status is that it makes one deserving of consideration and protection, then in a way it would be ironic to afford higher moral status to beings that are *less in need* of consideration and protection by others. When we moral agents perceive rationality and autonomy in others, we do feel a commonality with them, and this commonality does generate an affective response. We empathize with other autonomous agents when their freedom is restrained or when their faculties decline. And this sense of commonality does cause us to accept that others are worthy of consideration, as much as we believe our own autonomy – our own forming and pursuing of ends and our own striving for meaning – commands respect and consideration. Others' autonomy also generates a certain amount of awe; we are impressed by the ability of other beings to think and act independently and rationally.

It is not clear, however, that perception of rationality and autonomy in others plays a larger role in our recognition of commonality with others than does the perception that others experience pleasure and pain as we do or that others have a will to live as we do. Nor is it clear that others' autonomy generates greater awe in us than do other traits, such as beauty or prodigious physical and intellectual growth. Any affective response to others' situation, any caring about their fate, can, as suggested earlier, actually be muted by a perception that they are autonomous; we think they can fend for themselves, so they command less of our attention. A greater affective response would seem to arise from our perception of others' vulnerability to suffering than from a perception of their strong capacity for self-determination.

From a more objective, less self-serving perspective, then, higher cognitive functioning does not appear to be a stronger basis for attributing moral status than all the other bases considered, let alone so important as to outweigh all the factors that favor children. We can therefore feel some confidence in provisionally concluding that children have a higher moral status than adults. An entirely plausible way of viewing adulthood is as humanity in a state of decline, with its principal redeeming feature being the enhanced autonomy it typically entails, though few adults actually make much good use of.

Although this conclusion might seems counterintuitive, it is consistent with several significant aspects of our moral heritage. For example, in the Old Testament, a basic moral and cultural text for most Westerners, acquisition of knowledge of good and evil and of the capacity and freedom to choose between them is not treated as a great accomplishment or an advance in humanity's situation. It is, rather, viewed as a decline, a fall from grace.[31] And in the New Testament, Jesus manifests a special solicitude for children, because of their innocence, saying "Let the children come to me. For the Kingdom of Heaven belongs to such as these" (Mk 10:14; Matt 19:14; Luke 18:15–17). Childhood innocence has often been cited as a condition adults should try to recapture, as in the Shakespearean sonnet at the beginning of this chapter. Thus, adults have at times recognized that they are lacking in some respects relative to children, respects that are relevant to moral standing. As noted in Chapter 1, there are competing visions of and attitudes toward childhood in our culture, and we might ask whether those entailing a denigration of childhood reflect more a selfishness and self-serving defensiveness among adults than a well considered and objective moral assessment.

It is worth revisiting at this point the egalitarian, all-or-nothing view of moral status. A proponent of that view, such as Peter Singer, might react to the preceding analysis by saying that I am confusing moral status with magnitude of interests at stake. His position would be that a child and an adult are of equal moral status, because both pass his all-or-nothing sentience-only test, but that a child has more at stake than an adult in life-or-death situations. All humans have an interest in realizing their potential for future positive sentient experience, and that interest of

[31] There are contrary elements in the Bible as well, such as Abraham's willingness to kill his son when asked to do so by God.

children is of greater magnitude because they have the potential for more future experience, with more of their lives ahead of them. The criteria I have considered could easily be understood as rubrics of interests rather than of moral standing; to the extent children manifest greater aliveness, they have more to lose from dying, and to the extent children have more acute senses, they have more to lose from anything that deprives them of pleasure or causes suffering.

To say that children are of higher moral status, Singer would point out, would have to mean that their interests trump equally great interests of adults. The standard "whose life is more valuable" hypothetical does not present a good test case, because children will generally have greater interests at stake in remaining alive. One might respond to Singer that we would prefer the life of the child even if we know that the child, perhaps because of a terminal illness, has no greater potential for future life than the adult in question (suppose both have a life expectancy of ten more years). But then Singer could say that in that case we prefer the child out of fairness, not superior moral status; the adult has already enjoyed a great number of years, and the child is getting a raw deal no matter what, but it is fairer to give the child more years, to bring him or her closer to enjoyment of a full life, even on the supposition that the child and the adult are of equal moral considerability. Similarly, when dividing a pie, after giving a slice to one person, it is simply fair to give the next slice to another person, not a matter of treating them as of superior moral worth.

Singer is correct that an egalitarian view of moral status can produce the same conclusions in many conflict-of-interest situations as does a view that moral status is a matter of degree.[32] But it hardly follows from that partial coincidence that the egalitarian view of moral status is superior. And the coincidence is only partial, because there are many situations in which the two views would produce different results. Getting away from life-or-death hypotheticals to more realistic situations helps to demonstrate that. One situation when which view is adopted would matter is when a child and adult have equal but mutually incompatible interests at

[32] He might have to struggle to reconcile it with some strong intuitions about specific cases. For example, in this egalitarian view, it seems he would have to say that aborting a five-month-old fetus (which studies suggest is a sentient being) requires stronger moral justification than killing a ten-year old child. The fetus presumptively has more life ahead of it than does the child, so the fetus has greater interests at stake in living, and if the two human lives are of equal moral status, then the fetus has a stronger moral claim to life than the child.

stake and fairness considerations do not dictate a particular outcome. In everyday family life, such conflicts arise often. My daughters prefer one activity or dinner choice or vacation destination and I prefer another. My daughters want me to buy them some new play equipment, but I would prefer to use the money to buy myself a new mountain bike or kayak. There is no fairness argument of the sort discussed previously to support them; when I was a boy, I had little or no say in my activities, meals, and vacations, and my parents bought me only a small fraction of the playthings my daughters already have. No fairness argument *against* my daughters seems plausible either; "You should be deprived because I was deprived" is just mean. There are surely other bases for resolving the conflict of interests, but one way is to say that their interests just matter more than mine because they occupy a superior moral status. Some parents act as if this were the case, being generally inclined to be self-sacrificing for the sake of their children, whereas other parents act as if the opposite were the case, generally satisfying their own desires first and foremost. As discussed in Chapters 1 and 3, moral-status egalitarians really have no positive theory to support their view in the face of the obvious fact that every commonly cited basis for moral status is manifest to different degrees in different beings. The hierarchical view I offer is more consistent with general beliefs about what matters morally, the workings of our moral psychology, and the empirical reality that each characteristic of moral status comes in degrees.

I would again emphasize, though, that the analysis I have presented is subject to challenge on many fronts – for example, that there are other bases I have failed to consider, that I have not fleshed out some of the bases well enough, or that I have ignored certain facts about children or adults. I have no doubt that the analysis could be improved and I welcome that sort of criticism. What I present here is an initial stab at a more complete account of children's relative moral status than has been given before, with an effort to be even-handed. If nothing else, it illustrates what an adequately full-fledged conversation about moral status would entail.

My provisional conclusion, of course, will be counterintuitive for many people. The prevailing, though not universal view, throughout history, has been that adults are more important in every respect, and children are nonpersons or semipersons who rise in status as they age. Is there a way to explain to those people what they have been missing? The most persuasive, shorthand explanation for them might go something like this: "Look, you probably have not thought much about moral status at all, and when you have you probably accepted conventional wisdom, which has always been promulgated by adults, who would be naturally inclined to put themselves at the top of any hierarchy. If you ever attempted to articulate why children occupy a lower status, you probably focused solely on humans and on just one trait assumed to be valuable in humans – that is, our cognitive abilities. You probably didn't think about other species or about human infants, but if you had you would likely have recognized that something other than just higher cognitive functioning must be a basis for moral status. Now I'm telling you that there are in fact many things. I am also telling you that philosophers' and theologians' reports of humans' great rational capacities and participation in the divine through moral agency are greatly overblown. We're not so unlike other animals as has long been supposed, and even if we are born with the potential to attain advanced levels of morality, few adults actually achieve that potential, as is evident from the predominantly self-centered lives that they lead. Look at what adults are actually like rather than at the rarified ideal supposed by philosophers. Compare them with children on measures such as vitality, growth, engagement with the world, sensory acuity, intensity of experience, importance to family members, beauty, virtue, and capacity for future experience and projects. Face it, you were at your prime decades ago. If you refuse to accept it, then your choices are: (1) refute enough of the empirical suppositions I have made to tip the calculus in favor of adults, (2) reject some or all of the criteria other than those that favor adults, and then abandon a number of other, important specific beliefs you hold that can be supported only by reference to those criteria, or (3) continue to live with rationally inconsistent beliefs."

I have said little in this chapter about prebirth human beings, babies, infants, preschoolers, high-schoolers, young adults, and the elderly. Each of these other groups manifests relative strength with respect to some criteria and relative weakness as to others. Fetuses have few capacities, but they grow rapidly, are greatly affected by how they are treated, and have enormous potential for future life and experience. I noted that newborn babies score highest on the "object of care" criterion and very high as well on criteria of potentiality and nonsexual beauty. In addition, their neurological development is greater than at any other period of life. But their sense organs are in a relatively primitive state, they have no conception of themselves as distinct beings, and little or no rational capacities. Preschoolers' engagement with the world around them, their curiosity and attentiveness, and their cognitive development are quite impressive. But they have no moral independence from their parents. High-schoolers are in a period of tremendous growth psychologically and socially and of intense identity formation, but they also tend to be self-absorbed herd animals. Young adults might be at the peak of sentience (having stronger sense organs than middle-aged adults and greater processing capacity than children), creativity, transcendence, and sexual beauty. But their physical, intellectual, and moral growth is pretty much done and they are in between the periods of being recipients of care and givers of care. The elderly contribute knowledge, wisdom, culture, and family history to the community, and many adopt new charitable causes postretirement. But they manifest less physical and mental aliveness, their sensory capacities are seriously diminished, they need to receive assistance again rather than give it, and they have the least potential for future life. What a plausible chart of moral status over the course of a normal lifetime would look like could take several books to work out, and that is why I have confined my more extended remarks to a comparison of just two narrow age groups.

In the next chapter, I consider possible practical implications of the ranking I have arrived at in this chapter. In order to cover a broader range of situations, I am going to take the liberty of supposing (contrary to the truth) that I have in fact established more broadly that children as a whole, from birth to adulthood, are of superior moral status relative to adults as a whole. I would again point out, though, that it is not age per se that influences moral status in the account I have given, but rather traits that we might refer to collectively as youthfulness and that happen to correlate roughly with age. Adult readers who believe they have remained youthful can thus feel more elevated than their peers. For purposes of recommending changes in social practices, laws, and moral attitudes, however, it is necessary to think in terms of age categories, as has long been done.

6

Legal, Policy, and Moral Implications
of Children's Superiority

How would it matter to social existence and the law if children were, in fact, of superior moral standing? Even if one is not persuaded by the case presented in the previous chapters for viewing children as such, one might find it illuminating to consider what the practical implications would be. Imagining a world in which children occupied the top of a moral hierarchy might reveal something about assumptions embedded in current practices.

In this final chapter, I first identify some more general or abstract implications and then a number of more specific consequences in various areas of social existence. The more general implications follow conceptually, so are fairly definite. Identifying, with any confidence, specific implications of reversing the hierarchy of children and adults would require quantifying the difference in status between the groups, measuring all the interests each group has at stake in various situations, and then weighting those interests in accordance with the status-difference multiplier. Because I cannot undertake such a complicated calculation even in a rough way in this book, the specific implications I offer are speculative. It is worth noting, though, that adults are generally not very demanding of exactitude in determining when it is appropriate to subordinate others' interests, such as those of animals, children, and fetuses, to their own interests; many simply view their own interests as trumping those of all other creatures except when the interests other beings have at stake are huge and their own are rather trivial (and even in some such situations most decide in favor of their own interests, carnivorous eating being an obvious example).

GENERAL IMPLICATIONS

At the most basic level, superior moral status should translate into a greater weighting of the superior being's interests relative to identical interests of an inferior being. If children are superior, then legislators should give greater weight to children's interests than to identical interests of adults. How much greater, as I just noted, would be difficult to specify.

Of course, some favoring of children in making policy trade-offs would be justified even if they were of equal or lesser moral status relative to adults, on the grounds that children simply have more extensive interests at stake or greater needs in connection with particular policy decisions. For example, children unquestionably have greater interests at stake, on the whole, in connection with education policy than adults have, so adults' preferences per se (as opposed to their input into what is best for children) should receive little or no deference. But children's superior moral status would mean favoring children even when adults have as much at stake. For example, in allocating limited funds between welfare programs directed at identical interests of adults and children, such as alleviating illness or hunger, legislators might allocate more funds to children simply because children are more deserving. They might treat children's hunger as worse than adults' hunger just because children matter more.

Children's superior status might even mean that they will sometimes be favored even when adults have more at stake. For example, a custodial parent might stand to gain a great deal in terms of career advancement and lifestyle by relocating far from the noncustodial parent, at a modest cost to the child, but the child's greater moral considerability might preclude the relocation; it might be morally worse to cause the child a modest welfare loss than to cause the custodial parent a substantial welfare loss. (The welfare interdependence of parent and child makes such situations empirically complicated so, again, I am not offering any definitive conclusions as to such specific issues.)

Another more general implication of children's higher status might be that we could justifiably force adults into the service of children. As noted at the outset, one way in which adults' supposed superior moral status has been expressed in the law is in legal rules that entail an instrumental treatment of children – for example, giving parents a legal entitlement to deny their children a secular education, as a matter of the parents' free exercise of religion. Even on the assumption that children and adults are of equal moral status, the notion of parental entitlement to possession of their biological offspring and to control their upbringing is anathema; parenthood should be seen as a fiduciary role enjoyed as a matter of privilege rather than a right, bestowed only to the extent that it is best for a child (Dwyer 1998). Flipping the hierarchy might also make permissible the state's treating adults instrumentally, using adults to serve the interests of children. Following Kant, moral theorists generally accept that it is wrong to treat beings of the highest moral status merely instrumentally, but if human adults are not in fact beings of the highest moral status, then it might be permissible to treat them as means to advancing the interests of those beings, human children, who are of the highest moral status (if that is the case; I have not considered other beings). This might extend to pregnancy; the argument that pregnant women have a right against the state forcing their body and lives into the service of another human being would have less purchase if the most plausible account of moral status substantially elevates the moral considerability of fetuses and lowers that of adults.

Of course, parents already do serve the interests of children, generally devoting much of their income and attention to promoting their children's well-being. But this is something they do willingly and by their own choice, and arguably they gain more in return from the opportunity to associate with their children and the reciprocal attention their children typically give for the rest of the parents' lives. To treat adults instrumentally would mean *compelling* them to devote their time and resources to advancing their children's welfare and projects whether they want to or not, and even in situations where they do not receive a reciprocal, compensating benefit. An example might be forcing biological parents who prefer not to have a relationship with a child nevertheless to spend time with the child, if the child wished and if it is likely on the whole, despite the parents' reluctance, to be beneficial for the child (sometimes it will be and sometimes not), just as today children are routinely compelled against their interests or wishes to spend time with, and even live with, their biological parents. Compulsory parenting classes might be another example; parental complaints that attendance was inconvenient or contrary to their religious beliefs would be irrelevant, because their interests are simply relatively unimportant. Apart from parents, other adults might also be put in the service of children. For example, family members other than parents might also be legally compelled to assist financially with the rearing of a child. More broadly, taxing adults heavily to fund programs for children would require no other justification than that it is good for the children.

Attitudinally, a ranking reversal might lead us to encourage adults to emulate children, contrary to the exhortation traditionally given children that they should become like adults (in some ways) as quickly as possible. We would criticize people for "adultishness" rather than for childishness. Of course, treating youthfulness as an aspiration would not be something entirely new; even now it is common for adults to be criticized for lacking playfulness and spontaneity, for being too rational and disciplined. And today there is greater recognition of the inherent value of childhood, so that parents do not focus their spending and choices exclusively on preparing children for adulthood. The attitudinal shift would thus not be stark, and might just make more explicit what many already believe, but it might also lead to new social policies and public programs to discourage adultishness and encourage childlikeness in chronologically older people. For example, the law might compel adults to play (i.e., take vacations from work) just as it has compelled children to work toward adulthood (i.e., go to school), and the state might pay children to teach adults how to be youthful. A linguistic change might even be in order; because today "child" has pejorative connotations and "adult" has honorific connotations, we might choose to dispense with those terms and instead characterize people just as young or old. Age minimums for some activities, such as driving and drinking, would still be proper, but there would be no need to maintain global categories of "child" and "adult" in law or in social discourse.

SPECIFIC IMPLICATIONS

The interests of children and adults conflict in innumerable specific contexts in law, public policy, and social life. I address some specific possible implications of children's superior moral status here by proceeding through several categories of interest-conflict situations.

Family Law

There is a widespread misconception today that in any area of family law or juvenile law involving children a "best interests of the child" standard controls. The reality is that this standard is controlling in very few contexts, and even in some of those contexts it is only nominally controlling; adult interests influence decisions in ways that detract from children's welfare. I have explained in other writings how that is so. Here, I will simply suggest how the law might work if children's interests were more often controlling. In doing so, I consciously gloss over some complicating factors that would need to be considered in a more sustained analysis – in particular, the reality that children benefit from their parents' being happy and satisfied in their role.

Parentage

Even if children and adults were equals in moral standing, the notion that biological parents have a right to be in a legal and social relationship with their offspring regardless of whether this is best for the child, a notion that the law today embodies, is indefensible (Dwyer 2006). The sole aim of legislation creating general rules for parentage and of judicial decision making when individual cases require special attention should be to secure for a given child the best available parents, all things considered (including the child's interest in a biological connection to parents), among those who are willing. If the hierarchy were reversed, the state might go farther and impose parenthood on some reluctant adults even if they are not biological parents, though such reluctance obviously makes the adult's parenthood presumptively not best for the child.

CHILD REARING

Substantial child support obligations could be imposed on biological parents (and perhaps their adult family members) even if they do not become legal or social parents to the child and even if the child has two other adults acting as parents (i.e., if the child is adopted). Fairness objections (e.g., "I did not make the child worse off by creating it" and "I do not get the benefits of family life with the child") would be impertinent. The only legitimate objection adults could make to imposition of child support obligations might be that it would detract from their ability to provide for other children.

As noted earlier, even if adults and children are moral equals, the law should not attribute to parents control "rights" over children (they should, as indicated previously, exercise authority in a fiduciary role as a matter of privilege), and child welfare laws (abuse, neglect, education, medical care) should focus exclusively on what, from a secular perspective, is best for children in general. Any parental objections to compliance with school regulations or medical care requirements should have to be couched in terms of contrary evidence of what is best for children; parents' wishes and religious beliefs should, in and of themselves, be irrelevant (Dwyer 1998). Leaving religious schooling and home schooling virtually unregulated (as it is today) would become unthinkable, as would reclusive rearing of children in cult compounds. Reversing the hierarchy might mean that the law should deem children entitled to some greater control over their parents' lives, to serve the children's interests. For example, the law might give children a right to restrict the work hours of their parents, unless the parents can show this would, on the whole, be bad for the children.

Absent overwhelming evidence that corporal punishment is absolutely necessary to secure important child welfare aims, the law would prohibit hitting children more strongly than it prohibits spousal violence, rather than the opposite. Parents might be compelled to take classes in alternative ways of instilling self-discipline in children. In contrast, parents who abuse or neglect their children might be publicly flogged.

Divorce

When parents divorce, they impact their children's interest in stability in many ways – stability not just of relationships, but also of physical environment. Existing legal rules allow for first satisfying the interests of the adults in not spending time with each other and in establishing separate residences. Each parent gets his or her own permanent household, but the children must shuttle back and forth between houses, which might be some distance apart, to spend a few days with one parent here then a few days there with the other. This situation can be just as disruptive for children as it would be for the adults, if they had to go back and forth between two residences.

Reversing the hierarchy might mean first satisfying the interests of children to the greatest extent possible, then satisfying the adults' interests only to the extent compatible with the arrangement that is best for the children. This might mean, in the first place, increasing existing obstacles to getting divorced at all when a couple has children – for example, compulsory marriage counseling and longer separation periods. It might mean imposing a financial penalty on the parents to compensate the children for the suffering the parents cause them by failing to make their marriage work – for example, by requiring that children take a share in equitable distribution of property, in addition to receiving child support, with the children's share put in trust for them. This might be used to pay for college when the time comes, something for which most states do not now require custodial or noncustodial parents to pay.

Hierarchy reversal might also mean a quite different approach to custodial arrangements, one in which, when financially feasible (perhaps requiring extended family members to contribute), the court requires the parents first to establish a single permanent residence for the children, preferably the home they have been living in, where the children will remain and which can also accommodate a parent. The court could then require and authorize the parents to alternate in living in that residence. Where the parents stay when they are not in the children's home would be their problem; they can share an apartment with each other if they like (in which case the financial burden would be no greater than under current practices), or each rent their own apartment, or make some other arrangement. The consequence might be that neither parent can afford as large an accommodation for himself or herself as might be possible if they did not also have to share in the cost of the children's separate residence. It might also make it more difficult for the parents to form new relationships, if they have to keep switching residences and living in space shared with an ex-spouse. This rule could be conceptualized as simply requiring parents to compensate for the harm they have caused, in which case we need not posit that the children are morally superior. But if it seems that under such a regime parents' interests were being sacrificed inordinately for the sake of the children – inordinate, that is, if one assumes the parents' interests should count for as much as the children's – the justification would be that the parents' interests, in fact, should not and do not count for as much as the children's, because the children occupy a superior moral status.

In making custody awards after a divorce or parentage proceeding, courts would be freer to consider any parental choice or characteristic that could impact the child. Today, courts are prohibited from or reluctant to consider such things as a parent's choice of a new partner (e.g., of a different race or of the same sex) even when that could have an impact on the child (e.g., getting beat up on the playground). They are also reluctant to impose restrictions on parents' conduct (e.g., smoking, religious practices). Such adult-protective inhibitions on best-interests decision making would disappear.

Public Policy

In public welfare spending, child welfare would always receive highest priority. For example, if allocated funds are insufficient to cover similar medical needs of both children and adults, the funds would go to children.[1] We might adopt as an operating principle that no public money can be spent on other projects until all basic needs of all children are met.

---

[1]   The opposite sometimes occurs today. See, e.g., Gardiner Harris, "Money for Vaccinating Children is Diverted, Officials Say," *New York Times* (Dec. 16, 2004).

(Of course, some needs, such as national defense, are public goods that cannot be targeted to specific groups.) No child would live in poverty, in the sense of lacking basic goods because parents' lack resources. There would be universal health care for children, universal preschool, much greater public investment in schools in poor neighborhoods, free meals at schools, vouchers for purchasing children's clothing, and other forms of targeted or in-kind aid. Objections on the grounds that some groups of adults are losing out because of the spending on children or on the grounds that taxpayers should not be forced to pay for the care of other people's children would have little or no purchase. Fairness to adults might become a consideration only in cases of their extreme deprivation, the remedy for which would be interadult transfers rather than reduction of spending on children.

In addition, we might pay more attention to the thoughts and opinions of young people. Instead of evoking their views just to improve or guide them, we might take seriously the possibility that their views are worth adopting. This change, too, might not be so stark as it might at first seem. There are plenty of references in popular culture already to "the wisdom of the children," to the idea that children see the world with a certain clarity that later gets lost to adult rationalizations and self-deceptions. The change might entail some concrete new policies, though, such as a major shift of social resources for communication – including arts and entertainment – from adults to youths. At least before the Internet/cell phone era, the vast bulk of messages children received, even from other young people, were filtered through adults, many of whom were disposed to exploit youths or view them as simply consumers from whom money could be extracted. This seems still true of mass communication, as through television, radio, and print media. Young people should be able to communicate directly to each other and on a larger scale, so their own ideas germinate unfiltered and they can create a collective consciousness themselves rather than having one foisted on them by adults. To further a phenomenon already reflected in text messaging, e-mail, and socializing Web sites, the state might subsidize these and other avenues of communication, such as entertainment outlets run by youths, or might require radio and television stations to hand over some of their programming time and resources to youths. There are some existing examples of this being done voluntarily and of youths producing excellent programming, programming that one might judge to be more meaningful, less exploitative, and more positive than much of the programming that adults provide for young people.

Education policy would be reformed to eradicate tendencies to propel students toward sober professionalism and exclusively rationalistic ways of viewing the world, and to let students' views and interests dictate to a somewhat greater degree the content of class discussions, with teachers adopting a more deferential attitude, being open to learning from students. Teachers' role might be viewed as ensuring that students receive basic information and guiding discussion insofar as necessary as to ensure that, whatever the course students take in discussing the information, they develop essential intellectual skills and acquire essential knowledge, otherwise allowing them freedom to pursue their own lines of inquiry. It should be welcomed rather than resented and quashed when students challenge fundamental assumptions in the subject matter of their courses. Students can get much of what they need out of school through guided analysis of their own ideas; they do not need the worship of hoary authority that is now encouraged or the piles of inessential information that we now force them to digest and reproduce on standardized tests.[2]

Another way in which we could pay more attention to the views of young people is to allow them a direct voice in government and politics. Among the arguments advanced for maintaining the voting age at eighteen are some that suppose minors' views about social existence and public governance are insufficiently formed, which one could interpret to mean we have not had enough time to ensure that they think the way we adults do. But if we took seriously the notion that the interests of young people should receive more weight than our own, it should seem nothing sort of tyranny to exclude their views altogether from the process by which we most effectively express views about societal governance – namely, voting. Another means of empowering children politically, already adopted by some European nations, would be to establish an ombudsman office that invites children to express their views and has power to introduce legislation and otherwise influence public policy.

Social Life

In social practice, we might treat as more sacrosanct the activities of children. Adults' interfering with children's play would be more condemnable than children's interference with adults' work or hobbies, rather than vice versa. Parents would need better reason for saying "it's time

---

[2]   See, generally, "Symposium: School Accountability and 'High Stakes' Testing," 2 *Theory and Research in Education* (Nov 2004).

to go" than their own boredom or tiredness. Family activities might be structured to conform to children's natural or preferred daily rhythm of life and approach to carrying them out rather than with what adults find comfortable. For example, we might set up an eating station next to play areas and allow grazing at whim, rather than imposing a regimen of sitting down at a table for three meals a day. Prevailing current practices regarding meals match adults' lifestyle and are convenient for adults; we do not want to have to cook more often and forcing children to sit with us while we eat kills two birds with one stone. (We want to/are expected to spend time with them, and we have to eat, so why not combine them?) But if they are not optimal for children, we might just have to sacrifice that convenience, devoting more effort to food preparation and finding other times and ways to interact with our children, perhaps at the expense of our personal hobbies.

In addition, we might pattern our norms of social interaction after children's natural behavior rather than forcing them to adopt our highly stylized conventions. For example, we might come to admire, or at least be more tolerant of, children's honest expressions of opinion about others (or at least about adults), no matter how negative, rather than encouraging them to be embarrassed and disingenuous. Failing to squat when talking with a small child would be a great insult. An adult interrupting a child would be as much a breach of proper etiquette as a lawyer interrupting a judge.[3] An adult declining a child's invitation to get in the dirt and play would be as unheard of as a student declining a professor's invitation to discuss a shared intellectual interest over coffee.

CONCLUSION

Once again, I emphasize that these thoughts as to specific implications of children's superior moral status are merely speculative suggestions, food for thought. In many ways, they entail adults behaving the opposite of the way most now do, and so they reveal some ways in which we might now, even if unconsciously, suppose an inferiority of status in children. In those respects, then, change might be in order even if one adopted and endeavored fully to operationalize the more moderate position that children are adults' equal in moral status.

[3]   For an argument that rules of etiquette are a component of morality and that failing to show proper manners to another constitutes moral disrespect, see Sarah Buss, "Appearing Respectful: The Moral Significance of Manners," 109 *Ethics* 795–826 (1999).

Importantly, none of the discussion of practical implications in this chapter entails that, in a world reflective of children's superiority, adults would impose no constraints on children nor direct their development to a substantial degree. Respecting children does not mean abandoning the responsibilities of child rearing. Even from a perspective that views children as the pinnacle of humanity and accords their interests and preferences great deference, it would be permissible and even requisite, for children's own long-term well-being and for the sake of mutually beneficial social existence, to train children in certain ways – for example, increasingly to exercise self-discipline, to refrain from harming others, to lay the cognitive and social foundation for full realization of their talents and abilities, and to prepare for the day when they will be put in service to the next generation of superior beings. What I am suggesting, rather, is instead that children's interests, short-term and long-term, would determine their lives and ours to a much greater degree than they now do, and that to a significant degree this might entail coming to perceive as good what we now view as bad, and vice versa.

Conclusion

The basic idea of this book has been that if we closely examine wide-spread intuitions about what entities in our world have some moral considerability, and why they do, we will recognize these intuitions are based on a multitude of basic criteria for moral status that, if rigorously applied to human beings, might on the whole result in youthfulness elevating moral status. Youthfulness involves a collection of traits including vivacity, growth, enthusiasm, engagement with the world, sensory acuity, intense feeling, adaptability, flexibility, having an open future, being cared about by others, transparency, innocence, beauty, and potential for future life and experience. Chronological adults can manifest many of these traits, by happenstance or conscious effort, but in general youthfulness characterizes children rather than adults. Recognizing that children are superior beings in the moral order, rather than inferior or equal, arguably should lead to significant changes in public policy, law, social life, and popular attitudes.

Some will find these conclusions neither surprising nor unwelcome. A significant percentage of the population today devote their lives to advancing children's welfare and rights, and, through working with or for children, have come to realize the many strengths and virtues children possess. This is no doubt true of some parents, those for whom child rearing is truly an altruistic, self-subordinating undertaking and who repeatedly experience awe in witnessing their children's growth, surprising abilities, purity, and beauty. Such parents might not recoil at the suggestion that their self-sacrifice for children is morally obligatory rather than supererogatory.

Others will find the conclusions greatly counterintuitive and depressing. Many of us who are middle aged have consoled ourselves, consciously or subconsciously, as we experience repeated frustrations and fears resulting from a decline in many of our capacities, or feel envy in beholding the energy, passion, and beauty of younger people, that we are now at the top of the world, in our prime, fully grown up and in charge, because we are strongest at the one thing that matters most morally – rationality. Perhaps we are hard-wired to associate might with right, power with superiority and therefore find it difficult to wrap our brains around the idea that even though we run social institutions, make the rules, and control the resources, we are of inferior status and should think of ourselves as servants to the young.

For a couple of reasons, it should not be startling to conclude that we adults have been collectively mistaken for a very long time in failing to recognize children's superiority over us. As noted in the Introduction, the past century has seen significant change in attitudes toward children, and today many, perhaps most, people would say that children are of equal moral status, which would likely not have been the case a few centuries earlier. Consider also the history of abandoning discriminatory attitudes among adults that were based on suppositions about moral status. That history reflects a well-known human tendency toward self-serving valorization of whatever is distinctive about us, and those who are in power have always used social norms for their own self-aggrandizement. They have based hierarchy on race, gender, sexual orientation, age, and cognitive capacity as well. Recognition of this phenomenon is implicit or explicit in most of the animal rights and environmental ethics literatures, which at base accuse humans of being arrogant and self-serving in their moral attitudes. So it is not difficult to explain why adults have been so wrong for so long.

A conclusion that children are of higher moral status than adults might be easier to accept if we ourselves had received our moral due when we were children; if government, law, society, teachers, and parents had treated us with the respect due superior beings – if they had celebrated our strengths and valued our youthfulness, rather than denigrating our differences, treating us as subordinates, and trying to propel us toward adulthood as rapidly as possible. Then we could look back fondly and wish the same for the next generation. By way of analogy, donations to universities are naturally higher among graduates who view their college experience as very positive, and part of what motivates their giving is a desire to provide a new generation of students with the opportunity for a similarly positive experience. Many view their college years as the greatest years of their lives, because for the first time they were treated with respect as equals, valued for their strengths, consulted for their thoughts, and given the freedom to be and create themselves. They felt on top of the world in a different, arguably richer and more transcendent, way then. Rather than wanting to deny younger people that experience out of envy, they get satisfaction from sacrificing to facilitate that experience for them. This same outlook might be extended to childhood after we transformed our attitudes and practices.

At the same time, to the extent the analysis of this book is persuasive, adult readers might feel a call to action in their personal lives. We need not accept aging passively, content with the thought that we get wiser as we get older, that our minds continue to improve as we allow the rest of us to decay. We can make a determined effort to retain our youthfulness, to remain physically, intellectually, and emotionally vigorous. We can consciously choose to open our minds to new possibilities for ways of thinking, developing talents, and satisfying curiosities. We can seek out association with children to absorb youthfulness, just as children have always absorbed "adultishness" by association (mostly compelled) with adults. There are exceptional examples today of individuals who have remained youthful in many respects throughout very long lives, persons who seem younger at seventy than most people in their forties, elderly individuals whose deaths are especially momentous, sadder because more has been lost than in most cases, but also cause for greater celebration of the life that was lived. In a world that recognized the moral superiority of youth, we might expect more such lives to be lived.

Bibliography

Almeder, R. F. (2004). 'Marginal Cases and the Moral Status of Embryos,' in *Stem Cell Research* (Humber, J. M. and Almeder, R. F., eds.) (Totowa, NJ: Humana Press).

Ariès, P. (1962). *Centuries of Childhood: A Social History of Family Life* (New York: Alfred A. Knopf).

Armstong, Susan J., and Botzler, Richard G., eds. (2008). *The Animal Ethics Reader*, 2nd ed. (New York: Routledge).

Attfield, Robin. (1991). *The Ethics of Environmental Concern*, 2nd ed. (Athens: University of Georgia Press).

Becker, G. K. (ed.). (2000). *The Moral Status of Persons: Perspectives on Bioethics* (Atlanta, GA: Rodopi).

Belshaw, C. (2001). *Environmental Philosophy: Reason, Nature and Human Concern* (Ithaca, NY: McGill-Queen's University Press).

Bird, C. (2004). "Status, Identity, and Respect," *Political Theory*, 32/2, 207–32.

Blum, Lawrence. (1980). *Friendship, Altruism and Morality* (Boston: Routledge & Kegal Paul).

Bradie, M. (1994). *The Secret Chain: Evolution and Ethics* (Albany: State University of New York Press).

Brennan, A. (1988). "Puzzles about Value," in *Thinking About Nature* (Athens: University of Georgia Press).

Brennan, S., and Noggle, R. (1997). "The Moral Status of Children: Children's Rights, Parents' Rights, and Family Justice," *Social Theory and Practice*, 23/1, 1–26.

Brocklehurst, Helen. (2006). *Who's Afraid of Children?: Children, Conflict and International Relations* (Burlington, VT: Ashgate).

Callicott, J. Baird (1989). *In Defense of the Land Ethic: Essays in Environmental Philosophy* (Albany, NY: State University of New York Press).

   (1999). *Beyond the Land Ethic: More Essays in Environmental Philosophy* (Albany: State University of New York Press).

Carruthers, Peter. (1992). *The Animals Issue: Moral Theory in Practice* (New York: Cambridge University Press).

Cohen, Carl and Regan, Tom (2001). *The Animal Rights Debate* (Lanham, MD: Rowman & Littlefield Publishers, Inc.).

Coles, R. (1986a). *The Moral Life of Children* (Boston: Houghton Mifflin Company).

(1986b). *The Political Life of Children* (Boston: Houghton Mifflin Company).

(1990). *The Spiritual Life of Children* (Boston: Houghton Mifflin Company).

Darwall, S. (2006). "The Main Ideas II," in *The Second-Person Standpoint: Morality, Respect, and Accountability* (Cambridge: Harvard University Press).

DeGrazia, D. (1996). *Taking Animals Seriously: Mental Life and Moral Status* (New York: Cambridge University Press).

Dombrowski, Daniel. (1997). Babies and Beasts (Champagne: University of Illinois Press).

Dwyer, James G. (1998). *Religious Schools v. Children's Rights* (Ithaca, NY: Cornell University Press).

(2002). *Vouchers Within Reason: A Child-centered Approach to Education Reform* (Ithaca, NY: Cornell University Press).

(2006). *The Relationship Rights of Children* (New York: Cambridge University Press).

Evans, D., and Pickering, N. (eds.) (1996). *Conceiving the Embryo: Ethics, Law and Practice in Human Embryology* (Boston: Martinus Nijhoff Publishers).

Feinberg, Joel. (1984). *The Moral Limits of the Criminal Law* (New York: Oxford University Press).

Ferry, Luc (1995). *The New Ecological Order* (Chicago: University of Chicago Press).

Fineman, Marth Albertson. (2004). *The Autonomy Myth: A Theory of Dependency* (New York: The New Press).

Fionda, Julia. (2001). *Legal Concepts of Childhood* (Oxford: Hart Publishing).

Francione, Gary L. (2008). *Animals as Persons: Essays on the Abolition of Animal Exploitation* (New York: Columbia University Press).

Frankfut, Harry. (1988). *The Importance of What We Care About: Philosophical Essays* (New York: Cambridge University Press).

Franklin, Julian H. (2005). *Animal Rights and Moral Philosophy* (New York: Columbia University Press.

French, Marilyn. (1985). *Beyond Power: On Women, Men and Morals* (New York: Summit Books).

Frey, R.G. (1980). *Interests and Rights: The Case Against Animals* (New York: Oxford University Press).

Frey, R. G., and Wellman, C. H. (eds.) (2005). *A Companion to Applied Ethics* (Malden, MA: Blackwell Publishing).

Freyfogle, E. T. (1990). "The Land Ethic and Pilgrim Leopold," *University of Colorado Law Review*, 61: 217–56.

Gauthier, David. (1987). *Morals by Agreement* (New York: Oxford University Press).

Gewirth, Alan. (1978). *Reason and Morality* (Chicago: University of Chicago Press).

Gilligan, Carol. (1982). *In a Different Voice* (Cambridge, MA: Harvard University Press).

Goodpaster, K. E. (1978). "On Being Morally Considerable," *The Journal of Philosophy* 75(6): 308–25.

Graham, George, and LaFollette, Hugh. (1989). *Person to Person* (Philadelphia: Temple University Press).

Guyer, Paul. (2000). *Kant on Freedom, Law, and Happiness* (New York: Cambridge University Press).

Haidt, J., and Bjorklund, F. (2008). "Social Intuitionists Answer Six Questions about Moral Psychology." In Sinnott-Armstrong (Ed.) (2008b) (pp. 181–217) at 203.

Harris, John (1985). *The Value of Life: An Introduction to Medical Ethics* (Boston: Routledge & Kegan Paul).

Higgins, R. C. A. (2004). 'Respect for Persons and Law,' in *The Moral Limits of Law: Obedience, Respect, and Legitimacy* (New York: Oxford University Press).

Hodgson, Lucia. (1997). *Raised in Captivity: Why Does America Fail Its Children* (Minneapolis, MN: Graywolf Press).

Hume, David. (2006). *An Enquiry Concerning the Principles of Morals* (Oxford: The Clarendon Press).

Kant, Immanuel. (1956a). *Groundwork of the Metaphysics of Morals* (H.J. Paton, trans.) (New York: Harper Torchbooks).

   (1956b). *Critique of Practical Reason* (Lewis White Beck, trans.) (Indianapolis, IN: Bobbs-Merrill).

   (1960). *Observations on the Feeling of the Beautiful and Sublime* (J.T. Goldthwait, trans.) (Berkeley: University of California Press).

   (1997). *Lectures on Ethics* (New York: Cambridge University Press).

   (2005). *The Moral Law: Groundwork of the Metaphysics of Morals* (London: Routledge Classics).

Korsgaard, Christine M. (1996a). *Creating the Kingdom of Ends* (Cambridge: Cambridge University Press).

   (1996b). *The Sources of Normativity* (Cambridge: Cambridge University Press).

Krinsky, Charles. (2008) *Moral Panics over Contemporary Children and Youth* (London: Ashgate).

Kuhse, H., and Singer, P. (eds) (1998). *A Companion to Bioethics* (Malden, MA: Blackwell Publishing).

LaFollette, H. (ed.). (2003). *The Oxford Handbook of Practical Ethics* (New York: Oxford University Press).

Lauritzen, P. (ed.). (2001). *Cloning and the Future of Human Embryo Research* (New York: Oxford University Press).

Leahy, Michael and Cohn-Sherbok, Dan (eds.) (1996). *The Liberation Debate: Rights at Issue* (New York: Routledge).

Leiter, Brian. (ed.) (2001). *Objectivity in Law and Morals* (New York: Cambridge University Press)

Linn, S. (2004). *Consuming Kids: The Hostile Takeover of Childhood* (New York: The New Press).

Macedo, Stephen. (ed.) (2002). *NOMOS XLIII: Moral and Political Education* (New York: New York University Press).

Macnicol, John. (2006). *Age Discrimination: An Historical and Contemporary Analysis* (New York: Cambridge University Press).

Maine, H. (1930). *Ancient Law* (Frederick Pollock, ed.) (New York: Henry Holt and Company).

Matthews, Garrett. (1994). *The Philosophy of Childhood* (Cambridge, MA: Harvard University Press).

McMahan, J. (2002). *The Ethics of Killing: Problems at the Margins of Life* (New York: Oxford University Press).

Melden, A. I. (1977). *Rights and Persons*, (Berkeley: University of California Press).

Mendus, Susan. (2002). *Impartiality in Moral and Political Philosophy* (New York: Oxford University Press).

Menninghaus, W. (2003). "Introduction," in *Disgust: The Theory and History of a Strong Sensation* (Albany: State University of New York Press).

Mill, John Stuart. (2003). *On Liberty* (New Haven, CT: Yale University Press).

Nagel, Thomas. (1970). *The Possibility of Altruism* (Princeton, NJ: Princeton University Press).

Narveson, Jan. (2002). *Respecting Persons in Theory and Practice* (New York: Rowman & Littlefield).

Nelson, Todd D. (ed.) (2002). *Ageism: Stereotyping and Prejudice Against Older Persons* (Cambridge, MA: The MIT Press).

Neugarten, Bernice L. (1996). *The Meanings of Age: Selected Papers of Bernice L. Neugarten* (Dail, ed.). (University of Chicago Press).

Nipkow, K. E., and Schweitzer, F. (1991). "Adolescents' Justifications for Faith or Doubt in God: A Study of Fulfilled and Unfulfilled Expectations," *New Directions for Child Development*, 52: 91–100.

Noddings, Nel. (1984). *Caring: A Feminine Approach to Ethics and Moral Education* (Berkeley and Los Angeles: University of California Press).

Nussbaum, M.C. (2000). "The Future of Feminist Liberalism." *Proceedings and Addresses of the American Philosophical Association* 74:47–79.

(2001). *Upheavals of Thought: The Intelligence of Emotions* (New York: Cambridge University Press).

(2002). *For Love of Country: Debating the Limits of Patriotism* (Boston: Beacon Press).

(2004). *Hiding from Humanity Disgust, Shame, and the Law* (Princeton, NJ: Princeton University Press).

Oakley, J. (1992). *Morality and the Emotions* (New York: Routledge).

Oshana, M. (2003). "How Much Should We Value Autonomy?," *Social Philosophy & Policy Foundation*, 2003: 99–126.

Ouderkirk, W., and Hill, J. (eds.) (2002). *Land, Value, Community: Callicott and Environmental Philosophy* (Albany: State University of New York Press).

Paul, E. F., Miller, F. D. Jr., and Paul, J. (eds.). (2003). *Autonomy* (New York: Cambridge University Press).

Perry, Micahel J. (2010). *The Political Morality of Liberal Democracy* (New York: Cambridge University Press).

Prinz, Jesse J. (2007). *The Emotional Construction of Morals* (New York: Oxford University Press).

Pritchard, Michael S. (1996). *Reasonable Children: Moral Education and Moral Learning* (Lawrence: University Press of Kansas).

Rawls, J. (1971). "The Basis of Equality," in *A Theory of Justice* (Cambridge, MA: The Belknap Press of Harvard University Press).

Regan, Tom. (1983). *The Case for Animal Rights* (Berkeley: University of California Press).

Rollin, B. E. (1992). *Animal Rights & Human Morality* (Buffalo, NY: Prometheus Books).

Rolston, Holmes III. (1989). *Environmental Ethics: Duties to and Values in the Natural World* (Philadelphia: Temple University Press).

Sapontzis, S.F. (1987). *Morals, Reason, and Animals* (Philadelphia: Temple University Press).

Scanlon, Thomas. (1998). *What We Owe to Each Other* (Cambridge, MA: Harvard University Press).

Schopenhauer, A. (1965). *On the Basis of Morality* (New York: Bobbs-Merrill).

Schweitzer, Albert. (1933). *Out of My Life and Thought* (C. Campton, trans., 1961). (New York: Henry Holt and Company).

(1965). *The Teaching of Reverence for Life* (New York: Henry Holt and Company).

(1985). "Civilization and Ethics," in *The Extended Circle: A Commonplace Book of Animal Rights* (Jon Wynne-Tyson, ed.). (London: Paragon House).

(1993). *Reverence for Life: The Words of Albert Schweitzer* (San Francisco: Harper San Francisco).

Shrader-Frechette, K. (2005). 'Environmental Ethics,' in *Philosophy of Science* (Sarkur, S. and Parker, J., eds.) (London: Routledge).

Singer, Peter. (1975). *Animal Liberation: A New Ethics for Our Treatment of Animals* (New York: Random House).

Singer Peter. (1979). *Practical Ethics* (Cambridge: Cambridge University Press). (1990). *Animal Liberation*, 2d. ed. (New York: Random House).

Sinnott-Armstrong, W. (ed.) (2008a). *Moral Psychology, Vol. 1: The Evolution of Morality: Adaptations and Innateness* (Cambridge, MA: The MIT Press).

(ed.) (2008b). *Moral Psychology, Vol. 2: The Cognitive Science of Morality: Intuition and Diversity* (Cambridge, MA: The MIT Press).

(ed.) (2008c). *Moral Psychology, Vol. 3: The Neuroscience of Morality: Emotion, Brain Disorders, and Development* (Cambridge, MA: The MIT Press).

Slote, M. (2004). "Autonomy and Empathy," *Social Philosophy & Policy Foundation*, 2004: 293–309.

Steinbock, B. (1978). "Speciesism and the Idea of Equality," *Philosophy*, 53(204): 247–56.

(1996). *Life before Birth: The Moral and Legal Status of Embryos and Fetuses* (New York: Oxford University Press).

Steiner, Gary. (2008). *Animals and the Moral Community: Mental Life, Moral Status, and Kinship* (New York: Columbia University Press).

(2005). *Anthropocentrism and Its Discontents: The Moral Status of Animals in the History of Western Philosophy* (Pittsburgh, PA: University of Pittsburgh Press).

Stratton-Lake, P. (ed.) (2002). *Ethical Intuitionism: Re-evaluations* (New York: Oxford University Press).

Sunstein, Cass R., and Nussbaum, Martha C. (eds.). (2004). *Animal Rights: Current Debates and New Directions* (New York: Oxford University Press).

Taylor, Paul W. (1986). *Respect for Nature: A Theory of Environmental Ethics* (Princeton, NJ: Princeton University Press).

Terrizzi, J. A. Jr. (2007). *Prejudicial Attitudes toward Homosexuals: The Competing Roles of Moral Reasoning and the Moral Emotion of Disgust* (thesis presented to the graduate faculty of the College of William & Mary).

Timmons, M. (ed.). (2002). *Kant's Metaphysics of Morals: Interpretative Essays* (New York: Oxford University Press).

Turner, Susan M., and Matthews, Gareth B. (eds.). (1998). *The Philosopher's Child: Critical Essays in the Western Tradition* (Rochester, NY: University of Rochester Press).

Walters, James W. (1997). *What Is a Person? An Ethical Exploration* (Chicago: University of Illinois Press).

Warnock, G.J. (1971). *The Object of Morality* (London: Methuen & Co.).

Warren, Mary Ann. (1997). *Moral Status: Obligations to Persons and Other Living Things* (Oxford: Oxford University Press).

Westman, Jack. (2001). *Licensing Parents: Can We Prevent Child Abuse and Neglect?* (Cambridge, MA: Da Capo Press).

Wood, Allen W. (2007). *Kantian Ethics* (New York: Cambridge University Press).

Woodruff, Paul. (2001). *Reverence: Renewing a Forgotten Virtue* (New York: Oxford University Press).

Index